The Psychology of Men

THE

PSYCHOLOGY

OF

MEN

Psychoanalytic Perspectives

LEARNING RESOURCES
CENTRE
Havering College
of Further and Higher Education

EDITED BY

Gerald I. Fogel, Frederick M. Lane, and Robert S. Liebert

Yale University Press   New Haven and London

Figure 1, *Man offering a cockerel to a youth,* figure 2, *Man titillating a youth,* and figure 7, *Homosexual group,* are here reprinted by permission of the Ashmolean Museum, Oxford.

Figure 3, *Man and youth copulating,* is here reprinted by permission of the British Museum, London.

Figure 4, *Satyr homosexual group (detail),* is here reprinted by permission of the Stiftung Staatliche Kulturbesitz, Berlin.

Figure 5, *Heterosexual group (detail),* is here reprinted by permission of the Archaeological Museum, Florence.

Figure 6, *Antinoüs,* is here reprinted by permission of the Museo Laterano, Vatican.

Figure 8, *Abduction of Ganymede,* is here reprinted by permission of the Kunsthistorisches Museum, Vienna

Figure 9, *The Rape of Ganymede,* is here reprinted by permission of Windsor Castle, Windsor.

Originally published 1986 by Basic Books, Inc.
Paperbound edition with a new preface published 1996 by Yale University Press.
Copyright © 1986 by Basic Books, Inc.
Copyright © 1996 by the Association for Psychoanalytic Medicine.
All rights reserved.

Printed in the United States of America.
Library of Congress Catalog Card Number
95-62214
ISBN 0-300-06620-1 (pbk.)

A catalogue record for this book is available from the British Library.

The paper in this book meets the guidelines for permanence and durability of the Committee on Production Guidelines for Book Longevity of the Council on Library Resources.

10 9 8 7 6 5 4 3 2 1

CONTENTS

III

Men Growing Up: Developmental Epochs

IV

Men Seeking Change: Men and Women Treating Men

Preface to Paperback Edition

When this work first appeared, in 1986, it was far ahead of its time. Reviewers pronounced it an instant "classic," praising it for the quality of its coverage as well as its lively readability and affirmation of the "relevance and vitality of contemporary psychoanalytic theory" (Simon, 1987). But has the rapid expansion of the field of gender studies in the past ten years created a need for revising and updating? The editors do not think so. In reviewing the papers that comprise this collection, we were impressed again by their currency and vitality. They may be even more relevant today than they were ten years ago.

Psychoanalysis is not quantum physics or brain imaging. New knowledge in psychoanalysis, unlike more strictly technological fields, when presented at a high level usually also contains wisdom and art. It can therefore be prescient—can anticipate what is not yet fully explicit. Reading the book now, one can see that these papers not only integrate classical and more contemporary psychoanalytic knowledge but also are deeply responsive to emergent trends in contemporary intellectual and cultural life. Some of these trends have become completely clear only since the book first appeared. As I explain in detail in the introduction, classical Freudian perspectives are expanded here by new findings and perspectives—object relations, self, and separation-individuation theories, for example. Changing perspectives on sexuality and sexual stereotypes, as well as the changing cultural context, are carefully considered. But in that introduction I also summarize trends that emerge throughout the book when I note that the main problem for many men (and psychoanalytic theorists) is *women*. Men must deal with women as objects of love, aggression, envy, and identification. They must deal as well with their own "womanish" or feminine aspects. Finally, men must deal with what women represent, which usually includes the "infantile"—the primal and archaic layers of mental life.

Psychoanalytic theory has to deal with its lost feminine half as well. This requires a confrontation with the primacy of the phallus as a sole psychic organizer in higher mental organizations, as well as the bias that locates the feminine in preoedipal stages, in the primitive or developmentally less mature aspects of the human psyche. The new frontier this book predicts is therefore the degree to which psychoanalytic studies of female psychology and feminist theory are shaping our understanding of the human mind in general, and therefore our understanding of men as well as women.

In a recent paper I noted converging trends in modern psychoanalytic and intellectual life that have a strong impact on our understanding of male psychology. There I note four areas that comprise the theoretical context for a contemporary reconsideration of the universality of bisexuality:

> The first subject area is the increasing legitimacy in modern psychoanalysis of the view that psychic reality is both our database and bedrock frame of reference. Constructionist, representational theories of psychic reality introduce problems that are mighty. Constructionism also frees us, however, from rigid, categorical, or sexist biological and anatomical conceptual constraints. A second area is our newer notions of how psychic structure evolves. We increasingly measure developmental maturity by assessing the complexity of structural organization and the degree of autonomy and integration, as well as the capacities for dialogue, relationship, and personal responsibility. The emphasis is upon process variables, not on linear-deterministic categories which refer to psychodynamic contents or simplistic historical stepwise phases. A third area is comprised of hermeneutic, linguistic, and feminist studies that establish pre- and protosymbolic language and gender templates—categories for the representation, construction, and reconstruction of gender, sex, and self. The fourth and last subject area is the recent psychoanalytic literature, mostly by women, that argues for a new complexity to our conception of female genital experience and its developmental evolution, and a small but significant literature on the *inner* genital experience of boys. (Fogel, unpublished manuscript, p. 5)

Only the fourth category is, strictly speaking, about (or mostly about) female psychology. But one can easily now see in retrospect that virtually every contributor to the book was working on all four of these frontiers, attempting to take them into account as they showed how they used modern psychoanalytic concepts to better understand their male patients. The problem of finding the place of the "feminine" and giving it full parity on a measure with its ubiquity in higher mental organizations and all human life is being carried on in all four of these important areas. Locating and defining this feminine aspect and its role in all mental life is a major challenge for modern psychoanalysis. In addition to demonstrating the richness and relevance of modern psychoanalytic theory for the understanding of male sexuality, every contributor to this collection, implicitly or explicitly, takes up that challenge.

This book was conceived in the aftermath of a symposium on the psychology of men sponsored by the Association for Psychoanalytic Medicine and the Columbia University Center for Psychoanalytic Training and Research. Although, by design, all three editors contributed equally to the book that was its final outcome, the laws of alphabetization may have given some readers the impression that I was the senior editor. Not so. In fact, the inspiration and much of the original organization of the whole were the work of Robert Liebert, a respected colleague and close friend who has since died. His taste, style, editing skills, and psychoanalytic excellence influenced every aspect of the book. We dedicate this new edition to his memory.

—Gerald I. Fogel

BIBLIOGRAPHY

Fogel, G. Inner genital space in men: What else can be lost in castration. Unpublished manuscript.

Simon, J. 1987. Review of *The psychology of men: New psychoanalytic perspectives. American Journal of Psychiatry*, 144:9, pp. 1226–1227.

CONTRIBUTORS

Arnold M. Cooper, M.D.
*Stephen P. Tobin and Dr. Arnold M. Cooper Professor Emeritus in
Consultation-Liaison Psychiatry, Cornell University Medical College; Editor
for North America,* International Journal of Psychoanalysis; *Training
and Supervising Analyst, Columbia University Center for Psychoanalytic
Training and Research.*

Gerald I. Fogel, M.D.
*Associate Clinical Professor of Psychiatry, College of Physicians and
Surgeons, Columbia University; Training and Supervising Analyst,
Columbia University Center for Psychoanalytic Training and Research.*

Richard A. Isay, M.D.
*Clinical Professor of Psychiatry, Cornell Medical College; Faculty, Columbia
University Center for Psychoanalytic Training and Research.*

Otto F. Kernberg, M.D.
*Director, Personality Disorders Institute, The New York Hospital-Cornell
Medical Center, Westchester Division; Professor of Psychiatry, Cornell
University Medical College; Training and Supervising Analyst, Columbia
University Center for Psychoanalytic Training and Research.*

Frederick M. Lane, M.D.
*Clinical Professor of Psychiatry, College of Physicians and Surgeons,
Columbia University; Associate Director for Student Affairs and Training
and Supervising Analyst, Columbia University Center for Psychoanalytic
Training and Research.*

Robert S. Liebert, M.D. (deceased)
Clinical Professor of Psychiatry, College of Physicians and Surgeons, Columbia University; Training and Supervising Analyst, Columbia University Center for Psychoanalytic Training and Research; Adjunct Professor of Psychiatry, Cornell Medical College.

Eugene J. Mahon, M.D.
Training and Supervising Analyst, Columbia University Center for Psychoanalytic Training and Research; Assistant Clinical Professor of Psychiatry, College of Physicians and Surgeons, Columbia University.

Donald I. Meyers, M.D.
Clinical Professor of Psychiatry, College of Physicians and Surgeons, Columbia University; Training and Supervising Analyst and Co-chair of Child Analysis Program, Columbia University Center for Psychoanalytic Training and Research.

Helen C. Meyers, M.D.
Clinical Professor of Psychiatry, College of Physicians and Surgeons, Columbia University; Training and Supervising Analyst, Columbia University Center for Psychoanalytic Training and Research.

Peter B. Neubauer, M.D.
Clinical Professor of Psychiatry, New York University, Psychoanalytic Institute; Former Director, Child Development Center, New York; Editor, Psychoanalytic Study of the Child.

Ethel S. Person, M.D.
Training and Supervising Analyst, Columbia University Center for Psychoanalytic Training and Research; Professor of Clinical Psychiatry, College of Physicians and Surgeons, Columbia University.

John Munder Ross, Ph.D.
Clinical Professor of Psychology in Psychiatry, Cornell Medical Center, New York; Training and Supervising Analyst, Columbia University Center for Psychoanalytic Training and Research.

Roy Schafer, Ph.D.
Training and Supervising Analyst, Columbia University Center for Psychoanalytic Training and Research.

Arthur H. Schore, M.D.
Clinical Assistant Professor of Psychiatry, New York Hospital-Cornell Medical Center; Training and Supervising Analyst, Columbia University Center for Psychoanalytic Training and Research.

George Stade, Ph.D.
Professor of English and Comparative Literature, Columbia University.

The Psychology of Men

Introduction:

Being a Man

GERALD I. FOGEL

Stand up straight and act like a man. Face it like a man. Have they sent me a boy to do a man's job?

Am I man enough to do the job? Am I man enough for her? If only I felt more like a man.

I expect that such phrases exist abundantly in every language. Most of us react with intuitive understanding and acceptance of them. They serve purposes and carry personal meanings that are important to us and convey these meanings to others who share our assumptions and values. But usually we must not spell out in too much detail the behaviors and characteristics implied in our use of the word "man." This is especially true in recent years, where we have become aware of the use of such phrases in another sense, as sexual stereotypes. We are especially sensitive to stereotypes that dignify or idealize one sex at the expense of the other. It is likely, for example, that I would have offended many readers had I included within my list such equally evocative phrases as: *Stop acting like a girl,* or *Don't be such a sissy,* or even *Why can't you act like a* real *man?* although the spirit of such phrases is often not so far removed from those I chose as some would insist.

So the language of everyday life demonstrates that we all have and have need of strong opinions about whether someone is manly or masculine. We express these opinions, whether we are aware of it or not, when we use these pithy characterizations. We value and evaluate a man's character when we refer to him in these ways. We assess his strengths and limits, virtues and flaws. We examine his moral integrity, accomplishments, sexual desirability, self-control, reliability, courage, his largeness of spirit, and more—indeed, we determine whether he *has* character, and whether or not he is worthy of admiration and emulation, rivalry and envy.

This does not mean, however, that two people making such an assessment of a particular man in a particular instance would necessarily agree. For example, in a recent Norman Mailer novel, *Tough Guys Don't Dance* (1984), the protagonist sees in his own father a mythic male—the toughest, the most street-smart, and the most self-contained. He is given a mythic history and portrayed as able to easily handle any man, woman, or situation, no matter how terrifying, repellent, or bizarre it might appear to us. Many readers might agree, but others would find the father less admirable, less heroic. They might note, for example, that he never kisses a woman, including those he loves or makes love to. This avoidance (not clearly labeled so in the story) is entirely consistent with the counterphobic ethos of heroic masculinity extolled in this book.

That appearances may deceive is equally true, of course, of many of the men who reject such narrow, "macho" ideals. Some of them have been influenced by feminist and other cultural currents in recent years and have cultivated more sensitive, tender, and thoughtful aspects of themselves; they have altered their views about work, competition, aggression, feelings, sexual roles, parenting, and their relationships with both sexes. And many are better men for it. But poet Robert Bly (1982) sees something missing among these improved model males. Many such men, he says, have lost touch with an essential aspect of their deepest nature—a mythic "wildman"—a hairy, archetypal quintessence of something that is definitely not what most of our grandmothers thought of as a nice boy. Bly argues that this fierce, terrible, and awesome primal essence of maleness must be faced, worked with, and integrated for a man to fully realize himself.

I emphasize what most readers already know. Stereotypes can mislead as well as guide. On close inspection, one person's model for everything a man can aspire to be might appear to another as nothing but a shallow parody of a man. Our prototype may be gentle or fierce, tender- or tough-minded. Our ideal psychologically evolved man may be an adventurer in outer space or a voyager in inner space, master of all he surveys or able to yield to and learn from what he cannot be or control. But if we think too simplistically, we may easily err, mistake style for substance, fail to detect a mask or a pose pretending to be the right stuff.

Obviously, a superficial or reductionistic approach to this vast subject of masculinity will not suffice. Psychoanalysts are not immune from the general human tendency to need at times to oversimplify such a difficult and ambiguous subject, and our theoretical models may also be applied stereotypically or become mere stereotypes. But psychoanalysis at its heart rejects such a stance. The purpose of this book is to present the best current psychoanalytic thinking on male psychology. In so doing, not only will major psychological, sociocultural, and scientific assumptions be questioned and issues reappraised from the psychoanalytic point of view, but psychoanalytic theory itself will be reassessed and reformulated to take into account the major advances that have occurred within psychoanalysis and in other major fields of study in recent years.

The controversy, anguish, and doubt that has for many thoughtful persons accompanied the acquisition of new insights and perspectives into female psychology alerts us to the fact that a useful approach to our subject is more than a simple uncovering of new facts, in the ordinary "objective" sense. On the subject of men and women, many passionate voices clamor to have their say, often seeming to be at odds with each other. Conflict exists not only within individuals but also among individuals, the sexes, the generations, and a multiplicity of competing value systems, ideologies, and theoretical systems.

Given this complexity, the psychoanalytic approach can be especially useful. Although psychoanalysis has been attacked for

; volume demonstrates the willingness inherent in
ɔ search out biases as an important aspect of scruti-
ita. Additionally, there is a commitment to not turn
ard truths because they are unpopular or out of favor
ustic or other worthy trends in the scientific or cul-
tu.... unity. The psychoanalytic approach to a patient, to a
theoretical subject, or even to the theories themselves will always
strive to be nonreductionistic. Schafer (1983) and others have
characterized as centrally important the analyst's attitude to his
or her subject of study, never merely the subject matter itself.
There will be a rigorous attempt not to let moral or ideological
judgments intrude; there will be a respectful tolerance for ambiguity and contradiction, and even confusion; there will be a willingness to embrace, respect, and try to integrate multiple perspectives. Thus the psychoanalytic approach is not useful to us here
only because of its familiarity with the subject matter. It is also
temperamentally well suited to the task of taking a close look
while at the same time keeping its head among conflicting
factions.

So there will be few easy answers in this volume. No reader
should be disappointed, however. Our authors use familiar psychoanalytic tools, but they supply information and insights that
are fresh, rich, varied, and often provocative. Some of their
findings and conclusions overlap, some common themes and
trends emerge, and differences also. They reflect upon what men
are, can be, and are commonly afraid to be; they examine fantasies, realities, wishes, fears, conflicts, and defenses—conscious
and unconscious; they describe some of the developmental tasks
and problems common to all men and typical neurotic bargains
by which they attempt to solve them—the measures that men
and societies take to reinforce and protect their often too vulnerable masculinity; they consider the particular dilemmas prevalent
today, a time of changes in sexual standards and models, in psychoanalytic theoretical perspectives, and in the kinds of problems
most psychoanalysts see in their clinical practice.

Freud's view of male sexuality is often summarized in a few
sentences. The recognition of the differences between the sexes
is one of the crucial events that accompanies and influences the

phallic-oedipal phase, which is characterized in the boy by a wish to obtain exclusive sexual possession of the mother by defeating and eliminating the father. Under the threat of castration by his powerful, forbidding rival, the little boy renounces his incestuous infantile claims and solves his dilemma by identifying with his father, who is internalized as the psychic agency of the superego. Castration anxiety and the importance of the relation to the father is central. Successful oedipal resolution correlates with a strong, healthy sexual identity and the consolidation of a more mature, autonomous psychic structure.

It is commonly agreed that there is a phallocentric bias in this model and that this partly reflects a personal and cultural legacy from Freud and his later followers. Freud conceptualized the most fateful problems and important tasks in any individual's psychological destiny from the point of view of a little boy at the phallic and oedipal stages. Human psychology was insufficiently distinguished from male psychology; certain characteristics of male psychology were idealized in comparison to female psychology; female psychology was derived from that of the male.

Stated so succinctly, however, the model may be deprived of its actual richness and complexity. In both his theoretical and clinical studies, Freud places this drama between father and son at a pivot point around which an enormous array of psychic forces and players congregate and interrelate. The complete oedipal complex contains both a positive and a negative complex, both resolved by multiple identificatory processes. Bisexuality, orality, anality, and narcissism inevitably contribute to, shape, and limit the oedipal configuration. The presence of psychic conflict, regression, fixation, compromise formation, and overdetermination reveal that in any particular complex, developmental sequences are condensed and hidden which have to be taken into account. Both constitutional factors and early object relations importantly contribute. The possibilities are numberless. Every oedipal solution is a unique, infinitely complex achievement. The succinct version of male sexuality has the advantage of capturing metaphorically a dramatic and fateful universal moment in every life history, but the disadvantage of representing traditional views in a way to make them appear more reductionistic and stereotyped than they usually are when actually applied in the clinical setting.

Freud's vision was limited, partly by his and his culture's perspectives and values but primarily because knowledge had not yet become available that would later add to, correct, alter, or replace the old. Generations of ego psychologists, object relations theorists, self-psychologists, child observers, and others would follow. Sometimes without being aware of it, the average psychoanalyst using the adjective "oedipal" today usually means something quite different from what an analyst applying the same term fifty years ago meant. The term "triadic" is interchangeable with the term "oedipal" in many contexts. These terms now imply phenomena and concepts that were virtually unexplored in a systematic way in Freud's time. They imply stages in the capacity for object relations and stages on the path to ego autonomy, self-cohesion, separation-individuation, and object constancy. They imply typical constellations of wish and defense, an assessment of the capacity to experience or resolve psychic conflict, stages in the acquisition of psychic structure, types and degrees of stability of various internalization processes, and types and flexibilities of defensive processes. They imply an assessment that takes the multiple relationships among these and other factors into account and tells us something of the way the psyche is organized as a whole—the degree to which certain achievements and integrations have taken place or not.

So in bringing our knowledge of men up to date, all of the studies in this volume will take advantage of the vast amount of new data we have accumulated since Freud's formulations. Much of this data has come by way of observational research and clinical work with children as well as through psychoanalytic studies of the so-called difficult patients—those with prominent preoedipal or narcissistic characterological features. We have also reexamined the subjects of homosexuality and perversion, especially from the point of view of their relations to character structure and character formation in general, and discovered that these studies throw new light on the developmental sequences on the various paths to masculinity in boyhood. We have learned a great deal about such factors as the fateful importance of early object relations, especially the powerful role of the early relationship with the mother in shaping both sexes; the significance of preoedipal stages and conflicts; the stages of separation-individuation, and what threatens these achievements later in development; the importance of the self developmentally and of healthy narcissism in adult life; and of the complex interplay of the preoedipal, narcissistic, and oedipal in shaping adult character. Additionally, we have discovered many new complex variables—biological, intrapsychic, and sociocultural—that influence very early gender identity and behavior, and new data that bears on the subject of the relationship between the separation-individuation process and core gender identity.

Armed with this new data, our authors map out an expanded psychology of men. It is not surprising that so many of them tell us that for most men the problem is women. Masculinity is often defined in relation to and in contrast to women; as boys and men we are dependent upon, threatened by, vulnerable to, and envious of women—in far more conscious and unconscious ways than we can ordinarily bear. Not only must men struggle with the real and fantasy-distorted powers of women as objects, but also with those qualities and impulses within themselves that are perceived as womanly or womanish. Thus men's view of women becomes further twisted and confused. If women are not enough of a problem in their own right, they become so in their assigned role as the bearers or symbolic representatives of various disavowed, warded off, projected, degraded, unacceptable aspects of men.

Add to this potential confusion another factor. There are sexual differences—at least some irreducible anatomical and physiological ones. There is even good scientific evidence that some traits or behaviors traditionally called masculine or feminine are statistically more easily or frequently elicited in one sex than the other, and that biology probably plays some role here (Money 1980). But most of what is called masculine or feminine is common to both sexes and is assigned a more restrictive sexual meaning for various reasons. Thus, "feminine" in our culture often stands for the infantile: for being childish or dependent; for lacking control of appetites or emotions; for irrationality; for incompleteness, emptiness, and longing; for helplessness, passivity, greed, jealousy, and envy. A man's relationship to the primitive and primal —his more archaic longings and fears—are often cunningly condensed and controlled by locating these qualities in women—at least the "lower," demonic, and darker side of them. Thus it is in their relationships to women and in their comparisons of themselves to women that many men commonly play out their struggle to become and to securely feel that they are good and manly men.

Traces of the bias that links the preoedipal and narcissistic to women may be found in the theoretical oversimplification which finds the source of all psychopathology that is preoedipal and narcissistic in the earliest mother-child bond. However, even if the next theoretical corrective leads us to the importance of early fathering, for now few of our authors fail to note the importance of the early relationship with the mother. And most stress the important roles that preoedipal conflict, narcissistic vulnerabilities, and the struggle to attain separation-individuation commonly play in the psychology of men.

Many of them also believe that castration anxiety and the importance of the relation to the father in the resolution of the oedipal conflict commonly either are given too exclusive an emphasis or are too narrowly understood to do justice to the complexity and full range of wishes, fears, developmental levels, and relationships observed in working clinically with men. Many argue that the clinical or theoretical emphasis on the oedipal father and castration anxiety serve the purpose of defending a male-oriented psychology from a multiplicity of additional anxieties, some related to the mother, and often related to earlier or additional stages.

Thus men fear loneliness, abandonment, and death. They long for and envy powerful protectors, female and male, and fear they cannot defend themselves from or satisfy powerful and needed female protectors and validators of their self-esteem. They envy and blindly hate what they cannot be or fully control and further dread the consequences of their inability to control this primitive aggression. Phallic narcissism often defends fears of loss, vulnerability to narcissistic injury, and wishes for and fears of engulfment, merger, devouring, bodily invasion and control, fragmentation and annihilation, and so forth. The list is extensive, and understandably horrifying.

As long as our culture has tended to support the anatomical illusion that men are haves and women are have nots, it has been possible to manipulate psychological configurations to misrepresent the childhood situation as one in which possession of, protection of, envy of, or compensation for the lack of a penis is of exclusive, or even central, concern. However, every child, male and female, grows up in a world dominated by powerful figures of both sexes—loving, hating, fearing, envying—and vulnerable to the strengths and weaknesses, capacities, and limits of both parents or their surrogates.

In these chapters, men are seen to love, envy, fear, and identify with mothers and sisters as well as fathers and brothers. For better or worse, such factors add complexity to their adult personalities and lend a more varied, rich, and flexible range of positive potentialities to them as well as the special vulnerabilities commonly noted. A healthy adult male identity is potentially strengthened and expanded. A boy will still long for and need a strong father for his ideal development and to know and feel pride that he is a man like his male models and peers. But fathers and other models should not need to be constructed along lines dictated by sexually restrictive categorizing.

Our contributors offer us a more complete and less distorted view of male development. To recapitulate, three interrelated and overlapping areas—each with its own special problems—emerge again and again from these chapters. The first area is that occupied by women—a man's relations with women in childhood and adult life. Also importantly involved is his relationship to the woman within—to his own femininity. The liberation and dread of a man's bisexual or androgynous nature is a central focus here. Being a man requires an encounter with the feminine—with women and the woman within.

The second area is that occupied by the primitive or primal—a man's relationship with the more archaic components of his infantile psychosexuality. Most men (and too many psychoanalytic theorists) wish simply to regard these elements of a man's inner or outer world as something beneath him, something less good, to be disavowed, denied, and forgotten, or outgrown and left behind. The liberation and dread of a man's preoedipality and narcissism is in central focus here. Being a man requires an encounter with the primitive.

The third area is that occupied by men and men alone—a man's relationship with the external world, other men, and himself as man, distinct from woman or child. The inevitability and universal importance of the sexual distinction and the distinction between the generations and the necessity for every man to come to terms with these in his own historical time and place are central here, as are his deep needs, wishes, and fears in relation to the archaic father of earliest childhood. Being a man requires an encounter with the masculine.

An immediate need exists for further research into this third area. Earlier I referred to Robert Bly's observation that many modern men need, long for, and fear an encounter with their "wildman," the primal father and the father within. Bly reminds us that in myths, a young man must follow the wildman into the dark woods, outside the safe circle of mother, parents, home, and hearth in a risky search for his manhood, and if he returns, life can never be for him as it was. He draws a modern parallel. A man can learn important things about himself in the lessons of the women's movement, expand his view and deepen his respect for the power of women and the feminine within. He is thereby enriched. But he must finally venture forth with only his "wildman" to guide him. Without mastering the pain, grief, and dangers in this encounter he cannot fully realize his power and creative potential as a man.

By analogy, a psychology of men is enriched and expanded by giving full weight to the importance of women and the feminine. Our revision of female psychology has forced us to begin to fully grasp the importance of these factors in shaping a man's character and his masculinity. But I do not think that a psychology of men can ever entirely dispense with phallocentrism, although to retain (or regain) a central place, no doubt it must be redefined and new forms found that allow for its healthy expression and for its rightful place in a more complete hierarchy of behavioral, emotional, and ideological values. Blos (1984) has written of the im-

portance of the boy's oedipal love for his father and of the hereto-
fore relatively neglected important dyadic father complex—the
earliest relationship between father and son. He urges us to examine the important narcissistic and preoedipal ties that exist in
this relationship, notably the protective and facilitative closeness
that is so significant for the psychic health of males and the
painful, challenging issues that inevitably arise out of this bond
that must be resolved and integrated to achieve full adult manhood. Confusion of the primitive—the early and the deep—with
the feminine may have delayed our discovering the full range of
the archaic forerunners of masculinity and the full significance of
fathers for the psychic health of their sons. Perhaps this is the
direction to look further to discover, or to rediscover, the awesome, wondrous, and terrifying primal male—the masculine
counterpart of the primal mother of the infant-mother dyad.
Otherwise we might fall into the ironic error of deriving male
psychology from the female!

The chapters in this book are a fine beginning. I hope that the
man that emerges from these pages will be both a worthy ally
and, when necessary, a worthy adversary for his female counterpart, and that society will help provide forms which challenge
and provide means of expression for such healthy masculine
aspirations. Men, after all, must aspire to be men, and although
a man may be many different things, being a man, *whatever* that
means, seems always to be of crucial importance.

The Plan of the Book

The book is comprised of four sections. Part I is entitled "What
Men Want—Men View Themselves, Women, and Each Other."
The emphasis here is on delineating the male experience. What
makes a man feel like and act like a man; what goals must he
satisfy, conflicts must he solve, fears and problems must he overcome, ideals must he live up to, and societal tasks must he accomplish? What challenges his masculinity, measures it, contributes

to a false sense of it, or makes him think he lacks it, even when he only imagines he does?

The section opens with George Stade's chapter, "Dracula's Women, and Why Men Love to Hate Them." Stade is our only nonpsychoanalyst author, but do not be fooled by his protestations that he will leave learned explanations to the psychologists. His thesis is that much can be learned about the psychology of men in our culture by looking at the women they create in popular fiction. In his witty and elegantly crafted chapter, he demonstrates much of the ground that will be covered in the book.

Those readers who need to be reminded of what we actually mean by the term "primitive" will have a vicarious experience of thrills and chills as Stade makes us shudder deliciously along with him and clarifies how easily most men confuse the primitive with the feminine. These women—the dark side of the safe and idealized Victorian ladies in the book—represent the unknown, madness, primal lusts, infantile sexuality unbridled, primitive greedy devouring seductive passion unleashed without mercy. The Victorian masculine ideal—reason, self-control, and courageous defender of womanhood's purity—is revealed as a weak match for the unabashedly androgynous Dracula and his bloodthirsty seductresses, just as our beleaguered modern male often feels overmatched by the primitive lusts and aggressive self-interests that lurk beneath the surface of the women in his life and by the bestial impulses, threats, and contradictions that threaten to emerge from his own unconscious mind.

John Munder Ross and Ethel S. Person apply psychoanalytic theoretical conceptual tools to the ground Stade has dramatically mapped. Both speak of the phallocentric bias that has constrained both male psychological development and psychoanalytic theory. Ross's chapter is entitled "Beyond the Phallic Illusion: Notes on Man's Heterosexuality." He asserts that maternalism or femininity is necessary to the identity of the whole man and, further, that "the seemingly contradictory desires to employ one's penis, to be a woman, and to be a babe in arms constitute a paradoxical unity at the hidden core of a boy's and man's heterosexual impulses and identity with regard to them." He reviews the boy's developmental psychosexual stages and demonstrates how phallic narcissistic modes can be a caricature of masculinity, functioning defensively and counterphobically against an ambisexual sexual identity and fears of intimacy, fatherhood, nurturance, empathy, and infantalism.

In her chapter, "The Omni-Available Woman and Lesbian Sex: Two Fantasy Themes and Their Relationship to the Male Developmental Experience," Person examines two common male sexual fantasies and the reasons they have been relatively neglected in the literature. One of her conclusions is that the phallocentric bias of traditional psychoanalytic developmental theory is as wrong for men as we have discovered it to be for women. She argues that the traditional model deemphasizes the mother-son relation at all developmental stages and idealizes the phallic narcissistic solution. In theory as well as in life, the prominent role granted to the powerful oedipal father and castration anxiety denies ubiquitous male fears of genital inadequacy and rejection, the important place of the deeply dreaded and envied powerful woman, and the wish for a feminine identification as common dynamics in male psychology.

In chapter 4, "Men Who Struggle Against Sentimentality," Roy Schafer reports on a complex character trait—sentimentality —and reflects upon the reasons that men (and, increasingly, women also) fear it. Schafer characterizes sentimentality as among those "key words" that are value words for both sexes and that are frequently assigned to one sex or another. These key words and the images in which they are embodied refer to major values and ideals and "transcend easy categorization." The infantile prototypes and unconscious meanings and conflicts assigned to them, however, will be an important part of any analysis.

After reviewing the various ways our culture and our analysands commonly, but unreflectively, overvalue nonsentimentality, Schafer argues that a struggle against sentimentality can be viewed as a struggle against regression and a turning away from what he calls inner reality. Of the many processes and phenomena that may be struggled against, he singles out five: daydreaming, being a baby, identification with one's mother, anality, and latency-age boyishness. He closes with a brief description of a common family constellation especially conducive to the development of antisentimentality and a description of various countertransference attitudes that often emerge in work with such men.

Part II is entitled "What Men Fear: Male Vulnerabilities and Solutions." Of course, one cannot separate the subject of male attitudes, ideals, and aspirations from male fears, vulnerabilities, and adaptive solutions, as part I made clear. But in these chapters the stress falls more heavily on the latter, and several chapters contain detailed clinical examples.

Arnold M. Cooper's chapter, "What Men Fear: The Façade of Castration Anxiety," opens part II. He argues that castration anxiety has a special and central place in male psychology and in psychoanalytic theory, but that today psychoanalysts are alert and attuned to a wide variety of fears—largely preoedipal and narcissistic—while castration anxiety is primarily an oedipal event or a final form of expression of the earlier losses and fears. He offers an exhaustive catalog of the terrors he alludes to: those arising around issues of bodily and narcissistic integrity, separation-individuation, preoedipal aggression, orality, anality, and more. A vivid case example demonstrates how manifest psychological configurations may serve multiple functions and disguise compromise formations in which oedipal, preoedipal, and narcissistic issues are condensed and intricately layered, often in defense of each other. An analyst who focuses too exclusively on the "higher" defensive configurations based on castration anxiety often will miss the more frightening, primitive, and centrally important fears.

Frederick M. Lane agrees with Cooper and, in his chapter, "The Genital Envy Complex: A Case of a Man with a Fantasied Vulva," puts to rest the traditional analytic dogma following Freud that stressed the centrality of castration anxiety in the development of the boy and penis envy for the girl. Lane argues that genital envy is central in all sexual development. We all have a mother and a father, bisexuality, a positive and negative oedipal complex; we all identify with, love, and fear both parents, and the differences between the sexes and the generations will dictate envy as an inevitable current. In his case report, the strengths and aggressivity of the patient's mother powerfully shaped his unconscious aspirations and fears, and his envy of and identification with her emerged in his analysis in a particularly dramatic form: the uncovering of a childhood fantasy that he had a vulva.

Otto F. Kernberg and Robert S. Liebert examine sexual behavior—homosexuality and perversion—that traditional psychoanalytic theory regards as regressive adaptive solutions to sexual conflict. Both chapters widen our views of these subjects by taking into account new data, and both utilize their findings to deepen our understanding of male sexuality in general.

In "A Conceptual Model of Male Perversion," Kernberg demonstrates the crucial functions that polymorphous perverse infantile sexuality plays in normal erotic life. A perversion exists where such behaviors "have a *habitual* and *obligatory* character, which excludes a broad spectrum of behaviors and fantasies characteristic of normal sexuality."

The content of the perversion is an insufficient frame of reference, however. For example, there may be far greater differences between two individuals where one's perversion or homosexuality exists at a neurotic level of personality organization and the other's at a borderline or narcissistic level than between a heterosexual and a homosexual who are both organized at a neurotic level. So the level of personality organization is the important analytic question in terms of analyzability, prognosis, depth and quality of relationships, ego and superego capacities, and so forth. Kernberg reserves the term "perverse structure" for the prognostically more guarded diagnostic categories—those with borderline and narcissistic organizations.

Although he deepens our understanding of the necessary role that perverse and homosexual elements play in healthy adult erotic life and love relations, Kernberg believes that "the boundary between male homosexuality and normal polymorphous perverse sexual trends is sharper than we would expect theoretically." Male homosexuality "presents itself clinically as linked to significant character pathology."

In chapter 8, "The History of Male Homosexuality from Ancient Greece Through the Renaissance: Implications for Psychoanalytic Theory," Liebert takes a different view from Kernberg regarding the possible etiologies and significance of the homosexual "solution" and its relation to male sexuality in general. Using data from a number of recent scholarly historical studies, Liebert argues that any individual's sexuality is a complex outgrowth of biological, social, and intrapsychic forces. In any given culture and historical period, "universal homosexual potential is coded and expressed throughout a range of behavioral enactment, fantasized possibilities, and repressed and unconscious thoughts." These vary greatly according to a particular culture's definitions of deviance, whether it is alleged to be on a moral basis or a psychopathological one. "In any given society, some patterns of resolution of conflict and behavior will be facilitated and others impeded." Liebert advises, therefore, a great deal of caution in presuming what is "normal."

In fact, however, he discovers ambiguity. History does not allow him to conclude that exclusive homosexuality either is or is not "normal." For he finds that an "iron law of history" is that males must conform to male gender roles. Even in those societies, such as ancient Greece and Rome, where homosexual behavior was acceptable, such behavior either was not allowed between dominant males in the society or was ritualized and only one component in a total gender identity and role that included sexual relations with women, marriage, and family. In most cultures exclusive homosexuality has most often been practiced by a disenfranchised group; when such sexual activity has been acceptable behavior by dominant males, it was most often allowed only with a member of the disenfranchised group. Liebert considers some of the reasons why our society has allowed exclusive homosexuality to become more acceptable in recent years and has also granted the heterosexual man an opportunity for a fuller expression of his bisexual potentials.

In part III, "Men Growing Up: Developmental Epochs," the authors of both chapters invite us to reconceptualize the richest phases of psychological growth—early childhood and adolescence—in a way that transcends our familiar developmental and sexual categories.

In chapter 9, "Reciprocal Effects of Fathering on Parent and

Child," Peter B. Neubauer has drawn interesting conclusions by observing fathers who have, in the liberated spirit of the times, become more involved in preoedipal parenting. Their participation allows them a "regression under the auspices of caring," with a resultant opportunity for reworking preoedipal aspirations and conflicts and for ego enhancement and identity enrichment. He also notes that these fathers provide a libidinal, ego-enhancing object for their young children, before aggression and conflicts emerge in the phallic and oedipal stages.

He goes on to challenge aspects of current developmental theory. In particular, he challenges the idea of an orderly sequence from dyadic to triadic. It oversimplifies a complex subject, says Neubauer, to propose that first there is a dyadic phase in which self-object organization and separation-individuation are formulated simply and reductionistically as mother-child interaction experiences, then followed by a triadic phase, in which a three-person relationship becomes possible, which then can include the father. All Mahlerian subphases and transitional objects need to be more widely reformulated, he says, to account for the fact that the preoedipal child has the capacity for early multiple relationships and that such varied good relationships, when they are reliable, tend to enhance, even repair, the primary mother-infant bond rather than dilute it. He suggests that rather than speak of preoedipal triangulation, we might speak of an early capacity for broad multiple object choices that allow for many individual variations, and that these primary object ties, and the envy, rivalry, and longings that accompany them, precede, prepare, and lead into the stage of the oedipal primacy of the parents and its higher level of intrapsychic organization. He also advises us to avoid a theoretical predisposition to lay too great a stress on the mother.

In "The Contribution of Adolescence to Male Psychology," Eugene Mahon argues that both instinct and gender are devoid of chauvinistic distinctions. The biological necessity of sexual differences is transformed and distorted in every boyhood by inevitable instinctual pressures and infantile fantasies into something that is believed to be "a consequence of castration, loss, crime and punishment" and where the relations between the sexes are seen as some version of a dangerously exciting and distorted primal scene. Adolescence, says Mahon, is the place where a young male has his first opportunity to throw aside "the chauvinism that years of latency development seem to demand of him" and attain a level of psychic organization that is the true beginning of maturity. He reviews the work of Erikson, Anna Freud, Blos, and Piaget as well as several literary authors and demonstrates and integrates what we now know of the difficult but essential psychological tasks of adolescence and the developmental tools that become available at that time to cope with them. In the adolescent male's reverential discovery of women and the idea of woman, and in his new capacity to search and find meaning that may transcend self-centeredness, Mahon sees important keys to a capacity for maturation as a man.

In part IV, "Men Seeking Change: Men and Women Treating Men," the focus shifts to the realities and soul-searching of everyday clinical practice. Donald I. Meyers and Arthur H. Schore's chapter, "The Male-Male Analytic Dyad: Combined, Hidden, and Neglected Transference Paradigms," reviews the phallocentric bias of our culture and our theories from the point of view of the possible transference distortions that can be observed when a male analyst works with a male patient.

They observe that the following transference elements are commonly neglected or insufficiently emphasized: the early nurturant and facilitating role of the preoedipal father, the facilitating role of the oedipal father, the early maternal transference, and the impact of early maternal and parental imagos on each other. Working with such early transference elements does not allow stereotypical sharp distinctions, for at such stages, many transferences are composites, derived from stages in development when mother, father, and self are less clearly differentiated.

In chapter 12, "How Do Women Treat Men?" Helen Meyers observes that the sex of the analyst often affects the sequence, intensity, and inescapability of certain transferences, and elucidates the many reasons that might account for her observation that intense oedipal and preoedipal "good" maternal transferences are prominent, more inevitable, and less easy to miss in the analysis of a man by a woman. She believes, however, that countertransference often prevents the full emergence and/or recognition of certain transferences. Commonly, female therapists have trouble experiencing themselves as (in increasing order of difficulty) the "bad" preoedipal mother, the competitive-oedipal father, and the homosexually loved or supportive preoedipal father. She observes that as times change, men seem more able to accept their homosexuality and dependence on women, and these may be used as defenses against other fears.

In the final chapter, "Homosexuality in Homosexual and Heterosexual Men: Some Distinctions and Implications for Treatment," Richard A. Isay distinguishes between two groups of patients. The first are heterosexual men who may use homosexual fantasies and behavior as a defense against conflicts about assertiveness, including heterosexual assertiveness. In contrast, he argues, most homosexual men should not be viewed as defended from "normal" heterosexuality. Their sexual orientation is fixed, probably through some combination of infantile preoedipal origins and constitutional factors. Attempts to change that orientation are misguided and destructive and are usually based on the false preconception that only heterosexuality is normal and on an internalization of the social prejudice against homosexuals. Isay believes that meaningful analytic work—work that includes analysis of the origin of the patient's sexuality and that leads to significant structural change—may be accomplished with homosexual men if the countertransference difficulties in therapeutic work and theory-building can be corrected.

I believe that these chapters are unusually consistent in their high levels of scholarship and readability. Profoundly important and deeply problematic issues are confronted without polemics or simplification. Good psychoanalytic observation and thought is inevitably enriched by and in turn enriches the significant intellectual and sociohistorical currents of its times, and this is true here. Additionally, the scholarship and articulateness of these chapters is rooted in the clinical realities of everyday analytic practice. They are thus grounded in personal experience, and are accessible and direct. Male psychology is a subject ripe for psychoanalytic exploration, and, as I said earlier, this rich and diverse collection is a fine beginning of a dialogue in depth.

BIBLIOGRAPHY

Blos, P. 1984. Son and father. *Journal of the American Psychoanalytic Association* 32:301–324.
Bly, R. 1982. What men really want. *New Age Magazine* (interview) May.
Mailer, N. 1984. *Tough guys don't dance.* New York: Random House.
Money, J. 1980. *Love and love sickness.* Baltimore: Johns Hopkins University Press.
Schafer, R. 1983. *The analytic attitude.* New York: Basic Books.

I

What Men Want:
Men View Themselves,
Women, and Each Other

1

Dracula's Women, and Why Men Love to Hate Them

GEORGE STADE

Introduction

I think I can fairly claim one distinction from the other contributors to this volume. Unlike them, I have no expert knowledge of male psychology—nor do I want any. Expert knowledge has a way of exploding myths, and at this late stage of the game I am in no condition to get by without the *mythos* of masculinity. We men, nowadays, have all the ontological insecurity we can handle. I don't see why we should go around looking for more of it, even for the sake of the truth.

For the sake of the truth, however, I will confess to more anxious reading in the psychology of men than can possibly be good for me. And certainly there must have been a time when I half-consciously studied other males for cues as to how men are supposed to perform. I know for sure that there was a later time when I obsessively read whatever narratives came my way, from the *Iliad* to *The Idiot*, from *Tropic of Cancer* to *Tarzan of the Apes*, for similar cues—and found them, too. For the sake of the truth, I will even confess to thirty-five years of queasy introspection. I am happy to report, however, that all this reading, observation, and introspection has not resulted in anything that you could dignify by the word "knowledge." The sole fruit of my wild-eyed glancing about, a fruit that was already worm-eaten in 3,000 B.C. when the Sumerians pressed their yarns about Gilgamesh into clay, is this sour gripe: when it comes to women, all men are fools.

The father of psychoanalysis, in this respect no different from other men, notoriously asked "What do they want?"—it being understood that (as usual) by "they" we mean women. For our purposes the more appropriate question is "What do we want from them?"—it being understood that (as usual) by "we" we mean men. That question leads inevitably to another, which is "Why do we want it?" Thus we move, question by question, from the psychology of rumor to the psychology of men.

I base this large claim on a suspicion that in the equations of both academic and folk psychology women still occupy the position of an unknown. Any confident assertion about an unknown reflects the speaker more than what he is talking about. Such assertions have the logical force more of exclamations than of testable propositions. For the diagnostician of male psyches, then, women are inkblots, the Rorschachs of everyday life. The maleness of a man, as distinct from his humanity, is never more exposed than in his attitudes toward women. More specifically, what men say about women reveals what ails men (see Wolff 1972). To the practitioners among you I offer free of charge this infallible diagnostic instrument: just ask your male patients what they think about women.

So far I have been pretending to write about life, but that was just to get the ball rolling. From the mere fact that the editors asked me to contribute this chapter I assume that psychoanalysts, too, have had it up to here with life. The equivalent in literature to male discourse about women in life is not what male characters say about women, but how male writers depict them. How male writers depict women exposes what ails the male in a writer, as distinct from his humanity. To pile assumption upon assumption, as you might pile ice cube upon ice cube in a 500-degree oven, I assume that any literary work written by a male, of enduring interest to male readers, and in which women are lovingly or loathingly lingered over, will expose what ails men in general.

For evidence and instance I might have chosen many works, from the *Odyssey,* in which dangerous and nubile mother-goddesses preside, to *Ulysses,* in which before going to bed Leopold Bloom worries over the problem of "what to do with our wives"and then gives it up as unsolvable. But I wanted a work that (1) readers have long chosen to read for fun, rather than because it was alleged to be improving or assigned in a course; (2) was naive rather than sophisticated, its symptoms neither undercut by irony nor displaced by self-consciousness; (3) was modern, just in case it is really true that human nature changes; but (4) was pre-Freudian, to avoid putting myself in the position of the man who tried to hold himself at arms' length by his own hair; (5) appealed neither to the specific prejudices of highbrows or lowbrows, but to the prejudices they have in common; (6) subjected stock female characters to extreme situations, because stock female characters are refractions of a group's professed ideal woman, whereas extreme situations reveal what we would really like to do to her; and (7) was polymorphously sexy, because that's wherein lies the fun—and because to talk about what ails men without mentioning their baffled and raging lusts is like talking about the last days of Pompeii without mentioning the volcano.

Dracula

The book that most conveniently fits my case is Bram Stoker's *Dracula.* Unlike many greater works, it has never been out of print, although it was published way back in the dark ages, in 1897. Its avid readers have ranged from people like T.S. Eliot and Dylan Thomas to the kind of guy you couldn't flog into reading more than one book every other year. The British stage version of 1923 broke record after record for performances, attendance, and take. So did the American stage version of 1927 (Ludlum 1962). During these performances, according to an actor of the time, it was mostly men who fainted. Nurses and ambulances attended every performance to cart them away. The film version of 1931 bailed out a sinking Universal Studios (McNally and Florescu 1982). The one hundred or so other *Dracula*-derived movies puffed the sales of lesser craft; there are as many *Dracula*-derived novels. And *The Night Stalker,* in which an immigrant Dracula romps through Las Vegas, was, last time I looked, the most popular made-for-TV movie ever shown. Dracula, along with his near contemporaries Sherlock Holmes, Wister's Virginian, and Tarzan, was invented by an individual but co-opted by the group mind. If figures like this can be taken, at least half-seriously, as aspects of a single personality, Dracula's position among them is that of a repressed wish.

And just as we can study the unconscious only through its effects, so the shaky focus of Stoker's novel is not on the vampire, but on his victims. These are all women, except for Renfield, who is a madman; but his madness, in this novel's system of equivalences, makes him very like a woman. What Dracula does to and for women we never see directly; the novel has no omniscient narrator; its action comes to us through letters, diaries, newspaper clippings, a ship's log, bills of lading, and other such documents, only one of which describes (in an emotional haze) an attack by Dracula on one of his victims. He casts no shadow because he is one, a darkness round the periphery of the mind's inner eye. He is at best a reflection, not in mirrors but in the reactions to him of the other characters. We can sum it up by saying that women react to him by becoming sexy; men, by going or getting mad. Our first job is to put together what we know of Dracula's attributes; these ought to tell us what it is about him that appeals to women.

Dracula's Women, and Why Men Love to Hate Them

Dracula's Traits

Dracula's attributes, as we fit together the scattered bits and pieces, amount to those of a negative Eros, not the plump, dimpled, and cuddly babe of love, but an ancient, lean, mean demon of lust made kinky by repression. He is rank of breath, hairy of palm, livid of lip, and anemic, all of which, according to cautionary old wives' tales, are what you get and deserve for self-abuse and sexual excess. His brows meet over his nose; his teeth are sharp, his ears pointed—all signs of his animal nature. He has a "grip of steel," which means that once he gets a hold on you, he doesn't let go. On the other hand, he does not embrace you without an invitation: he will not cross your threshold or sill unless you ask him in. When early in the novel Jonathan Harker visits Dracula's castle, he is at first left standing outside the door. The count, from inside, greets him like this:

> "Welcome to my house! Enter freely and of your own will!" He made no motion of stepping to meet me, but stood like a statue, as though his gesture of welcome had fixed him into stone. The instant, however, that I had stepped over the threshold, he moved impulsively forward, and holding out his hand grasped mine with a strength which made me wince. . . . (P. 16)

Once you have entered his house or he has entered yours, he will hypnotize you. Under his penetrating glare you will become passive, submissive, or, as we used to say, feminine; your will and intelligence, all your inhibitory faculties, become subservient to what they normally inhibit. "I know that when the Count wills me I must go," says Mina Harker after Dracula has had his way with her. "I know that if he tells me to come in secret, I must come by wile; by any device to hoodwink—even Jonathan," who is her husband. Mina sounds like a philandering wife, but Jonathan ought to be understanding. He had nearly come under Dracula's spell himself. Renfield, who succumbs entirely, explains how it feels: "His eyes, they burned into me and my strength became like water." Dracula has the evil eye—which means that his gaze is a projection of your guilt; you see him seeing in you what you have tried to hide from yourself.

Most often he visits his victims when they are asleep, when hypnosis would be redundant, for to sleep is to dream, and to dream is to become passive before those fantasies we normally inhibit. Dracula's victims, when they awake, remember him, if at all, as a dream of suffocation and blood. After he has visited her a few times, Lucy Westenra, for example, begins to think of sleep, in her words, as "a presage of horror." "What do you mean?" asks her doctor. "I don't know," she answers; "oh, I don't know. And that is what is so terrible. All this weakness comes to me in sleep; until I dread the very thought." But after a while her dread turns to something else, and she sleeps as much as her interfering friends will allow. Though finally on her deathbed, Dr. Van Helsing tries to keep her awake: "It will be much difference [*sic*], mark me, whether she dies conscious or in sleep"—for if she dies in her sleep, she will awake as a vampire; if she dies conscious, she will simply die. Much later, Mina Harker, after a few nocturnal visits from Dracula ("tainted as she is with that vampire baptism"), keeps in touch with him telepathically while she sleeps. To find out where he is, Dr. Van Helsing, Dracula's opposite and opponent and alter ego, puts her into a hypnotic trance. "Where are you?" he asks. "Sleep has no place it can call its own," she answers, thus letting in the chill of interstellar space.

The night, starlit or moonlit, is a chiller in itself, and not just because that is when we sleep and dream. "No man knows till he suffers from the night how sweet and how dear to his heart and his eye the morning can be," writes Jonathan Harker in his diary. One of Dracula's many advantages over us is his ability to see in the dark, his native element. "I love the shade and the shadow," he says. Dr. Van Helsing provides a partial explanation: "His power ceases, as does that of all evil things, at the coming of the day." But during the night he can materialize out of mists, dust motes, and moonbeams, things there and not there, but there enough to prod an agitated imagination into connecting the dots. And at night he can transform himself into a wolf or a bat; he can call up or command legions of animals such as these, animals that

Dracula's Women, and Why Men Love to Hate Them

fit Freud's definition of the uncanny, animals that are nocturnal, familiar, and alien. A wolf is an uncanny dog; a bat is an uncanny bird; a rat is domestic and wild, *heimlich* and *unheimlich*. Dracula's bite is equally uncanny. Although his canines are wolfish, the holes he leaves in Lucy's neck look to Mina "like pin-pricks," as though made by the pin of a brooch pushed accidentally through a tiny fold of skin. Dracula's bite, in short, is that of a serpent, author of all our woes.

Like Satan, Dracula is a dark parody of Christ, whom he quotes: "The blood is the life!" he says, reminding us that he, too, participates in a kind of Eucharist—for Dracula not only drinks his victim's blood, but he also makes Mina, at least, drink some of his, from a vein he opens in his breast. And as Dracula recapitulates Satan, so do his victims recapitulate Eve. Late in the novel, after Jonathan Harker discovers that Dracula has begun to visit his wife, Mina, he comes to a resolution:

> To one thing I have made up my mind: if we find out that Mina must be a vampire in the end, then she shall not go into that unknown and terrible land alone. I suppose it is thus that in old times one vampire meant many; just as their hideous bodies could only rest in sacred earth, so the holiest love was the recruiting sergeant for their ghastly ranks. (Pp. 314–315)

If Mina is going to play Eve, he will play Adam as, bite for bite, the repressed slowly returns.

In Harker's mention of sacred earth there is even a sign of some dim awareness on Stoker's part (and their names rhyme for a reason) that puritanical Christianity produces prurient fantasies, of which Dracula is an instance. In the movies, Dracula must sleep in his own coffin; in the novel, it is enough that he sleep in consecrated ground. "This evil thing," says Van Helsing, "is rooted deep in all good; in soil barren of holy memories it cannot rest." When Dracula travels from Transylvania to London, he brings with him fifty crates of consecrated earth, to make sure he isn't caught short. Van Helsing and his comrades render these coffin-crates, one by one, unfit for Dracula's repose through a kind of homeopathic magic, by sprinkling them with holy water and bits of consecrated wafer. Van Helsing's explanation is not impressive for its logic:

> And now, my friends, we have a duty here to do. We must sterilise this earth, so sacred of holy memories, that he has brought from a far distant land for such fell use. He has chosen this earth because it has been holy. Thus we defeat him with his own weapon, for we make it more holy still. It was sanctified to such use of man, now we sanctify it to God. (P. 315)

Dracula and Madness

I must outline one more of Dracula's attributes, one that explains why women can't resist him. That attribute is Dracula's multiplex relation to madness, especially in men. Nearly all the male characters, as they watch Dracula's effect on women, wonder whether they are going or have gone mad. Jonathan Harker actually comes down with brain fever and has to do time in an asylum. Dr. Seward has to take chloral hydrate to sleep: "I sometimes think we must all be mad and that we shall wake to sanity in straitjackets," he says. Even the stalwart Van Helsing gives way to what Dr. Seward calls "a regular fit of hysterics," during which he "laughed and cried together, just as a woman does," babbling all the while how he and his three male comrades are all Lucy's husbands because they have given her transfusions of blood and how "this so sweet maid is a polyandrist," thus implying what we had already guessed, that the exchange of blood is a metaphor for sexual intercourse.

When Dracula comes to England he selects for his first base of operations the grave of a young man who killed himself to spite his mother. A local gaffer tells Lucy and Mina the story:

> He hated her so that he committed suicide in order that she mightn't get an insurance she put on his life. He blew nigh the top of his head off with an old musket that they had for scarin' the crows with.

Dracula's Women, and Why Men Love to Hate Them

> ... I've often heard him say masel' that he hoped he'd go to hell, for his mother was so pious that she'd be sure to go to heaven, an' he didn't want to addle where she was. (P. 71)

The grave of this young mother-hater (to whom Stoker has given a number of his own feelings)[1] looks over the harbor; Lucy and Mina often sit on a slab that covers it for the breeze and the view. That's how Dracula gets his teeth into Lucy. One night, under his influence, she sleepwalks to the grave, where Dracula is waiting for her. Her habit of sleepwalking is given in the novel as evidence of her lack of character and will. ("Lucy is so sweet and sensitive that she feels influence more acutely than other people do.") It is also evidence of an impulse she doesn't know she has.

But the novel's prize madman is of course Renfield, an inmate in Dr. Seward's asylum, located next door to Dracula's main London address. According to Dr. Seward's unconventional diagnosis, Renfield is "a zoöphagus (life-eating) maniac; what he desires is to absorb as many lives as he can." He first spreads sugar on the windowsill of his cell to attract flies, which he eats. He then feeds his flies to spiders, a more concentrated form of nourishment, in that they each contain the lives of numerous flies. From spiders he advances to sparrows. But Dr. Seward, unlike our more advanced medical experimenters, knows when to stop: he turns down Renfield's wheedling request for a pet cat. Like Mina later on, Renfield is in telepathic communication with Dracula; he sees his "Master" in visions and knows what he wants. He opens his window sash a crack so that Dracula can pour in, solidify, and find his way to Mina, who with her husband is visiting Dr. Seward. Thus in each case Dracula gains access to his two female victims through the intermediary of a madman.

The nature of Dracula's affinity for madness is explained in a impromptu lecture that Van Helsing bestows on Mina and Dr. Seward (and here his accent, which is supposed to be Dutch, becomes a trial):

1. "Central to the structure and unconscious theme of *Dracula* is, then, primarily, the desire to destroy the threatening mother, she who threatens by being desirable." So argues Roth (1982, p. 123). See also Farson (1975, chap. 19, "The Sexual Impulse") for Stoker's relation to his wife.

33

To begin, have you ever study the philosophy of crime? "Yes" and "No." You, John [Seward], yes; for it is a study of insanity. You, no, Madame Mina; for crime touch you not—not but once [when Dracula attacked her]. . . . The criminal has not full man-brain. He is clever and cunning and resourceful; but he be not of man-stature as to brain. He be of child-brain in much. Now this criminal of ours is predestinate to crime also; he, too, have child-brain, and it is of the child to do what he have done. . . . (Pp. 360–361)

This passage, and others like it, sets up a series of equivalences: to be insane is to be criminal is to be childlike is to be a monster of appetite is to be piggy about sex is to have an undeveloped brain.

In setting up these equivalences, the distinguished Dr. Van Helsing is not shooting from the hip: he is internationally renowned for having "revolutionized therapeutics by his discovery of the continuous evolution of brain-matter." He is qualified, therefore, to recognize in Dracula the paradox of the primitive: Dracula is both older and younger than we are, younger because older, a centuries-old case of arrested development, of incomplete moral evolution, victim of a culturally undernourished environment, namely Transylvania, where nothing is up to date. He is where we once were, but he has come to London expressly to feed his brain, to grow up: "With the child-brain that was to him he have long since conceive the idea of coming to a great city. What does he do? He find out the place of all the world most of promise for him. . . . It help him to grow as to his brain. . . . What more may he not do when the greater world of thought is open to him."

He will then be pretty near invincible, although he is hard to resist as it is. We are susceptible to him because he is already in us, which is why, as Dr. Van Helsing puts it, "all men are mad in some way or the other." In the continuous evolution of brain-matter, that is, nothing is discarded. The old is merely overlaid with the new, one function of which is to keep the old in its place. The primitive brain that makes Dracula what he is lies dormant even in cultured British gentlemen, but in them it is entombed in an overlay of new brain-matter generated by progressive Victorian culture. The overlay manifests itself as a kind of self-control or self-denial, a resistance to temptation, what in the novel is called "bravery." It is what distinguishes Victorian gentlemen from Victorian ladies, in whom the overlay is thin.

Dracula's Women

Women are so much more susceptible to Dracula because very little stands between them. Their beauty is skin deep: right beneath it, they are crazy, criminal, selfish, and sexy, half-evolved monsters of appetite. Dracula merely releases something in them that is already raging to get out—and they know it. "Why are men so noble," Lucy writes to Mina, "when we women are so little worthy of them?" And women fear what they know about themselves—which fear sends good women looking for husbands. "I suppose we women are such cowards," Lucy writes, "that we think a man will save us from our fears, and we marry him." A woman needs a husband to keep her in line; she has nothing in her of her own with which to resist Dracula. And to be bitten by Dracula is to become abandoned to lust, a kind of moral rabies. And that is what it is about Dracula that appeals to women.

Take the three lovelies Jonathan Harker meets early in the novel. He has come to Dracula's castle on business. Soon he finds himself a prisoner, of whom or what he can't quite figure out. One night, looking for a means of escape, he wanders into a ladies' boudoir, "where in old times possibly some fair lady sat to pen, with much thought and many blushes, her ill-spelt love-letter." He decides to sleep there, rather than in his own spartan chamber. He dozes off on a couch, then awakes to find that he is not alone. Under his lashes he sees three beautiful young ladies, two dark, with aquiline noses and red eyes. "The other was fair, as fair as can be, with great wavy masses of golden hair and eyes like pale sapphires. I seemed somehow to know her face, and to know it in connection with some dreamy fear, but I could not recollect at the moment how or where." The women have prominent teeth and "voluptuous lips." "I felt in my heart a wicked,

35

burning desire that they would kiss me with those red lips," Harker confesses. The women seem ready to oblige. "Go on! You are first, and we shall follow," says one of the brunettes. "He is young and strong; there are kisses for us all," answers the blonde. Here's what happens next:

> I lay quiet, looking out under my eyelashes in an agony of delightful anticipation. The fair girl advanced and bent over me till I could feel the movement of her breath upon me. Sweet it was in one sense, honey-sweet, and sent the same tingling through the nerves as her voice, but with a bitter underlying the sweet, a bitter offensiveness, as one smells in blood.
>
> I was afraid to raise my eyelids, but looked out and saw perfectly under the lashes. The girl went on her knees, and bent over me, simply gloating. There was a deliberate voluptuousness which was both thrilling and repulsive, and as she arched her neck she actually licked her lips like an animal, till I could see in the moonlight the moisture shining on the scarlet lips and on the red tongue as it lapped the white sharp teeth. Lower and lower went her head as the lips went below the range of my mouth and chin and seemed about to fasten on my throat. Then she paused, and I could hear the churning sound of her tongue as it licked her teeth and lips, and could feel the hot breath on my neck. Then the skin of my throat began to tingle as one's flesh does when the hand that is to tickle it approaches nearer —nearer. I could feel the soft, shivering touch of the lips on the super-sensitive skin of my throat, and the hard dents of two sharp teeth, just touching and pausing there. I closed my eyes in a languorous ecstasy and waited—waited with beating heart.
>
> But at that instant, another sensation swept through me as quick as lightning. I was conscious of the presence of the Count and of his being as if lapped in a storm of fury. (Pp. 39–40)

In a tremendous rage, the count hurls the fair lady behind him. "How dare you?" he says; "this man belongs to me." But "with a laugh of ribald coquetry," she sasses him back: "You yourself never loved; you never love!" They both know better: "Yes, I too can love; you yourselves can tell it from the past. Is it not so?" In a conciliatory spirit he promises the women that when he finishes his business with Harker, they can kiss him at will. Meanwhile he throws them a bone, or rather a sack containing a child he kidnapped from a nearby village. Writing in his diary the next morning, Harker notes "that of all the foul things that lurk in this hateful place the Count is the least dreadful to me; that to him alone I can look for safety." In general, "nothing can be more dreadful than those awful women," but just the same, they make him think of his angelic fiancé, later his wife: "I am alone in the castle with those awful women. Faugh! Mina is a woman, and there is nought in common. They are devils of the pit." At this point we might allow ourselves the venerable psychoanalytic stunt of reading denial as affirmation; certainly later events would bear us out.

There is much to mull over in this episode, in particular the equal and opposite emotions of attraction and revulsion, one revolving around the other; the familiar look of the blonde; and the implication that you have to be strong to hold up to a kiss, that for a woman to kiss a man is to drain his strength, although the blonde seems to be getting herself ready more for one of the common oral perversions than for a kiss. But what in retrospect seems most curious is that Stoker never allows us to enjoy through Harker the dangerous caresses of these femmes fatales. Perhaps the idea was too horrible to contemplate. In any case, such scenes of interruptus must have occupied a good portion of Stoker's fantasy life, for they occur throughout the novel.

Lucy, for example, a few minutes before she is to expire (for the first time), lies in a coma watched over by Dr. Van Helsing, Dr. Seward, and her fiancé, Arthur Holmwood. Then suddenly she awakes:

> Her breathing grew stertorous, the mouth opened, and the pale gums, drawn back, made the teeth look longer and sharper than ever. In a sort of sleep-waking, vague, unconscious way she opened her eyes, which were now dull and hard at once, and said in a soft, voluptuous voice, such as I had never heard from her lips:—
> "Arthur! Oh, my love, I am so glad you have come! Kiss me!" Arthur bent eagerly over to kiss her; but at that instant Van Helsing . . . swooped upon him, and catching him by the neck with both hands, dragged him back with a fury of strength which I never thought he could have possessed, and actually hurled him almost across the room.

"Not for your life!" he said; "not for your living soul and hers!"
And he stood between them like a lion at bay. (Pp. 168–169)

The scenes are structurally akin, but in the second Van Helsing, rather than Dracula, does the interrupting. The two men, after all, have a lot in common: both are old, both foreigners who speak with an accent, and both sum up the advanced thinking of their respective times. Van Helsing, what is more, owes his life to benevolent vampirism—to the sucking (by Dr. Seward) of infected blood from his hand. Like Dracula, he lets out a sharp hiss when startled; his busy eyebrows, like Dracula's, meet over his nose. Van Helsing is to Dracula as Victor Frankenstein is to his monster, as Holmes is to Moriarty, as Dr. Jekyll is to Mr. Hyde, as Freud's ego is to his id. "Oh, unconscious cerebration," exclaims Dr. Seward, who is Van Helsing's pupil, "you will have to give the wall to your conscious brother"—which amounts to saying where id was, there let ego be. I conclude from all this that as women need husbands to save them from Dracula or themselves, so men need a partriarch, whether in his aspect of good father or bad, to save them from women. Van Helsing, by the way, shares his first name, Abraham, with Stoker and with Stoker's father, a retiring man who failed to protect his son from his much younger and aggressive wife, a feminist with a vengeance and a good friend of Lady Wilde, Oscar's mother.

We meet Harker's three would-be paramours only once more, at the very end of the novel, when Dracula is already cornered. Van Helsing is looking for their crypts, so that he can cut off their heads and transfix them with stakes, thus forever ridding the world of their menace. But as he lingers over his task, he pins their menace on their charms:

She lay in her Vampire sleep, so full of life and voluptuous beauty that I shudder as though I have come to do murder. Ah, I doubt not that in old time, when such things were, many a man who set forth to do such a task as mine, found at the last his heart fail him, and then his nerve. So he delay, and delay, and delay, till the mere beauty and the fascination of the wanton Un-Dead have hypnotise him; and he remain on and on, till sunset come, and the Vampire sleep be over.

Then the beautiful eyes of the fair women open and look love, and the voluptuous mouth present to a kiss—and man is weak. . . .

. . . Yes, I was moved—I, Van Helsing, with all my purpose and with my motive for hate—I was moved to a yearning for delay which seemed to paralyze my faculties and to clog my very soul. . . .

. . . She was so fair to look on, so radiantly beautiful, so exquisitely voluptuous, that the very instinct of man in me, which calls some of my sex to love and to protect one of hers, made my head whirl with new emotion. (Pp. 391–392)

But a despairing and distant wail from Mina breaks Van Helsing's spell. He steels himself to "the horrid screeching as the stake drove home; the plunging of writhing form, and lips of bloody foam," until his work is finished. Well, vampires are "undead" in the first place because the wages of sin is death. The vampire women are killed doubly dead for the same reason. The sin, in this case, is female sexuality. What is sinful about it is that it arouses men, who are weak. Why men should not be aroused, Stoker doesn't say, but one can guess.

The Light of the West

These notions are easier to laugh at—in a nervous sort of way—when abstracted from the novel's events than when left latent in them. Stoker's terrific sincerity is the very opposite of camp. Especially the novel's main event, Lucy's transformation, which is stretched as on a rack over two hundred pages, pulls you in by the lapels. Her full name is Lucy Westenra, which, as a number of critics have remarked, means roughly "Light of the West"; her decline into vampirism has about it the atmosphere of a world-historical catastrophe. Certainly she has the qualities of a daydream we can document in the writings of Western males straight back to Chaucer, at least. She is very fair, so gorgeous that three well-set-up males propose to her in a single day. She is virginal, innocent, inexperienced, sweet, defenseless, a damsel in distress, a stimulus to fantasies of sexual assault. And she has all the right attitudes: she regularly makes invidious comparisons between the sexes in favor of the male's greater nobility, bravery, generosity, fair-mindedness, competence, good sense, steadfastness of purpose, self-control, and all-around virtuousness. She has nothing but scorn for the "New Woman," the feminists of her day.

But this paragon, as she sleepwalks out to Dracula and thereafter night after night opens her window to him, proves that after all she is only a woman. One good effect of Lucy's assignations with Dracula is that it brings together the novel's main male characters, whose bonds of friendship to each other are made of better stuff than the love of a woman. When her fiancé, Arthur Holmwood, later Lord Godalming (a good name for a would-be savior), becomes alarmed over her lethargy and anemia, he calls in his friend, Dr. Seward, one of Lucy's former suitors. Dr. Seward brings with him Quincey Morris, an outdoorsy but housebroken American, Lucy's third suitor. Stumped by Lucy's symptoms, Dr. Seward then calls in his old teacher, Dr. Van Helsing, for a consultation. Now that the patriarch is in place, this primal horde comes close to saving Lucy from herself, from her openness to Dracula. Their treatment, in the main, is to make Lucy eat a lot, to decorate her person and her bedchamber with the symbols of Christianity and with garlic plants, and, above all, to give her transfusions of blood. "A brave man's blood is the best thing on this earth when a woman is in trouble," says Van Helsing to Quincey Morris. "You're a man and no mistake. Well, the devil may work against us for all he's worth, but God sends us men when we want them."

That's what Lucy thinks, too. Flustered at having to turn down two of her three suitors, Lucy had prettily asked "Why can't they let a girl marry three men, or as many as want her, and save all this trouble?" She gets her wish, metaphorically speaking, as the men empty their vital fluid into her. Each time, the transfusion restores Lucy's rosy cheeks, but leaves the donor pale and limp. "No man knows, till he experiences it, what it is to feel his own life-blood drawn into the veins of the woman he loves," says Dr. Seward, with a sigh. And each time the sacrifices of the men are negated by women, as Lucy, her mother, or maidservants remove those smelly garlic plants or crucifixes, or sleep on the job of lookout while the depleted men try to revivify themselves with sleep, Death's brother. As Lucy inexorably sinks, all the parental figures die off—Lucy's mother, Arthur's father, Harker's foster father, even Gerald Swales, one hundred years old, who had taken Lucy and Mina under his wing. (Lucy had been fatherless and Mina had been motherless and fatherless to begin with.) Parental authority out of the way, Lucy dies into undeath.

Soon there are newspaper stories of a "Bloofer Lady," or beautiful lady, who kidnaps children and then leaves them where patrolling Bobbies find them dazed, weak, and with pinpricks on their necks. Dr. Van Helsing knows what is happening, but his comrades refuse to believe him. One night, at the stroke of twelve, he leads them to Lucy's grave, so that they can see for themselves.

Here, in Dr. Seward's words, is what they see:

a dark-haired woman, dressed in the cerements of the grave. We could not see the face, for it was bent down over what we saw to be a fair-haired child. There was a pause and a sharp little cry, such as a child gives in sleep. . . . My own heart grew cold as ice, and I could hear the gasp of Arthur, as we recognized the features of Lucy Westenra, but yet how changed. The sweetness was turned to admantine, heartless cruelty, and the purity to voluptuous wantonness. . . . We could see that the lips were crimson with fresh blood, and that the stream had trickled over her chin and stained the purity of her lawn death-robe.

When Lucy—I call the thing that was before us Lucy because it bore her shape—saw us she drew back with an angry snarl, such as a cat gives when taken unawares; then her eyes ranged over us. Lucy's eyes in form and colour; but Lucy's eyes unclean and full of hell-fire, instead of the pure, gentle orbs we knew. At that moment the remnant of my love passed into hate and loathing; had she then to be killed, I could have done it with savage delight. As she looked, her eyes blazed with unholy light, and the face became wreathed with a voluptuous smile. Oh, God, how it made me shudder to see it! With a careless motion, she flung to the ground, callous as a devil, the child that up to now she had clutched strenuously to her breast, growling over it as a dog growls over a bone. The child gave a sharp cry, and lay there moaning. There was a cold-bloodness in the act which wrung a groan from Arthur; when she advanced to him with outstretched arms and a wanton smile he fell back and hid his face in his hands.

She still advanced, however, and with a languorous, voluptuous grace, said:—

"Come to me, Arthur. Leave these others and come to me. My arms are hungry for you. Come, and we can rest together. Come, my husband, come!"

There was something diabolically sweet in her tones—something of the tingling of glass when struck—which rang through the brains even of us who heard the words addressed to another. As for Arthur, he seemed under a spell; moving his hands from his face, he opened wide his arms. She was leaping for them, when Van Helsing sprang forward and held between them his little golden crucifix. She recoiled from it, and, with a suddenly distorted face, full of rage, dashed past him as if to enter the tomb. . . .

Never did I see such baffled malice on a face; and never, I trust, shall such ever be seen again by mortal eyes. The beautiful colour became livid, the eyes seemed to throw out sparks of hell-fire, the brows were wrinkled as though the folds of the flesh were the coils of Medusa's snakes, and the lovely, blood-stained mouth grew to an open square, as in the passion masks of the Greeks and Japanese. If ever a face meant death—if looks could kill—we saw it at that moment. (Pp. 222–223).

Lucy's sweetness turns into heartless cruelty, her purity into voluptuous wantonness, her gentle orbs into unclean hell-fire, her beautiful color into a livid flush. And because of these changes, Dr. Seward's love turns into hate and loathing. "Had she then to be killed," he says, "I could have done it with savage delight." The single catalyst for these transformations is the element of sex. All that has been perceptibly added to Lucy is sexuality. "Come, my husband, come!" she says, like many an exasperated wife before her. But before Arthur can come, Van Helsing intervenes, as he had intervened once before, as Dracula had intervened between Jonathan Harker and the vampire ladies. And as though she were not already hateful enough, Lucy "with a careless motion" flings the child from her breast, where instead of nursing it, she had been feeding on it. An aroused female sexuality, that is, does not nurture children and husbands; it drains them dry and tosses them aside. Female sexuality is insatiable and selfish, indifferent to the decent self-restraint, the self-sacrifice and suppression of appetite upon which survival of the family depends. It is the very antithesis of Motherhood. Thus the Light of the West goes out. No wonder the men agree that the next day at noon they will put stop to the nonsense once and for all.

As they look down into Lucy's coffin, any qualms they may have felt are quenched by her debauched aspect, by "the blood-stained, voluptuous mouth—which it made one shudder to see—the whole carnal and unspiritual appearance, seeming like a devilish mockery of Lucy's sweet purity." As Lucy's fiancé, Arthur has best claim to do the honors—"the work of her destruction was yielded as a privilege to the one best entitled to it." He places the point of a sharpened stake over her heart, so that you can "see its dint in the white flesh," while Van Helsing reads a prayer for the dead. "Then he struck with all his might," and Dr. Seward's choice of words makes us see an even more primal scene behind the one he describes:

> The Thing in the coffin writhed; and a hideous, bloodcurdling screech came from the opened red lips. The body shook and quivered and twisted in wild contortions; the sharp white teeth champed together till the lips were cut, and the mouth was smeared with a crimson foam. But Arthur never faltered. He looked like a figure of Thor as his untrembling arm rose and fell, driving deeper and deeper the mercy-bearing stake, whilst the blood from the pierced heart welled and spurted up around it. His face was set, and high duty seemed to shine through it; the sight of it gave us courage so that our voices seemed to ring through the little vault.
>
> And then the writhing and quivering of the body became less, and the teeth seemed to champ, and the face to quiver. Finally it lay still. The terrible task was over.
>
> The hammer fell from Arthur's hand. He reeled and would have fallen had we not caught him. The great drops of sweat sprang from his forehead, and his breath came in broken gasps. It had indeed been an awful strain on him. . . . (Pp. 227–228)

The sympathy, which has a narcissistic ring to it, is all for poor Arthur, maybe because Lucy seems to be having the best orgasm in recorded history. Either way you look at Arthur's mercy-bearing stake, Lucy is the sole beneficiary, either of a saved soul or a satiated body. No doubt that is why high duty shone on Arthur's face—which only shows how easy it is to do one thing while your mind is on another, a slight of mind not restricted to bedrooms of the Victorian era. That high duty, we gather, is to give Lucy in spades the punishment she was asking for, but the trick lies in not letting yourself know that you enjoy doing it. The knowledge would cancel out the enjoyment. One therefore does one's duty, but the strain is awful.

That Stoker is not the only one who felt this strain we can tell from a medical text first published in 1857 and then regularly brought out in new editions, translations, and reprints until 1894, around when Stoker began to write *Dracula*. This text is evidence that the fears behind Dr. Seward's hate and Arthur's retribution had their public and scientific equivalents. The author of the text was William Acton, a reform-minded doctor known for his enlightened views on the problem of prostitution. The full title of his book is *The Function and Disorders of the Reproductive Organs, in Childhood, Youth, Adult Age, and Advanced Life, Considered in their Physiological, Social, and Moral Relations.* That seems to say it all, but the book has important omissions: only two very brief passages mention women at all, as though they had no reproductive organs worth mentioning. The longer of these passages reveals why Acton was anxious to keep these organs out of sight and out of mind. Here is how he reassures young men hesitating on the brink of marriage for fear that their bedroom duties will be too much for them[2]:

> I should say that the majority of women (happily for them) are not very much troubled with sexual feeling of any kind. What men are habitually, women are only exceptionally. It is too true, I admit, as the divorce courts show, that there are some few women who have sexual desires so strong that they surpass those of men. . . . I admit, of course, the existence of sexual excitement terminating even in nymphomania, a form of insanity which those accustomed to visit lunatic asylums must be fully conversant with; but, with these sad exceptions, there can be no doubt that sexual feeling in the female

2. The substance of this paragraph and the quotation that follows it come from Steven Marcus (1966).

is in the majority of cases in abeyance . . . and even if roused (which in many instances it never can be) is very moderate compared with that of the male. Many men, and particularly young men, form their ideas of women's feelings from what they notice early in life among loose or, at least, low and vulgar women. . . . Any susceptible boy is easily led to believe, whether he is altogether overcome by the syren or not, that she, and therefore all women, must have at least as strong passions as himself. Such women however give a very false idea of the condition of female sexual feeling in general. Association with the loose women of London streets, in casinos, and other immoral haunts (who, if they have not sexual feeling, counterfeit it so well that the novice does not suspect but that it is genuine), all seem to corroborate such an impression, and . . . it is from these erroneous notions that so many young men think that the marital duties they will have to undertake are beyond their exhausted strength, and from this reason dread and avoid marriage. . . . The best mothers, wives, and managers of households, know little or nothing of sexual indulgences. Love of home, children, and domestic duties, are the only passions they feel.

As a general rule, a modest woman seldom desires any sexual gratification for herself. She submits to her husband, but only to please him; and, but for the desire of maternity, would far rather be relieved from his attentions. No nervous or feeble young man need, therefore, be deterred from marriage by any exaggerated notion of the duties required from him. The married woman has no wish to be treated on the footing of a mistress. (Pp. 31–32)

Having argued that in the equations of medical science women are an unknown, I am in no position to say whether this passage is true or false, so far as it regards women. So far as it regards men, I can say a little, on the presumption of an insider's knowledge. That men are in general fearful and weak, for example, any woman who has been married to a man can testify. But most men, I think, would find it hard to locate within themselves Acton's specific shrinking horror and resultant denial of female sexuality. For myself, all I have ever consciously wanted, since about age eleven, is for some woman to take me as a sex object entirely. No doubt the horror is buried very deep, which may be why Stoker had to disguise it as a fear of vampirism. Quite likely, it is in part an elaboration of a still deeper fear of castration. After all, who wants to be castrated? But all that is for those of you with expert knowledge to say. For me the symptoms are enough, more than enough. I am not yet so far gone as to want to know the first cause of anything. That's where the real horror lies.

Mina, That Pearl Among Women

If Lucy becomes an epitome of what is horrifying about women, Mina is an exemplar of what women must become to avoid the mercy-bearing stake. Oh, she is enough of a woman to fall some distance into vampirism. ("I suppose it is some of the taste of the original apple that remains still in our mouths," as she herself observes.) But she does not go all the way. The traits that enable her to hold back from going all the way are the traits that make her an exemplar of feminine virtue. For one thing, she knows enough to put her fate into the hands of men. When the men decide to keep her in the dark about their plans for destroying Dracula—"It is too great a strain for a woman to bear," says Dr. Van Helsing—she agrees that they know what is best for her: "I suppose it is one of the lessons that we poor women have to learn," she says.

For another thing, she understands that her gender-specific purpose in life is to be of service to men. While still only engaged to Jonathan she studied shorthand, timetables, and business law, so as to be "useful" to her future husband. "I must attend to my husband" is her constant refrain. But if she is wifely to Jonathan, she is daughterly to Van Helsing, sisterly to Quincey Morris, and motherly to Arthur in his bereavement. "We woman have something of the mother in us that makes us rise above smaller matters when the mother spirit is evoked," she says; "I felt this big sorrowing man's head resting on me, as if it were that of the baby that some day may lie on my bosom, and I stroked his hair as though he were my child"—thus showing that, unlike Lucy, she knows what a bosom is for.

Again unlike Lucy, she is fully conscious of her taint, which she properly abhors. By way of introduction to a plea that the men do away with her should she become a full-fledged vampire, she says this:

> I know that all that brave earnest men can do for a poor weak woman, whose soul perhaps is lost—no, no, not yet, but is at any rate at stake —you will do. But you must remember that I am not as you are. There is a poison in my blood, in my soul, which may destroy me; which must destroy me, unless some relief comes to us. (P. 349)

Better yet, and still unlike Lucy, she knows how dangerous her taint is to men, how vigilantly she must suppress her passion to infect Jonathan. "Unclean, unclean!" she exclaims. "I must touch him or kiss him no more. Oh, that it should be that it is I who am now his worst enemy, and whom he may have most cause to fear."

It is not surprising, then, that prose poems in praise of Mina, that "pearl among women," flow from Van Helsing's lips: she is proof "that there are good women still left to make life happy." In fact, "she is one of God's women, fashioned by His own hand to show us men and other women that there is a heaven where we can enter, and that its light can be here on earth. So true, so sweet, so noble, so little an egoist—and that, let me tell you, is much in this age, so sceptical and selfish." Mina is a haven in a heartless world. That's much, but not everything. What above all enables her to resist Dracula, to conquer her own female nature, is that she is not entirely a woman. Morally speaking, that most important component in her makeup is masculine. She does not have the primitive and criminal brain of Dracula. She has the brain of a man. "Ah, that wonderful Madame Mina!" says Dr. Van Helsing. "She has a man's brain—a brain that a man should have were he much gifted—and a woman's heart," the perfect combination. It is through application of "her great brain which is trained like a man's brain" that she is able to organize a mass of documents so as to reveal to the men exactly what Dracula is, what his plans are, and how to track him down. Thus her better half helps to defeat her worser.

So there we have it: through Mina, we see what men want of women. Through Lucy we see what men both want and don't want. Men want women to be at once sexy and virginal, for example, and motherly to boot. They like their women to be womanly, but will kill them for it, at least in their imaginations. They also like their women to be manly. But it would take a far less easily fatigued pen than mine to itemize all that men want of women, for men are weak. I will skip the addition and guess at the sum: men say that women are this or that, rather than that or this, because they need women to be this or that—which has the sound of a tautology (like other statements about anything of importance). But between the first term and its return we pass through one explanation of misogyny. I would say that the size of a man's mysogyny is equal to the distance between the compliant creatures of his daydreams and the women he actually meets, who are different, to put it mildly.

One final word, for the last thing I want to be confused with is a feminist sympathizer. Although I know nothing about women, I believe that if you were to look at how women writers depict men, in, say, *Frankenstein* and *Jane Eyre,* you would find yourself in a separate but equal madhouse of fascination and dread, of displaced horror, misdirected violence, and abysmal longings. For although I know nothing about women, I am a firm believer in the equality of the sexes.

BIBLIOGRAPHY

Farson, D. 1975. *The man who wrote Dracula: A biography of Bram Stoker.* London: Michael Joseph.

Ludlam, H. 1962. *A biography of Dracula: The life story of Bram Stoker.* London: W. Foulsham, see Chap. 24: "Dracula as Play."

McNally, R. T., and Florescu, R. 1972. *In search of Dracula.* Greenwich, Conn.: New York Graphic Society.

Marcus, S. 1966. *The other Victorians: A study of sexuality and pornography in mid-nineteenth century England.* New York: Basic Books.

Roth, P. A. 1982. *Bram Stoker.* Boston: Twayne Publishers.

Stoker, B. 1897. *Dracula.* With an introduction by George Stade. New York: Bantam Books, 1981.

Wolff, C. G. 1972. "A mirror for men: Stereotypes of women in literature." *Massachusetts Review* (Winter-Spring):205–218.

2

Beyond the Phallic Illusion: Notes on Man's Heterosexuality

JOHN MUNDER ROSS

Introduction: What Does Man Want?

Freud's famous question (Freud 1933), formulated toward the close of his own working life, is now half a century old. It has assumed the status of an aphorism or proverb rather than remaining a mystery, and today we know it in its adulterated and truncated form: "My God, what does woman want?" It used to be that the problem found an age- or epoch-appropriate answer. Lacking anatomically and socially, woman wanted to be a man and wished for a penis of her own. Since she was not so endowed, her person wanting, she strove in convoluted ways to be him or get his. She trapped them, men and their phalluses, through her feminine wiles, by being a heterosexual woman.

In the current feminist era, such linear, chauvinistic formulations will not wash. In resonance with the times, analytic child observers countered what Ernest Jones had called the "phallocentric bias" of psychoanalysis (1933, 1935). The discoveries of inner genitality, core gender identity, primary femininity, and early motherliness vindicated many of the notions Karen Horney (1924, 1926) had derived from her adult patients on the couch. Girls are girls; women are women, and not would-be men. Discharged of their sexism, analysts could breathe easier.

Yet in this flurry of attention to women, what about *men?* They have been, it seems, pretty much left out of it all. It is assumed that men want what they already have: their penis and a relatively liberated use of it. Indeed, the male has an ironic advantage over his love object, according to Freud's and Ferenczi's early reflections, in that his phallus yields access to a womb, and therein union with mother, a feat denied to the possessor of the organ itself. All is thus well with men, in contrast to their female counterparts. And, I would add, more silent now, nonetheless the sexism persists.

In this chapter I will pose the question: What does man want? I will do so against a dialectical backdrop that emphasizes in psychosexual dimorphism a tension between asserting differences and seeking unity. Clinically, I hope to exemplify a dictum of Erik Erikson's, namely that a "sublimated maternalism (or femininity) is necessary to the positive identity of a whole man."

Some Personal Words

When I began to study fathers ten years ago, at the height of feminism and on the eve of the so-called new fatherhood, the realities of parenthood were not in the forefront of my concerns. Rather, I was more impressed with the mystery of what Lawrence Kubie (1974) was to call, in one of his last published writings, "the drive to become both sexes."

Beginning with Freud's story of little Hans (1909), I delved through the analytic annals (Ross 1975), rediscovering a literature on the wishes of boys and men to bear, suckle, and rear babies. According to Jacobson (1950), these writings had been repeatedly lost, largely because of the male analysts' defenses against their own womb and breast envy. These very undercurrents gave rise, perniciously and by way of reaction formation, to the phallocentric or, as Zilboorg (1931) put it, "androcentric" bias of psychoanalytic theory. More adaptively, they found sublimated expression in the psychological midwifery at the heart of clinical practice.

In everyday life, I further reckoned, men might find a resolution of the conflict between their efforts to maintain their masculinity and their anxiety-laden wishes to be mothers, and therefore women. And this without succumbing to a transvestite's delusion; or mutilating their genitals in the primitive rites of passage described by Bruno Bettelheim (1954); or subjecting their psyches to rigors of the Tantric mystery and its arduous course of training (Kakar 1982); or striving for the creative artist's inspiration, for an aesthetic and hermetic self-insemination (Kris 1952). They could do so simply and acceptably enough by becoming fathers—men who make, tend, and ideally delight in growing children—and, I would add now, by becoming lovers.

Spearheaded by Spitz (1965) and Mahler, Pine, and Bergman (1975), developmental research has demonstrated the unfolding of the infant's diffuse sensuous reactivity into, first, inchoate longings to possess what is no longer present and, subsequently, into discrete *wishes* for objects. These gain representation and enduring substance and constancy as a function of visual and subsequently symbolic and semantic capacities.

Their wishes for objects bring an individual full circle. Inevitably the desire for an object will imply union with it, partially reviving outmoded primary identifications. The little boy hungers for the mother whom he once, primevally, experienced as indistinct from his nascent sensed self. Failing to possess her at that point when he *first* begins to grasp the triangular relation of mother, father, and self (Abelin 1975), he would fill the void by way of two diverging identificatory routes. The male toddler assumes his father's perceived gender in stereotypical or, better, sensorimotor fashion, enacting the masculinity that distinguishes and separates him from mother and that provides a template for the unfolding of phallic strivings. At the same time, more covertly and eventually unconsciously, he also comes to replace mother as an unreachable object with a *secondary* and increasingly selective series of identifications with her person, her mothering, and her felt femininity.

In this sense the penis does indeed become a vehicle with which to regain what is at least retrospectively felt to be a paradise lost—the *post*partum womb of life before "psychological birth." Seemingly contradictory desires to employ one's penis, to be a woman, and to be a babe-in-arms constitute a paradoxical unity at the hidden core of a boy's and man's heterosexual impulses and identity with regard to them.

If we did not demur so from inquiring into the details of coital experience, we might discover this commingling of aims—which Ferenczi (1968) called an *amphimixis* of the genital and pregenital —along with some typical defensive strategies geared to eschew an immersion in sexual passion. Typically, however, clinicians have tended to accept rather easily their male patients' manifest and facile descriptions of intercourse as an act of penetration in which the status of a man's erection and its performance are stressed and evaluated. In so doing, the analyst or therapist often becomes complicit in the *phallic illusion.* Tumescence and entry are but penultimate achievements, after all. They usher in but fall short of (and, when concentrated on, may serve as masturbatory equivalents that guard against) a crossing over of sexual boundaries and the pervasive release and regression that occur at the height of orgasm—the climax equated by the French and Elizabethans like John Donne with a momentary "little death." That is, in ejaculating one's germplasm, the death of the self as a differentiated, sentient man is felt. Finally, when sexual intimacy assumes its biosocial goal of impregnation, these currents and the defenses against them are intensified.

With Aristophanes as his spokesman, Plato (415 b.c.?) put it this way: Humans began life as spherical creatures with eight limbs, two faces, and two genital organs facing in the opposite direction. These beings were so mighty and strong that they posed a threat to the Olympians. When they attacked the gods, Zeus retaliated against their *hubris* not by destroying them but by cutting them in two. From then on the two parts of human beings, each desiring his (or her) other half, "came together, and throwing their arms about one another, entwined in mutual embraces, longing to grow into one: they were on the point of dying from hunger and self-neglect, because they did not like to do anything apart. They were in the process of thus destroying themselves when Zeus took pity on them and turned their genitals around to the front so that they could at least embrace in intercourse. Thus they ". . . might be satisfied, and rest, and go their ways to the business of life: so ancient is the desire of one another which is implanted in us, reuniting our original nature, making one of two, and healing the state of man." (P. 145–46)

Phallic Narcissistic Defenses Against an Ambisexual Identity: A Clinical Overview and Illustration

Much attention has been paid to frank regressions from the phallic position in severe psychopathology and to the various hidden abdications of masculinity and acts of sexualized submission underlying neurotic symptomatology. The hypertrophy of martial masculinity and the sadistic narcissistic fixations typical of many men in our culture have been less well studied and conceptualized.

These are the individuals who are ultimately afraid of intimacy with women, terrified as they are of being united with them. They are "in and out like a shot," as the patient I shall describe once put it. They are also frightened by the prospect of fatherhood, which perforce calls upon their nurturance, taps their regressive empathy, and arouses fears of effeminacy and infantilism. When they do manage to produce children, they absent themselves or else tyrannize, exploit, and even sacrifice their own young in the service of self-aggrandizement.

A number of etiological factors may conspire in a boy's entrenchment in a phallic narcissistic holding position and the caricature of oedipal development that ensues upon this. Yet all in some way or another have to do with the unavailability early on of the father as a *libidinal* object and figure for internalization and identification in this regard. A father may be absent, emotionally or otherwise, thereby deferring to a powerful mother who fills up her son's life and invades the inner reaches of his emerging identity, sexual and otherwise. He may act like a brutal oppressor who invites an identification with a man merely as an aggressor. Or he may be so inhibited and ineffectual that his little boy must provide for himself—through the enactments of fantasy—age-specific but exaggerated, overcompensated versions of a "father principle." Mothers may disparage or fear men, further short-changing their actual relationship. In all events, the manhood thus achieved is a screen, a sheath, an artificially aggressivized, brittle, cardboard creation. It is unserviceable in negotiating the successive tasks of adult life, most important among them "husbanding" and parenthood. A brief vignette from a colleague in a study group on the father illustrates these phenomena.

"Good Sex" and "Getting Ready" for Fatherhood

The patient (HL) I am about to describe is a thirty-four-year-old man, then in the fifth year of his analysis. He initially presented an infantile, pan-phobic and severely obsessional picture. This was further characterized by an underlying devastating castration anxiety, with roots in separation-individuation failures, intense and projected oral rage, unneutralized (or modulated) aggressivity, marked homosexual fears (at times with paranoid trends), and a variety of narcissistic lacks and overcompensations. His sexual and work functioning were profoundly compromised, for HL's earlier difficulties subsequently infused his positive oedipal strivings with equally unnerving destructive aggression and fears of brutal retaliation. The revival of both preoedipal and oedipal struggles in adolescence was compounded by the traumas of his parents' divorce and grandfather's death.

He had been fired from one job and was intimidated by his

female boss at a new one when he began treatment. Nor had he had intercourse in a year. (He had masturbated but once as an adolescent.)

HL idealized his dead great uncle, who had reared his mother after her parents' death. He had seemed strong and manly, and resisted any notion or perception that might challenge and thereby "tarnish" his all-powerful, "perfect" image. Nor did HL mind fearing the great uncle and the thunderbolts that, Jovelike, were connected with his representation, HL learned later on. He bowed to these fears and the phobias in which they were manifest because he desperately needed "role models" whose fortitude and magnificence he could draw upon to feel both empowered and protected. HL's father had repeatedly disappointed him, and HL disparaged the fat, sloppy, loving, garrulous and affable man as "gassy," "dirty and weak," unable to stand up to his wife, the patient's mother.

As a boy he had both loved and unconsciously hated this volatile *strap-wielding* but beautiful mother, who had aggressively and libidinally overpowered him in toddlerhood and again in adolescence. She had emasculated his father as well, finally leaving him along with her two sons for another man (who subsequently fell prey to her vindictiveness). HL had lived with a great aunt and uncle since his parents' divorce since he was eighteen —two years before his great uncle's death. He complained that the old woman made him even more nervous, especially after her husband succumbed, fueling his phobias and hypochondria with her own incessant and unsuppressed worries about his safety and health. Still, Angie had been more motherly and soft than her harsh niece. Better a Jewish mother than none at all.

Significantly, HL lamented his own father's failure to discipline, even to "hit" him and the evident role reversal in his parents' relation to each other and to their children (him and a younger sister). What he partly meant was that his father had failed him as a guardian and a mentor. Nor had he acted to excite and then to modulate the patient's phallic aggressivity. Speaking of his mother, he told his analyst that "it's tough when the hand that loves is also the hand that hits."

During his first two and one-half years of analysis, HL ideal-

ized the male clinician variously as "stud," family man and professor. With his baldfaced oedipal fantasies about the "stable of
women parading through" his office, he roughhoused within the
transference, like Jacob with an angel of his own making. Rediscovering his oedipal competitiveness, as he did so he drank in
manliness in a more primitive mode. As a result, he made great
strides at work and school, eventually graduating at the top of his
class in the law school he had entered after two years of analysis.
He moved out of Angie's house and, in his words, bedded women
—"big ones" like mother, "not shrimps," like an earlier girlfriend,
K. He had enjoyed lifting her up, as if wielding her on his erect
penis, envisioning himself to be Superman. Indeed, as a latency
child, he remembered dreaming of flying home from the school-
yard, like the legendary comic-strip hero, in so doing psychically
compensating for the cruel fact that he was transported to school
in a bus for the handicapped. His seemingly "overprotective"
mother had been responsible for this arrangement, equating her
asthmatic son with the crippled children for whom the bus was
a necessity. At another point, he recollected, when he was three,
she had pointed to his exposed penis and remarked to a friend on
how small it was. In the transference, he and the analyst became
superheroes, reminding him of a photograph of the patient arm
wrestling with his potent great uncle, who could easily escape the
"clutches of females."

Many of HL's symptoms subsided in the heat of what initially
seemed to be a stark positive and negative oedipal transference
neurosis. But, alas, he was driven now, as he "paraded" his
"stuff." He was forever "on the go, go, go." The narcissistic and
aggressive strains in his character remained to be analyzed. So
impatient did HL become now that he made even his girlfriend,
S., who was fast finding her way into his affections in spite of
himself, sleep on a cot next to his bed so that she would not
"crowd him out."

In part, he was afraid of punishment for finding a woman who
loved him. Having intercourse in his sublet, he was literally afraid
the landlord or perhaps a neighbor would become enraged and
castrate him. When the analyst interpreted both the projection
and the real-life genesis of the threat, HL responded: "It's 99

percent probable you're right, but what about the 1 percent!" More than this, the uninterrupted intimacy was in itself terrifying. As Loewald (1951) long ago suggested, the threat of paternal castration served to fend off reabsorption. Cloacal fantasies abounded as HL became more interested in his girlfriend. And the patient, who had propped his feet on the analytic couch in the position of women during delivery, confessed that he was afraid that her womanliness was catching, that the secretions from a vagina he would have felt more secure in sadistically "scraping out" or "plugging up" would somehow contaminate him. When her sexual demands threatened him, he verbally abused her to hide his fears.

Gradually, however, he acknowledged his love of her, his fascination with oral sex. In the past, masturbation fantasies had involved a sequence wherein cunnilingus was followed by a reassuring near-rape. Fitfully, he spoke of "playing with her" pillow-like breasts, of his urge to melt into her, of his relish in the smells that had hitherto repulsed him. Even more tentatively, he admitted that on occasion, ejaculating, he had "squealed like a fuckin' baby." With this, fatherly ambitions also began to emerge.

I will excerpt approximately two weeks of sessions presented to our group from this period:

Your doorknob shocked me [an old bugaboo]. It made me furious. . . . I wouldn't be so angry if I had struck back when I was a kid . . . if I had a kid, I sometimes think I'd smash his brains too. . . . You gotta be tough— [The problems of abuse and HL's identification with the aggressing parent were also important subjects of analysis, the mother's violence having been screened by the threat of castration at God's (the father's), hands.] Maybe that is what's warranted in my old age—to get it out of my system. Women are like cats—they turn on you. . . .

In the next session:

My gay neighbors disturbed me last night, pounding all night in the closet. I still haven't gotten over those fears about the gays completely. [Later.] I'm rebellious. I didn't work on Saturday and stayed with S. S. and I are getting closer. She cried after intercourse. It scared me—I still don't stay in for long. She wants to marry me. But I got no models of good marriage. Maybe I'll get married next year. I imagine telling my uncle . . . I don't want to bend over backward no more—to submit. You know, nobody had control over my mother, not even my father. Maybe that's why I don't trust people. I think how my great uncle intimidated her, but so what. . . . You gotta have somebody to look up to. I used to put you in the godly role. . . . Being stubborn is masculine. I wanna be Superman. . . . With my coat behind me, I felt like Superman with his cape. [He had been deeply offended by the movie *Superman II,* specifically the scene where Superman cedes his superhuman powers to make love to Lois Lane.] Women are supposed to be gentle . . . passive. Female activity turns me off. Again I think about having kids. . . . I'm a baby inside and it scares me. S.'s breasts are so big; I sometimes think I like playing with them better than anything. How can you be a father if you're weak? A kid'll see right through you. [Another hour.] I read an article about fathers—they can be better parents than mothers. . . . I realize I like kids a lot. Sometimes I think my treating S. mean is a big coverup. I don't want to show her my fears. I'm real soft inside and care for her, and I get so scared for her [weeps]. I don't really think you should be involved with someone and not care for them. I'm thinking about kids a lot, like my [much younger] cousin. . . . I was mad she liked S. better. . . . [Later.] Sometimes I wonder whether I'll have children. I checked my old coin collection and trains to see whether they're still there. . . . One day I may have a son. [Pause.] My father wasn't good mechanically like my uncle [the great uncle], and he was subservient. . . . I wonder what traits make a good father? Mine never showed me how to make the football spiral. The best fathers do everything. . . . Still, he was always there when I was sick. And he hit a stickball a mile [an activity he had criticized him for until now]. If I had a son, what kind of father would I be? I could have conflicts. All that shit. Older toddlers are interesting, but then teens are pains again and turn around and stab you in the back. It's anticlimactic. . . . [Pause.] You know, I remember how excited I was when my brother Johnny was born [at six years]. And then teaching him things—he was a cute little doll. They say I really loved him. . . . [Later.] It seems like bullshit reasons to me, but they say men have kids to prove their masculinity and also relive their own childhoods. . . . Still, I can't imagine why a guy would want to be kidless . . . even Joe, this big guy [at work—an ex-football player], he's all caught up in his sons and daughters. It blows my mind. [Pauses; weeps.] That's what I mean about analysis! How can I go to the client like this!?

In a later session:

If I had a son, I'd name him after my uncle . . . but I'm scared he'd be defective, maybe . . . a daughter I'd like to shove back—like a booby prize. . . . Still, my friend's daughter is pretty cute. I don't know, it's all so scary. . . . When I think how much I really feel for women. You know, Bill really cares for his daughter—more than Uncle Nick did, he was less involved. My father—he cared for us a lot, though my mother put him down all the time. . . .

A later session:

S.'s irregular periods bother me—I haven't had sex with her for weeks. She felt so big inside the last time—it's scary, like there's a lot going on. I was reading an article about having kids when a woman's over thirty. . . . I'm thinking a lot about kids. . . . It can't be all biological. I'm thinking something . . . I don't want to say anything before I'm ready. . . . I guess the bottom line is I don't know what I want. . . . [Later.] I found these sex magazines unappealing [for the first time]. . . . It's not deep at all. How do *you* do it . . . having a family and working? I don't know . . . I just don't want to pass on my fears to my kids. . . . I guess I think you have to be perfect to be a father. . . . But there's no perfection. . . . There are no role models—not even you any more—and it pisses me off. I want things boom, boom, boom, not the complications. I don't want the gray stuff, but it's there. . . .

Later:

I had oral sex with S. . . . I like it . . . and screwing her, I thought how big she felt. But it wasn't too bad. [He at first had compared his penis in intercourse to "a pretzel in Boston's Callahan Tunnel."] But I had this fear the rubber might come off. . . . I'm thinking about giving her a very special present on her [thirtieth] birthday [a proposal, I later learned], but save that for another time.

Discussion: Particulars and Universals

Every analytic case is easily as interesting in its particulars as in its more general import. Obviously, a few brief excerpts cannot do justice to the complexity of this man. And even these few extracts point to his idiosyncracies, further modified and exaggerated by the impact of the particular analytic process—and analyst. To generalize about maleness and its development thus becomes difficult indeed.

One is struck, as it were, by the patient's mother. With her strap, obsessive cleanliness and biting tongue, her remarks leveled at her boy's autonomy and masculinity, she caricatured in real life the universal male fantasies of the phallic and vaginally abrasive and castrating mother. With a mother like this, one might well wonder, how was it that the patient achieved heterosexual functioning to the extent that he did? And in this vein, his father comes to mind as another fairly unique influence, perhaps the hidden hero in the patient's psychic drama, having been upstaged by the obvious and severe masculinity embodied by his revered Uncle Nick. Quite probably, it was paternal nurturance that quietly redeemed this man—his father's motherliness, in fact—sowing seeds to be watered in the transference and flowering first in the form of a latter-day phallic machismo and, more gradually and fitfully, in HL's unfolding capacities for genital love and potential fatherliness. His father's failures centered on his understimulation of aggression and on his inadequacies as a husband.

Apart from these particulars, a patient like this may indeed proffer some universal truths or suggestions about the psychic life of men in general. His development as an adult (albeit one in treatment) seems to suggest that encounters with women in late adolescence and early adulthood tend to revive a succession of phallic and paternal *motives* from the course of phallic oedipal development. It is frightening but ultimately thrilling for a young man and sexual tyro to experience the capaciousness and potential fertility of woman rather than merely to conquer her and to proceed through genitality into generativity.

Beyond the Phallic Illusion

Ultimately, as this patient himself suggests, though he cavils at it, the promise of procreation in intimacy is rewarding indeed. Participating in the succession of the generations, a man finds that his masculinity in the deepest sense is indeed memorialized. And, in loving and caring, he recovers through a reversal of voice the passive pleasures of a childhood lost and inevitably lacking.

During the year and a half following the sessions excerpted, HL was indeed able to propose to and marry S.—albeit not without regression, atonement, and propitiation. His tendency to see her as more maternal than sexual gave way to a fuller representation of her. He and his analyst now worked on the preoedipal *maternal* transference. As HL became more tolerant of his own "feminine" core, this came to replace the initial paradigm, in which the analyst had been subject variously to HL's rivalry, competitiveness, idealization, and, throughout, his "father hunger." Much was to be learned about HL's sufferings at his real mother's abusive hands. Memories of being slapped in early adolescence opened pathways to an early childhood and toddlerhood in which he had either been assaulted for being dirty or messy or else seemingly overprotected, his "stabs" at manhood and independence derogated or disallowed. In the process, HL came to recognize that he had striven to fortify his imperiled manhood by exaggerating and stereotyping it and by projecting a pure culture of maleness onto the therapist.

His rage and hostility within the transference became more heartfelt, no longer reflecting "pretense" to phallic bravado, as he himself put it. "It's real; I'm not strutting stuff." Italian food on his honeymoon, for example, set in motion gastroenterological symptoms. For some time he became preoccupied with feces. Only later, after he found himself smearing chocolate on the analyst's door, did HL recognize that in becoming "inflamed" he had been at once unconsciously defying his mother and breaking down the reaction formations she had prompted, propitiating the gods (composite images including that of his exalted grandfather) and making himself pregnant in the expectation that he would be a better mother than she. S.'s love and warmth and the genuine understanding tendered in the form of analytic interpretation set in relief his mother's intolerance for his masculinity and, ironically, her impatience with his infantile neediness.

HL could at last acknowledge his joy in cooking, food shopping, and housekeeping without "seeing [himself] as a sissy." He no longer needed to buy the biggest gifts to "prove himself" but chose instead symbolic small fruits and vegetables to present to his wife. More secure in his own masculinity, he even ceded the idealization of his uncle, which had suffused him with electrifying power [God and the burning bush, the Hulk, electrical storms had once obsessed him]. He felt freer in lovemaking and, to his surprise, found himself burrowing into his wife's soft enfolding contours along with her smells [though merger phenomena still eluded him]. He might just be a decent enough parent, after all, he further conceded, since, he confessed, he so enjoyed cuddling, rocking, and cooing to babies. He had more patience than his mother. He began to see her, himself, his future children within the generational cycle—all as limited, frail people. His mother, he realized, had suffered at *her* parents' hands. Periodically, of course, regression and resistance served to deflect his focus from insights such as these. In the midst of this painful growing up, the Monday following his wedding, HL asked the analyst to remind him that his "no-nonsense macho attitude is a *lot* of nonsense. . . . I feel things and like loving."

The Ontogeny of Sexuality and Fatherhood: Developmental Lines

I have sought to highlight how phallic nuclei can become hypertrophied and regressively clung to in an effort to "disidentify from mother," as Ralph Greenson (1966) put it, thereby shortchanging the future man's genital as well as generative functioning. I turn now to the interweaving of the developmental lines for male sexual and paternal identity.

The teleology of male sexuality, its phylogenetic function, is obvious, especially so among infra-human primates and in simple

societies. Its ontogeny is not so explicit—at least in a contemporary world where birth control, in freeing us, has also obscured
the purposefulness of pleasure—in re-creation and pro-creation.
Mothers bear, birth, and usually nurse their young, undergoing
a succession of body changes that are the underpinnings of a
psychological phase in the strict sense of the term (see Benedek
1959, 1970).

At the inception of life, in fact, it is not father but mother who
not only comforts and gratifies an infant but also embodies for
the child the power of an essentially parental universe. Once the
baby's solipsism gives way so that its mother becomes defined as
a being on the periphery of the inchoate self, it is woman, mother,
who soothes the savage soul of the drives and wards off no less
noxious stimuli from the surrounding environment—she who
seems to make things materialize as if at will. "Object" and
"environment" mother, Winnicott (1963) has dubbed her, a person in her own right and one who further holds the infant and
makes its life happen for it. Striving to embrace her nurturance,
omnipotence, and executive functions, the child, male or female,
eventually distinguishes and then identifies with what Van der
Leuw (1958) called the "active, producing mother."

At first, we might speculate, even the child's father may appear
to be one of a mother's many creations. How early his distinct
presence is felt remains moot. Abelin (1971, 1975) has suggested
that with symbiosis the adult male presence also becomes a pre-
object in the infant's world toward whom the child will turn for
increasingly *specific* refueling. In transactions with him, the baby
"thirsts or hungers" for some primal "male" or "father principle"
as fodder for psychological growth. Michael Yogman, collaborat-
ing with Brazelton (1982), has demonstrated what may be the
earliest behavioral indices of such psychic nutriment. From the
first weeks, infants reveal a greater synchrony of measurable
activity and excitation with *both* parents than with strangers.
Furthermore, mothers tend to envelop and equilibrate, soothing,
calming a baby, and reestablishing a tenuous homeostasis. Fathers engage in more intrusive, gross motor, high-keyed modes
of interaction for the most part. They stimulate their infants,
fostering a "base for play."

Implicitly, the baby and parents are behaviorally differentiated early on, anticipating what will evolve later as intrapsychic triangulation (Piaget's vertical decalage). Mothers are associated with being enfolded, quieted, kept close and potentially entrapped whereas fathers are linked to arousal, penetration, activity, and aggressivity. Mothers allow assimilation; fathers prompt accommodation. These trends further point to an early object relational basis for ambisexuality, which is at this point defined in terms of specific sensorimotor schemas (certain kinds of activities) tied to transactions with the child's two different primary objects, male and female. From the outset, mother is and means being female; father, male.

According to researchers, it is during the second half of the second year that boys and girls first become impressed with anatomical sex differences. They *consolidate* their core gender identity during the following year, from two and one half or so when one is no longer free psychically to choose or change his or her sex. This affective and cognitive revelation occurs just as a boy is struggling to disengage from a mother whom he still depends on and admires and whose person and qualities he longs to incorporate. He comes to cherish his masculinity, taking great pride in his penis as its prime, visible, and most sensible manifestation, at the same time he strives to be and be like mother, a female who can make and nurse babies and who, in his mind's eye, may or may *not* have a penis. He is thus confronted with a disquieting and abiding paradox: to be the all-powerful parent is to be castrated. Profound conflicts in gender identity are set in motion, then, with hermaphroditic promptings, evident during the second and third years, vying with the predestined thrust of phallic development.

Beset in this way, a boy seeks refuge in a father who offers himself up for adoration and emulation in various sex-specific guises. And in this regard, the mother's images of her husband in relation to herself and her child have influences that are both direct and subtle. Without a strong paternal presence, a mother's enveloping presence typically remains unchallenged and unmediated as far as both her son and *she herself* are concerned.

In any event, given good-enough parents, having consolidated their core gender identity, most boys assert its primacy and progress into the phallic phase between two and three years. The father's and son's upright urination is an initial organizer in this process (Tyson 1982). Penile tumescence also becomes elaborated in the fantasies of the three-year-old, who equates his penis with a spear. Being manly now means to be aggressive—to stand up tall, to possess and wield an intrusive weapon. In this vein, Freud (1905) referred to the boy's "obscure" (and, one should add, sadistically toned and therefore still anal) "urge to penetrate."

Women have not yet become the objects of desire. The first, or "proto-phallic," phase, to borrow from Jones (1933), in which a boy parades his masculinity, is thus also quintessentially phallic narcissistic. It is a dance whose aim it is to be applauded. The exhibitor reassures himself of the viability of his pretenses to virility while others reflect back to him and, in the process, magnify his machismo.

These displays must in fact be appreciated by both parents for phallic development to proceed optimally. The pathos of resolutions in which boys revert to feminine modes lies in the irony that the one way to be *at one* with woman is to possess her heterosexually. But the further trouble is that many boys, defending against more ominous possibilities, do not proceed beyond this stage into a genuine sexual relatedness. For them, as for HL, the sexual identity of a man remains bound up with conquest, even violence, with self-inflation through self-display.

As his interest in the mother who mirrors him grows, his curiosity moving him to fumble through the glass darkly, a little boy becomes intrigued and aroused by the protuberances and inner recesses of the mother who has admired *him.* He would somehow possess her now, get in there. He has entered the phallic *oedipal* phase proper. His sexual strivings, having been partly transformed into sexual researches, assume an object relatedness and a conflictual complexity.

They come to entail rivalry with the father. Earlier identifications with the productive mother are invoked and transfigured for purposes of defense and desire. Loving his father, as Freud initially reminded us (Freud 1909; see also Jacobson 1964), a son retreats in fear from his own intended mayhem as well as from the spectre of retaliation. He fortifies himself with fantasies of surrendering to and thereby passively receiving his father's manly fortitude. For these converging reasons, even the most "macho" of four-year-olds will also want to be a woman, Daddy's woman, yearning to submit and make love to his everlasting father and to bear and nurse his babies.

Nor does he understand as yet the procreative process and the male's part in it, except in the vaguest of terms. To be a man still implies aggression, a loss therefore of the tender and sensuous qualities equated with womanliness. Again, he would have mother by identifying with her—but now as a sexual and reproductive being related in these specific ways to father. Hence some of the many determinants and functions of the negative oedipal complex as a waystation en route to a paternal, heterosexual stance.

Subsequently, boys—the lucky ones—clarify their awareness of and deepen their identification with father as father. It is later during the *oedipal* phase that the father's sexual aspect and role within the primal scene and in procreation are first intimated to the child. With this, the father's penis can be transformed in a boy's unconscious imagery from a merely intrusive vehicle to a creative, life-giving organ—a source of parental power, pleasure, and sustenance. Maternal ambitions can then become integrated with masculine, phallic strivings in the form of a would-be fatherhood whose assumption helps resolve remaining conflicts in sexual identity—including the *wish* to be womanlike and, in so being, in a man's view, being castrated as well.

This is a point at which so many father-deprived and thus ill-informed boys of our culture have tended to founder—like Little Hans in Freud's Vienna (Freud 1909). Little Hans was, after all, never apprised of his father's and his own reproductive function, a void in knowledge that probably helped precipitate him into an abiding posture of homosexual submission. Soon enough in many cultures and throughout history (Aries 1962; Kakar 1982), boys will be wrested from the exclusive care of women and handed over to the tutelage of men. Thus it may be that *women* resist the loss of exclusive domination over their sons, compounding the reluctance of *men* to tender love for fear of effeminization. The failure of men to act as fathers and to be treated as such is, of course, a commonplace, and one that has deprived so many boys at a critical period of a developmental crescendo punctuating, synthesizing, and unifying their male sexual identity.

Let me skip a few years: As biological maturity is presaged in the rumblings of preadolescence, a boy is precipitated into an anal and quasi-homosexual regression, as Blos (1984) has shown. Disguised or frank homosexual activity and masturbation serve as rehearsals for heterosexuality. The teenager reassures himself repeatedly of the intactness of his body, his person, and his masculinity at the height of orgasm because in part he *wishes* the effeminization, emasculation, and dissolution he dreads. Preparing for the genitality that is now physically possible but still psychologically scary, the early adolescent's masturbation tactics and fantasies nonetheless cannot help betraying the maternal identifications still alive deep within him. Again and again a boy must rework the path toward manhood in the face of mother's and motherhood's great allure.

Indeed, more attention probably needs to be paid to a boy's first involuntary and then his induced ejaculations, and to the sensations, fantasies of body wastes, and fears of damage and sterility that accompany them. In contrast to menarche, these emissions of a boy's, harbingers of his capacity for procreation, are not ritually heralded but rather occur as private, often secret events. Nor do most boys anticipate their caretaking functions during adolescence to the extent that girls do, typically girding their loins in the phallic, combative camaraderie that characterizes the social life of the male adolescent.

The typical first experiences of actual intercourse described by male adolescents, their triumphs over body parts, reveal that theirs is most often not an image of sexual man as a sensual being. In sex, too, the aggressivity of desire—phallic conquest and anal sadistic control—guards against an accession to and dwelling in libidinal arousal and, with it, a loss of self in the presence of woman.

At no time is the interweaving of the psychosexual and psychosocial strains of identity more poignant than in adolescence.

The teenager aims to assure himself that he can perform as an adult man in arenas as seemingly discrepant as work and sex in order to verify that he remains in fact who he believes himself to be, wherever he is and whatever he is doing. It is probably only after achieving a sense of integrity in late adolescence that a young man can tolerate the disintegration of self-composure inherent in a fully realized sexual encounter. No longer self-absorbed, the postadolescent youth has become self-possessed and, with this, capable of yielding willingly, losing himself, and falling and being in love. Finding a woman with whom he can consider or at least imagine creating a mutually generative and caring life, a woman he loves, a man can discover at last his genuine sexuality and thus rediscover both the femininity and the fatherliness bound up with it.

BIBLIOGRAPHY

Abelin, E. 1971. The role of the father in the separation-individuation process. In *Separation-individuation: Essays in honor of Margaret S. Mahler,* ed. J. McDevitt and C. Settlage, pp. 229–252. International Universities Press.

Abelin, E. 1975. Some further observations and comments on the earliest role of the father. *International Journal of Psycho-Analysis* 56: 293–302.

Aries, P. 1962. *Centuries of childhood.* Trans., R. Baldick. London: Cape.

Atkins, R. 1982. Discovering Daddy: The mother's role. In *Father and child,* ed. S. Cath et al., pp. 139–149. Boston: Little, Brown.

Benedek, T. 1959. Parenthood as a developmental phase. *Journal of the American Psychoanalytic Association* 7:389–417.

————. 1970. Parenthood during the life cycle. In *Parenthood: Its psychology and psychopathology,* ed. E. J. Anthony and T. Benedek. Boston: Little, Brown.

Bergmann, M. 1971. Psychoanalytic observations on the capacity to love. In *Separation-individuation: Essays in honor of Margaret Mahler,* ed. J. McDevitt and C. Settlage, pp. 15–40. New York: International Universities Press.

Bettelheim, B. 1954. *Symbolic wounds.* Glencoe, Ill.: Free Press.

Blos, P. 1984. Son and father. *Journal of the American Psychoanalytic Association* 32:301.

Edgcumbe, R., and Burgner, M. 1975. The phallic narcissistic phase: A differentiation between preoedipal and oedipal aspects of phallic development. *Psychoanalytic Study of the Child* 29:161–180.

Erikson, E. H. 1969. *Gandhi's truth.* New York: Norton.

Ferenczi, S. 1924, 1938. *Thalassa: A theory of genitality.* New York: Norton, 1968.

Fox, R. 1982. Les conditions de l'evolution sexuelle. *Communications* 35: 2–14.

Freud, S. 1905. Three essays on sexuality. In *The standard edition of the complete psychological works*

Beyond the Phallic Illusion

of Sigmund Freud, 24 vols. (hereafter *S. E.*), ed. J. E. Strachey, vol. 7 (1953). London: Hogarth Press, 1953–1974.

———. 1909. The analysis of a phobia in a five-year old boy. In S. E., vol. 10 (1955), pp. 87–175.

———. 1926. Inhibitions, symptoms, and anxiety. In *S. E.*, vol. 20 (1959), pp. 87–175.

———. 1933. New introductory lectures on psychoanalysis. In *S. E.,* vol. 22 (1964), pp. 5–182.

Greenberg, M., and Morris, N. 1982. Engrossment: The newborn's impact upon the father. In *Father and child,* ed. S. Cath et al., pp. 87–99. Boston: Little, Brown.

Greenson, R. 1968. Disidentifying from mother. *International Journal of Psycho-Analysis* 49: 370–374.

Greenspan, S. I. 1982. "The second other": The role of the father in early personality formation and the dyadic-phallic phase of development. In *Father and child,* ed. S. Cath et al., pp. 123–138. Boston: Little, Brown.

Gurwitt, A. 1982. Aspects of prospective fatherhood. In *Father and child,* ed. S. Cath et al., pp. 275–299. Boston: Little, Brown.

Herzog, J. M. 1982. Patterns of expectant fatherhood: A study of the fathers of a group of premature infants. In *Father and child,* ed. S. Cath et al., pp. . Boston: Little, Brown.

Horney, K. 1924. On the genesis of the castration complex in women. *International Journal of Psycho-Analysis* 4:50–65.

Horney, K. 1926. The flight from womanhood. *International Journal of Psycho-Analysis* 7: 324–339.

Jacobson, E. 1950. Development of the wish for a child in boys. *Psychoanalytic Study of the Child* 5:139–152.

Jacobson, E. 1964. *The self and the object world.* New York: International Universities Press.

Jones, E. 1933. The phallic phase. In E. Jones, *Papers on psychoanalysis,* pp. 452–484. Boston: Beacon Press, 1961.

———. 1935. The early development of female sexuality. In E. Jones, *Papers on psychoanalysis,* pp. 438–451.

Kakar, S. 1982. *Shamans, mystics and doctors.* New York: International Universities Press.

———. 1982. Fathers and sons: An Indian experience. In *Father and child,* ed. S. Cath et al., pp. 417–423. Boston: Little, Brown.

Kernberg, O. 1977. Boundaries and structure in love relations. *Journal of the American Psychoanalytic Association* 25:81–116.

Kestenberg, J. 1975. *Children and parents: Psychoanalytic studies in development.* New York: Jason Aronson.

Kris, E. 1952. *Psychoanalytic explorations in art.* New York: International Universities Press.

Kubie, L. 1974. The drive to become both sexes. *Psychoanalytic Quarterly* 43:349–426.

Loewald, H. W. 1951. Ego and reality. *International Journal of Psycho-Analysis* 32:10–18.

Mahler, M. S., Pine, F., and Bergman, A. 1975. *The psychological birth of the human infant.* New York: Basic Books.

Parens, H. 1975. Report on workshop: Parenthood as a developmental phase. *Journal of the American Psychoanalytic Association* 23:154–165.

Plato. 415 B.C.. *The symposium.* In *The portable Plato,* ed. S. Buchanan. New York: The Viking Press, 1948.

Ross, J. 1975. The development of paternal identity: A critical review of the literature on nurturance and generativity in boys and men. *Journal of the American Psychoanalytic Association* 23:783–817.

———. 1977. Toward fatherhood: The epigenesis of paternal identity during a boy's first decade. *International Journal of Psycho-Analysis* 4:327–347.

———. 1979. Paternal identity: The equations of fatherhood and manhood. In *On sexuality: Psychoanalytic observations,* ed. T. B. Krasu and C. Socarides, pp. 78–97. New York: International Universities Press.

————. 1982. Oedipus revisited, Laius and the Laius complex. *Psychoanalytic Study of the Child* 37: 169–200.

Spitz, R. 1965. *The first year of life.* New York: International Universities Press.

Stoller, R. 1968. *Sex and gender.* New York: Science House.

————. 1975. Healthiest parental influences on the earlier development of masculinity in baby boys. *Psychoanalytic Forum* 5:232–262.

Tyson, P. 1982. The role of the father in gender identity, urethral erotism, and phallic narcissism. In *Father and child,* ed. S. Cath et al., pp. 175–187. Boston: Little, Brown.

Van der Leeuw, P. J. 1958. The preoedipal phase of the male. *Psychoanalytic Study of the Child* 13: 352–374.

Winnicott, D. W. 1963. Communicating and not communicating leading to a study of certain opposites. In *The maturational processes and the facilitating environment,* ed. D. W. Winnicott, pp. 179–192. New York: International Universities Press.

Yogman, M. 1982. Observations on the father-infant relationship. In *Father and child,* ed. S. Cath et al., pp. 101–122. Boston: Little, Brown.

Zilboorg, G. 1931. Depressive reactions related to parenthood. *American Journal of Psychiatry* 10:927–962.

3

The Omni-Available Woman and Lesbian Sex: Two Fantasy Themes and Their Relationship to the Male Developmental Experience

ETHEL S. PERSON

Introduction

The feminist movement's demand for a reevaluation of psychoanalytic sexual theories correctly pointed to erroneous concepts regarding female sexuality. However, the tacit and mistaken assumption was that these same theories exhaustively and accurately portrayed male sexuality.

We are now beginning to see that theories of male sexuality are incomplete if not skewed, focusing as they do primarily on the resolution of the positive oedipal complex through resolution of the boy's competitive struggle with his father. In this formula-

The first half of this chapter draws on and elaborates themes in my paper "Male Sexuality and Power" (in *Psychoanalytic Inquiry*, in press).

I would like to express my thanks to Drs. Gerald Fogel, William Grossman, and Eleanor Schuker, who read an earlier version of this chapter and offered many valuable comments.

tion, the boy avoids the threat of castration by renouncing his infantile wish for a sexual tie to his mother; he chooses the narcissistic cathexis of his penis over the libidinal cathexis of his mother, thereby preserving and strengthening his phallic narcissism. The fundamental sexual problem for boys is here viewed as the struggle to achieve phallic strength and power vis-à-vis other men.

This formulation is accurate as far as it goes, but by focusing predominantly on the father-son struggle, the threat of castration at the hands of the father, and the resolution through a powerful paternal identification, the importance of other developmental components of male sexuality is minimized.[1] In particular, the emphasis on the role of prephallic factors in influencing castration anxiety is erratic. And the contribution of adolescent sexuality to adult sexuality is only minimally theorized.

What is frequently missing is the impact of the mother-son relationship on sexuality at different developmental stages, making the traditional formulation an incomplete developmental scheme. Too often, the female is portrayed more as a prize rather than as both prize and protagonist in the boy's sexual development. There are important contributions to the psychoanalytic literature that focus on the effects of the mother-son relationship (beginning with Freud [1920] and followed up by Horney [1932]), but these studies—and the effects on male sexuality that they detail—tend to be neglected in the more recent literature. Even so, the ample evidence of everyday clinical practice and the perusal of the literature on male sexual fantasies emphasize their importance.

I propose to examine two sets of widespread male heterosexual fantasies—the omni-available woman and lesbian sex—the meaning of which draw our attention to an enlarged scheme of male psychosexual development. These fantasies are popularly acknowledged but largely unexplored in the psychoanalytic literature. At first glance, their meaning appears to be self-evident, no

---

1. Identification with the phallic father and his power and subsequent identifications with male sexual strength and independence form the psychological core of the collective male idea of male sexuality—namely, machismo sexuality. To the extent that my schematic formulation of psychoanalytic theories of male sexuality is accurate, the theories themselves reflect the cultural stereotype of male sexuality.

more than an expression of machismo sexuality. Yet they are not so simple as their manifest content would initially lead one to believe.

Psychological exploration of the omni-available woman fantasy reveals traces of those desires and frustrations directly referable to the boy's mother and his subsequent female sexual objects. It thereby draws our attention to prephallic factors in castration anxiety, to the narcissistic vulnerability of the sexual self, and to the impact of the adolescent experience. The lesbian fantasy frequently points to maternal envy and the wish for a feminine identification. It suggests certain parallels between homosexual and transvestite solutions as trial resolutions of the oedipal conflict anterior to "normal" resolution. Might these two groups of fantasies have been neglected precisely because they focus on aspects of male sexuality at variance with the cultural ideal of the "macho"?

Conscious Fantasies

Conscious fantasies are extremely varied, and sexual fantasies are no exception. The only major statistical analysis of sexual fantasies remains that of Kinsey and associates (1948, 1953). They discovered that both the content and the formal attributes of sexual fantasies vary with gender.[2] (The Kinsey group also noted some class differences, stressing that fantasies from any one sample cannot be safely generalized.)

Among men, a wide range in the content of sexual fantasies (even within this one culture) is well documented, both in popular books and professional journals. But despite variability among men, it appears that there are some general—and fundamental—differences in content between male and female fantasy life. For

2. For example, most males fantasize during masturbation. In contrast, fantasy accompanying masturbation is less consistent among females (Kinsey et al. 1948, 1953; Lukianowicz 1960). Females tend to fantasize about what has actually occurred; males more frequently fantasize about unfulfilled desires.

example, unlike female sexual fantasies, which are likelier to be diffusively romantic, male fantasies are more often explicitly sexual.

Another widely noted difference in content is that men more often entertain fantasies of domination, even sadism, and women fantasies of submission. Male fantasies are frequently impersonal; autonomy, control, and physical prowess are central concerns (May 1980). Male fantasies of rape, mastery, transgression, and bondage are widespread.[3] Although male fantasies may also be submissive or masochistic (Freud first described "feminine" masochism as it occurred in men [1924*b*]), domination is unquestionably a primary motif.

However, there are other male fantasies that are at least as common, possibly more so. Among these are the fantasies of "the omni-available woman" and "lesbian sex." In this chapter I will describe each fantasy, its variants and common enactments, and its meanings. I draw not just on my own patients' conscious and unconscious fantasies, but also on sociological and psychological studies of fantasies elicited by questionnaires and interviews, popular studies of write-in fantasies, and prevalent images in pornography. This variety of sources demonstrates the widespread presence of these fantasy preoccupations among a large population sample, not just among patients, and suggests a developmental continuum of related fantasies over the life span.

---

3. The Fantasy Project at the Columbia Psychoanalytic Center for Training and Research, designed to study sexual fantasies and behaviors, utilizing a questionnaire format, has analyzed data from 193 students. The results are quite striking. While there are only a few behavioral differences between the sexes, fantasy differences are significant. Our results thus far confirm the male predilection for dominance more than the female for submission. The following comparison between males and females is revealing. Eleven percent of the men reported fantasies of torturing a sexual partner and 20 percent of whipping or beating a sexual partner, but 44 percent fantasized forcing a partner to submit to sexual acts. The comparable figures for women are 0 percent, 1 percent, and 10 percent. (Person et al. N.D.).

The Omni-Available Woman and Lesbian Sex

The Omni-Available Woman

The omni-available woman is totally sexually accessible. She is often fantasized as lying on a couch awaiting the protaganist's arrival, forever lubricated, forever ready, forever desiring. From my patients' reports and my reading of the popular and scientific reports of fantasies, I conclude that, for men, it is the woman's availability, ready sexuality, and unqualified approval that is a major common thread. Her availability and enthusiasm bolster his virility.

Barclay (1973), in a study on the sexual fantasies of men and women at Michigan State University, found that

> male fantasies sounded like features of *Playboy* magazine or pornographic books, and included elaborate descriptions of the imagined sexual partner . . . they were stereotyped . . . without personal involvement. Women are always seductive and straightforward, ready to have intercourse at any given time . . . [with a] major emphasis on visual imagery. (P. 205)

In such fantasies, women are viewed as desirable but dispensable. In contrast, as Thorne (1971) points out, women see themselves as both desirable and indispensable.

Shaved pudenda are a surprisingly regular feature of male sexual fantasies. (Comparable fantasies in women are extremely rare.) This may reflect one variant of the wish for the woman to be completely exposed, to conceal nothing whatsoever. In fantasy, men can have all the girls they want and possess them fully —visually as well as sexually.[4]

A young boy's sexual fantasies seem to be largely involved with exploration and discovery of female anatomy. They are colored by a literal preoccupation with girls. As a variant of this fantasy, young boys, prepubescent and pubescent, commonly have fantasies about naked girls in such powerless situations as being tied to a bed (Thorne 1971). These need not contain ele-

4. The meaning of the fantasies of shaved pudenda is often more complex. For example, it also substitutes a nonthreatening little girl in the place of a grown, dangerous, potentially castrating woman. It may also be counterphobic.

ments of sadism, but often do (Lukianowicz 1960). In general, boys seem to fantasize about the sexual compliance of girls or about sexual advances from girls. In these fantasies, girls do not complain about the bad treatment they may be getting; they gratefully accept the status of sexual playthings.

The same themes continue to be found in young men, although the overt force may be less pronounced. The change in male fantasies as boys grow older—the partial replacement of physical dominance as a theme by that of the presence of a bevy of willing females—suggests a continuum of developmental significance. The common feature is the certainty of the sexually available female. In the fantasy, it may be more exciting if the woman consents to sexual handling despite her "coolness." The wish is that girls are really panting for sex. But the constant is that she really does not, cannot resist.

Nancy Friday (1980), in her study of write-in fantasies, found that the largest single fantasy category for men was that of sadomasochistic sex. But she noted that the intent was usually not to hurt the woman, only that she enjoy the encounter. Forcing a partner is one way of ensuring her presence. I find this fantasy, in its intent, to be on a continuum with the fantasied presence of a woman in a perpetual state of sexual readiness, with no other purpose than to receive the man's sexual advances.

The male preoccupation with the omni-availability of the sexual female, irrespective of his own availability, is enacted in myriad small ways by men. There is the legendary example (fact or fantasy) of the business magnate famed in his industry for having a woman perform fellatio on him under the desk while he does business, or examples of men who idly fondle women while doing business on the phone. The constant sexual availability of a woman, in which she serves virtually no other function than the sexual one, is part of the attraction to men of "keeping" a woman. Furthermore, the repetitive recourse to naked, erotic women in advertising appears to speak to the male's unconscious need to be surrounded by sexually available and willing females. One could even argue that it is this need which provides a good deal of the market for prostitution.

A man with this fantasy preoccupation may ask a woman not

to wear panties or a brassiere under her regular clothes, an obvious symbol of her sexual readiness and availability. However, the most common translation of such fantasies into real life is the obsessive urgency with which some men fill every spare evening with an erotic encounter, even when they have ongoing satisfactory or superior emotional and sexual relationships (as self-reported). I have heard many so-called bicoastal businessmen boast that they have a wife on one coast and a girlfriend on the other.

As I have already suggested, these fantasies and their enactments are often taken at face value, seen as requiring no further understanding. The male interest in multiple or simultaneous partners is accepted as part of his sexual voraciousness (rapaciousness?). These sexual enthusiasms enter into the collective male ego ideal as part of an idealized macho sexuality. But a darker and more problematic reality underlies. There is something haunting in the fantasies—a denial and reversal of the realities of female sexuality, a magically exaggerated picture of male sexual prowess, and a wistful desire for a different sexual world.

Many male sexual fantasies are essentially magical repairs of male sexual fears. While wishful fantasies are about size, hardness, endurance, skill, and willing females, fears and fearful fantasies are about penis size, impotence, lack of skill, fear of female rejection, female damage to the male (vagina dentata fantasies), and homosexual dread (Goldberg 1976; Zilbergeld 1978). Corresponding to these major male anxieties are core sexual concerns: adequency and intactness of the penis, performance issues (control or lack of control of the penis), and availability (or control) of the female sexual partner.

Fantasies of the omni-available woman reveal not only the pressing desire for female availability, but the simultaneous desire to erase any one woman's individuality or importance. This provides reassurance about virility, the "on-call" availability of the sexual object, and the inherent importance of the man vis-à-vis a woman. While the fantasies may be contaminated by the need to discharge aggression, they are not always fueled by it. These are not domination fantasies per se but are more subtle, revealing the widespread need to bolster the male's subjective sense of control and command. They counter the dread of personal inadequacy, male subordination, and female rejection or harm. They suggest an overabundance of women whose primary interest and sole function is sexual, ensuring that the man will never be humiliated by the absence of a sexual object.

Fantasies of the omni-available woman are reassuring insofar as they guarantee female sexual availability and approval—a state of affairs somewhat at variance with Everyman's actual experience. These fantasies also portray a female sexuality at variance with the actuality of female sexuality in another way. Like male fantasies of women making love (happily) to animals with gigantic penises, or women masturbating with dildoes, this group of fantasies portrays unusually sexually energetic women. Such women cannot accuse men of being beasts, barbarians, or dirty; they are female versions of the man's own sexual self-image. (Consequently this set of fantasies denies the meaning of sexual differences.) And such women are ready to be sexually satisfied. Through their easy excitability they foster a male's excitement and assuage his sexual self-doubts. Because they are easy to please and experience great pleasure, these women are not viewed as potential castrators.

Ultimately, the fantasies focus on female compliance. The women do not surrender to their own desires; their desires are seen simply as extensions and mirrors of male desire and, therefore, essentially irrelevant and nonthreatening. The woman's voraciousness is seen as in the service of his needs, not in opposition to them and not primarily as a means to her own gratification.

In actuality, I have heard many women complain that men are frightened by active female sexuality. And men have confirmed that observation. Some men resent the "work" sometimes needed to arouse women, and also resent women they regard as voracious in their demands, women who require "servicing." Sexually active women sometimes find themselves in the position of having "withholding" partners, men who would prefer to think that what pleases them is exactly what pleases (or should please) the woman, as it is in the fantasy of the omni-available woman. It is this wish that, in part, fuels the fantasy of simultaneous orgasm as the *sine qua non* of successful sex—the complete mutuality or mirroring that is effected in fantasy. At one level, such a wish serves simply as a denial of the sexual distinction (Brunswick 1943; Person 1983). At another level, the strength of this wish suggests some psychic continuity with the longing for a preoedipal ministering and "feeding" mother.

My clinical impression is that men for whom behavioral derivatives of the omni-available woman fantasy are urgent (for example, those men who *never* permit their wives to wear underpants) often camouflage intense oral and dependent needs under the guise of sexual ones. In addition, the narcissistic use of the object may bolster phallic narcissism as a defense against a sense of phallic vulnerability. Clinically, one sees that when such men are sexually frustrated by their wives, their fantasies and dreams frequently veer to images of degradation of women or vengeance and violence directed against them.

On the one hand, fantasies of the omni-available woman appear continuous with earlier demands for instant gratification. On the other hand, the fantasies appear compensatory to specific anxieties engendered in the normative crises of male psychosexual development: anxieties about virility, the availability of female objects for sexual gratification, and the sexual difference.

Because these fantasies and their enactments reflect desires and counteract anxieties that appear to be widespread among men, one must look for their antecendents in common male experiences, not in the idiosyncratic experiences of a few.

Developmental Sources for Feelings of Sexual Inadequacy and Fears of Female Unavailability

From where does a sense of sexual deficiency and potential "starvation" arise? Traditional accounts of male sexual fears focus largely on castration anxiety referable to the fear of the father implicit in the oedipal triangle. Oedipal themes and fears are explicit and ubiquitous in male fantasy life; they are copiously revealed in conscious fantasies, dreams, and free associations, and leave little doubt as to their centrality to the male experience. Unfortunately, as I have already noted, they have been emphasized without sufficient attention to a series of developmental issues that affect their intensity.

Castration anxiety (if construed as only deriving from the oedipal struggle) is not a sufficiently broad category to account for all the fears one sees in adult men. It is difficult, for example, to accept castration anxiety as the sole explanation for the clinically frequent fears of female rejection and genital inferiority. There are clearly other sources that contribute to these anxious preoccupations either directly or by intensifying castration anxiety. One source derives from significant developmental experiences with females, another from the nature of the male's sexual realities at different points in the life cycle. A third source, though more variable, relates to the ambiguous masculine identification seen in some men and the degree of feminine identification that may obtain.

Freud (1920), Horney (1932), and, more recently, some of the French theorists (Chassequet-Smirgel 1985; McDougall 1980) have suggested that the first blow to the boy's sexual narcissism is his *inability* to secure his mother's sexual love. In other words, fear of his father and the threat of castration (at the hands of his father) are not the only factors in the boy's renunciation of his mother. As Freud (1920) suggests, the boy also withdraws his libidinal investment from his mother because he feels he does not have the genital endowment to compete with his father. His sense is that his mother rejects him in favor of his father because his penis is too small. Many men never recover from this literal sense of genital inadequacy. One might say that many men are destined to suffer lifelong penis envy.

It was Horney (1932) who most fully elaborated this formulation of male sexuality, and I shall quote her at some length.

The anatomical differences between the sexes lead to a totally different situation in girls and in boys, and really to understand both their anxiety and the diversity of their anxiety we must take into account first of all *the children's real situation* in the period of their early sexuality. The girl's nature as biologically conditioned gives her the desire to receive, to take into herself; she feels or knows that her genital is too small for her father's penis and this makes her react to her own genital wishes with direct anxiety: she dreads that if her wishes were fulfilled, she herself or her genital would be destroyed. (Pp. 355–356)

The boy, on the other hand, feels or instinctively judges that his penis is much too small for his mother's genital and reacts with the dread of his own inadequacy, of being rejected and derided. Thus he experiences anxiety which is located in quite a different quarter from the girl's; his original dread of women is not castration-anxiety at all, but a reaction to the menace to his self-respect. (P. 356)

As Horney notes, the boy suffers a blow to his sense of genital adequacy and consequently to his masculine self-regard. At the same time, he is reminded of earlier frustrations (oral, anal) at the hands of that same mother. Consequently, in accordance with the talion principle, "the result is that his phallic impulses to penetrate merge with his anger at frustration, and the impulses take on a sadistic tinge." If the anger and sadism thereby generated are sufficiently great, the female genital (again by virtue of the talion principle) will itself become the source of castration anxiety and the mother, along with the father, will be seen as a potential castrator.

However, Horney observed that sexual sadism and fear of the female as castrator were not invariable among her patients, whereas the anxiety connected to masculine self-regard was almost universal. As she puts it, "According to my experience the dread of being rejected and derided is a typical ingredient in the analysis of every man, no matter what his mentality or the structure of his neurosis" (1932, p. 357).

Horney quotes Freud (1923) to the effect that the boy "behaves as if he had a dim idea that his member might be and should be larger" (1923, p. 358). She points to the continuity between the narcissistic blow to the oedipal boy and the adult man's ongoing anxiety about the size and potency of his penis. This mental set has several different components: fear that his genitals are inade-

81

quate, the corollary fear of female rejection, and a sense of the superior endowment of his rivals.

I believe that this formulation delineates one important developmental strand in male sexuality. However, it remains difficult to substantiate the continuity between these hypothetical childhood events and adult fears.[5] We do know though that the conjectured events are recapitulated in adolescence by virtue of the male and female adolescent's *real situation* and again by the adult's *real situation*.

The boy's narcissistic wound—his inability to secure the object of his childhood sexual desire—is recapitulated in adolescence by the frequent unavailability of female sexual partners. The typical male adolescent experience is a sense of perpetual sexual arousal, with only masturbation as a primary outlet. The boy's arousal and desire comes at a time when he is not psychologically or realistically equipped to achieve a secure sexual relationship easily. This reinforces any fears he may have about securing a sexual object and his own genital adequacy. Yet he may well resent the unavailability of a female partner. Since he often assumes other males are doing better (a derivative of his oedipal defeat), his feelings of inferiority compared with other men are intensified.

Furthermore, the ambivalent uncertainty about his control over his genital equipment and sexuality can be traced to physical aspects of the adolescent induction into genitality. An adolescent boy is frequently overcome by sexual arousal over which he feels he has little control. While spontaneous erection and ejaculation may be best understood as release phenomena, the subjective experience is an ambivalent one. The boy's anxiety arises out of a contradiction in the sexual experience: pride in the pleasure and power of the phallus, but the simultaneous sense that the phallus is not really owned by him, not under his control. The idea that the penis has a separate life is reflected in the common tendency of young men to personify the penis by, for example, bestowing pet names upon it. Adolescent boys feel shame at inopportune

5. Although I have noted many associations in analyses of men that demonstrate the male's sense of inadequacy vis-à-vis women and their sense of inadequate endowment, I have found it difficult to definitively establish the genetic source of the anxiety. It appears to me to stem from different developmental levels.

erections and some live in dread of the humiliation of having a visible erection at the wrong time. Wet dreams betray the boy's sexuality to his parents, particularly his mother. He often feels he has no privacy.

The adolescent's sense of lack of control over the penis is almost never completely resolved. This feeling may frequently become a locus for symbolic elaboration and thereby a key factor in shaping male fears. It predisposes men to fears of impotence or premature ejaculation, the subjective evidence that they may not be fully in charge of their members.

Insecurity about his sexual adequacy and his ability to please a woman are reinforced by another of the vagaries of sexual reality—a lifelong distinction between the sexes. There is a basic imbalance in sex—men are stuck with the fact that their sexual excitement is visible. There is no hiding the failure to achieve an erection and, simultaneously, no certain way to gauge the woman's sexual arousal or orgasm. That he is a good lover is difficult to ascertain, and many men are unable to accept a compliment or reassurance from women. The fear surfaces in some men's obsessions about their partners' past lovers—"Was he better?" "Did she have more orgasms? Better orgasms?" and so forth. Of those men apparently confident in their performance, some are so intent on controlling the female by ensuring her pleasure that their own participation lacks spontaneity. Some men feel comfortable pursuing their own pleasure only after they have brought the woman to orgasm; some attain full erection only when the woman is sated. For some men, the need to please the woman first is a means of disarming her, of protecting against the threat of castration by the female.

How do men cope with these anxieties about performance and female rejection? Collectively and individually, men submerge their fears into an overestimation of male sexuality. Horney (1932) speculates, and I concur, that the boy's remedy to the narcissistic mortification implicit in the renunciation of his mother is a defensive phallic narcissism. This is reinforced by the boy's compensatory identification with the phallic power of his father. His phallic narcissism, intensified by his adolescent's pride in the erectile power of the penis, coalesces with the magical sexual properties with which he has endowed his father and other rivals. Out of this emerges the individual and collective male pride in some version of "machismo" sexuality, no doubt reinforced by male gender socialization or "male bonding."

Men attempt to assuage their sexual self-doubts through active sexuality or fantasies of it, in which control over the penis is sought through sexual mastery and control over the sexual object. In his fantasies, the male reverses his self-doubts and anxieties. He endows his penis with supernatural powers and size (those he once attributed to his all-powerful father). As described by Zilbergeld (1978), the collective male fantasized penis is "two feet long, hard as steel, and can go all night" (p. 23).

Fear of female unavailability and rejection leads to compensatory fantasies about a cornucopia of sexually available women, and the male projects his own sexual desires onto his fantasy females. It is they who are forever randy, perpetually aroused and ready. Most important, they are always available and never rejecting. The assumption is that women are automatically satisfied and require no special stimulus; they take their pleasure from his pleasure. But the fact that the omni-available female (even in fantasy) is often viewed with condescension, contempt, or even sadism bears witness to the underlying experience of frustration at the hands of the mother (and subsequent female objects) and resentment at the rejecting female.

Consequently, men may be internally driven to conquer women, to possess them, and to do so repeatedly. They may also split their sexual desires between a number of different women, usually those seen in a somewhat inferior position, who can therefore be readily dominated. This allows men to control the source of sexual gratification and ensures the availability of one sexual object if another vanishes. In fantasy, it will be the woman, not the man, who is humiliated. It is she who will serve him, admire his penis, and submit.

Control of the sexual object serves as a compensatory device that defends against the male child's sense of inadequacy and inferiority in relation to both parents and the humiliation of the unavailability of a sexual object at different points in his life. Out of revenge, the man reverses the humiliation implicit in both his infantile and his adolescent experience: he stands ready to demand sexual availability and fidelity while disavowing it himself.

Thus far I have focused on the male need to fantasize the availability of sexually available women ready to submit to his needs, wishes, and demands, and its relationship to anxieties about his genital adequacy and to his dread of female rejection. I have suggested in passing that the fantasy of the omni-available woman also reveals the male wish to disavow the sexual distinction. The centrality of this latter dynamic—and the feminine identification that may be related to it—appears more clearly in the underlying structure of the lesbian fantasy.

Lesbian Sex

The erotic fantasy life of many heterosexual men contains lesbian themes. Although heterosexuals of both sexes fantasize homosexual sex with members of their own sex, usually only heterosexual men also fantasize homosexual sex involving the opposite sex. Some heterosexual women may be aroused by male homosexual sex, but these are relatively few.

Fantasies of lesbian sex have two major variants. In the first, the sexual encounter is exclusively between the women; in the second, the women are joined either by a male onlooker or a male participant. These fantasies appear to be on a continuum; the transitional fantasy between lesbian sex and threesome sex is the fantasy in which the male is initially an onlooker, then joins in the sex play.

In the second variant (in which a male is present), what is remarkable is the cooperation among the players. Jealousy and possessiveness are nowhere in evidence. There is sexual sharing of the highest degree, plenty to go around, and no one feels excluded.

Lesbian sex is so much a part of pornographic movies intended for heterosexual men that it is almost a convention of such films. Some men are surprised by their arousal in response to a film sequence of female lovemaking. In other words, the visual depiction of lesbian sex arouses some men who do not generate the fantasy independently.

Even though the lesbian fantasy does not appear to occupy as prominent or conscious a place in the typical man's fantasy life as that of the omni-available woman, a study by Mavissakalian and associates (1975) revealed that heterosexual male arousal to lesbian images was as high as the response to either female auto-erotic or heterosexual erotic images. (Homosexual men were not aroused by lesbian sexual encounters.) In a significant minority of men, it is not only a fantasy preoccupation but a major pursuit.

Lesbian fantasies, like those of the omni-available woman, are often enacted in derivative forms. The most common way to introduce a second woman into the bedroom is in conversation —in love talk, not in the flesh—though watching two women make love and threesome sex have become more popular practices in recent years (or so it seems from the reports of my patients). Another derivative of the fantasy is a man's insistence that his different lovers know of one another's existence, though the women may decline to meet.

One of my former patients, a call girl, reported that call girls were frequently requested in pairs. They may be required to make love to one another while the client looks on and masturbates or the three may engage in sex together. (The irony within this configuration is that so often the call girls are thereby allowed to satisfy their real homosexual proclivities.)

The most facile exploration of the meaning of lesbian sex as a fantasy theme is that the heterosexual male has concocted a fantasied harem for himself. This explanation obscures the subtler and deeper meanings of the lesbian fantasy behind the façade of a voracious macho sexuality. In order to understand the fantasy, one must consider why the women need to make love to each other rather than simply awaiting the man (the omni-available fantasy) and why, so often, the male subject is not himself ostensibly part of the conscious fantasy.

In part, the male preoccupation of sex with two women simultaneously is probably frequently related to an underlying anxiety about potency. Although there may be the lurking fear that women can do without him (as in the lesbian film sequence), in the fantasy the male feels powerful because he controls two women and believes, despite their mutual erotic involvement, that only he can satisfy them. At another level, the women protect him. They do part of the erotic work for him (with each other), even satisfy each other, so that the performance burden on him is lessened. To some degree, a voyeuristic impulse is obviously implicated, though the question remains as to why "lesbianism" is favored. From clinical data, it appears that the lesbian image is often linked to residual incestual impulses and to an unconscious female self-identification.

Desire, Envy, and Identification

One woman is often significantly older than the other in the lesbian fantasy, perhaps suggesting the simultaneous satisfaction of the man's desire for a teacher/nurturer and his wish for someone to initiate, the virgin he can claim as his conquest and who will be eternally grateful to him. In pornographic films, the older woman often initiates the younger in the wonders of lesbian sex. When the male appears, however, the attention is focused primarily on him. The presence of the two women together suggests superabundance and a connection with the omni-available fantasy vis-à-vis compensatory male dominance.

But insofar as one woman appears to represent a powerful maternal figure whose presence lends potency, these fantasies appear to reflect incestual fantasies and oedipal desires. The older woman appears to be a representation of his own mother, sometimes represented in his fantasy life as his mother-in-law. For some men, the incest theme is disguised by their unconscious identification with the younger woman in the lesbian fantasy, though I have been surprised that some male patients have an intuition of the meaning of the identification even prior to any analytic work.

In the course of her analysis of K., McDougall uncovered the existence of "a powerful and immutable fantasy whose meaning eluded him" (1980, p. 26). "The cast of characters frequently included two women in which the elder, perhaps the mother, was beating her daughter on her bare buttocks" (p. 26). This took place in front of an unnamed spectator. K. also engaged in sex in which he beat his young mistresses's buttocks and sometimes beat himself in front of a mirror. In her extended analysis of these fantasies and behaviors, it appeared to McDougall that K. identified both with the mother with the whip (the phallic woman who possessed the paternal phallus) and the girl who eroticized the welt marks (representing castration). For McDougall, the presence of the unknown onlooker established the transformation of the primal scene and of the oedipal constellation. That is, it undid the boy's discovery of his parents' sexual pleasure together.

Although McDougall's patient reports a perverse elaboration of the lesbian fantasy, I believe some of the dynamic elements may have more widespread applicability. What is especially remarkable in lesbian fantasies is the absence of the oedipal rival of childhood. In some, the triad becomes a dyad. Insofar as there is a triangular configuration, there is a reversal in the makeup of that triangle. Two males and one female have been replaced by two females and one male. In both dyadic and triadic lesbian fantasies, the rival father has simply vanished.

An important, common dynamic function of the fantasy is that the boy solves the oedipal competition by disavowing his father. In part, he disavows the genital distinction as well. In analysis, however, it is often revealed that one or the other woman in the lesbian fantasy is phallic, thereby symbolically preserving the man's own hidden phallus. Whether the man identifies with the woman viewed as phallic (and thereby incorporates her phallus) or whether the phallic female is the disguised man himself (disguised to elude the castrating father), the oedipal constellation has been rearranged. The boy has solved the problem of his envy of one or both parents. He usurps his mother as libidinal object and incorporates her power as well.

Both these dynamics—identification with the phallic female and self-disguise—resonate with those found in the full-blown transvestitic syndrome (Ovesey and Person 1976; Person and Ovesey 1978). But it ought not be assumed that these fantasies have reference just to evasion of the competitive and castrating father. Importantly, they also reveal a feminine identification, originating in the preoedipal period, that persists or is reinvoked for dynamic and defensive reasons.

The lesbian preoccupation appears to be restricted to heterosexual men; some researchers even consider the erotic response to lesbian sex as diagnostic of male heterosexuality. In contrast to homosexual men, the fantasy life of transvestic men is known to be permeated with lesbian imagery. Consequently, the "lesbian" fantasy promises to shed some light on the divergence and convergence of sexual development among "normal" heterosexual men, homosexuals, and transvestites.

Freud (1924a) argued that the sexual distinction was not a matter of grave consequence for the boy until he had entered into the positive oedipal constellation. Only then does he conceive the idea that castration might be the punishment for coveting his mother. In other words, it is then that the sexual distinction appears to have any personal meaning for him. In response to the imagined threat, he renounces his mother and identifies with his father.

However, the transvestite and homosexual resolutions allow two different solutions to the problem of two sexes and its inevitable concomitant problem, sexual rivalry. Both homosexuals and transvestites are uncomfortable in a world made up of two sexes, but each group solves this problem in diametrically opposed ways. Each eliminates one sex. Homosexuals live their intimate lives in a world of men, whereas transvestites eliminate men—to some degree in reality and to an extensive degree in fantasy. Both solutions resolve the dilemma of oedipal competition by eliminating one sex; if there is no sexual distinction, there can be no oedipal competition.

The homosexual solution is familiar analytic territory, but I will elaborate somewhat on the transvestic solution. It is traditionally understood as a simultaneous identification with and love for a phallic woman (Fenichel 1930). In transvestites (heterosexual cross-dressers) there is evidence of an unusually intense and ultimately unresolved oedipal struggle in which the incestual object persists and oedipal rivalry is perpetuated. The female clothes simultaneously symbolize the mother as a transitional and incestual object (Ovesey and Person 1976; Person and Ovesey 1978).

The transvestites' fantasy (two women, albeit with penises, making love together) symbolically destroys the father. At the same time, clothes (or feminine self-identification) represent a defensive posture in the oedipal constellation (Ovesey and Person 1973; Person and Ovesey 1978). They magically protect the transvestite in two ways: (1) they symbolize an autocastration, a token submission to his male competitors, which wards off their retaliation; and (2) they disguise his masculinity and serve to disarm his rivals. The clothes conceal his penis, the symbol of masculine power, and deny his hostile intent. He therefore feels safe because his rivals do not know that secretly he is plotting their demise. He avoids detection by passing as a woman, which makes it possible for him to risk assertion and thus validate himself as a man.

I would suggest that on the route to the "normal" resolution of the oedipal complex, most (all?) boys transiently attempt anterior (prior) solutions. It is here that the boy's penis envy (sense of inferior genital endowment) plays a role. Insofar as he feels he must renounce his mother because of his meager endowment, he has three choices.

The first alternative, of course, rests on the boy's temporary renunciation of his erotic ambitions, his projection of his ego ideal onto his father, identification with his father and the promise that identification will eventually prove its own reward (Chasseguet-Smirgel 1985). Second, he can assume the feminine role and hope to incorporate the paternal phallus in a homosexual resolution. Last, he can declare the father's penis nonexistent, that is, he can construct a world made up solely of women—or a world of women in which he is the only male. This is a solution that eliminates oedipal rivalry and is clearly related to the transvestic solution. I would suspect that the lesbian fantasy, pronounced as it is in heterosexual men, reflects back to a transient transvestic resolution (analogous to the transient homosexual resolution found alongside "normal" oedipal resolution in so many analyses). The weaker the boy's authentic father-identification, the more pronounced the transvestic solution appears to be.

In part, female identification reflects envy of women and their prerogatives, but it also masks the negative oedipal constellation. The boy, in essence, envies both parents. Though I have stressed transient female identification as a solution to oedipal anxiety, there is, of course, a deeper layer. Regression to preoedipal roots, particularly merger or incorporation fantasies with mother that are reparative to separation anxiety, may be the more important dynamic. Ovesey and Person (1973, 1976) have reported such fantasies as prominent in studies of transvestites and the cross-gender disorders. These same fantasies, to a lesser degree, are regular features seen in the psychoanalysis of male patients. The lesbian fantasy becomes one way of simultaneously achieving security through incorporation or merger while preserving (hetero) sexuality.

Person and Ovesey (1978) reported transient transvestic episodes in adolescence (similar to transient homosexual episodes in adolescence) that resolve without clinical sequelae, though distinctive unconscious conflicts and constellations persist. The lesbian fantasy remains as the residue from an attempted transvestic resolution of the threat posed by the fact of two sexes, a resolution that is anterior to the conventional oedipal resolution and that may persist alongside it.

Discussion

That the theoretical discussion of male sexuality has been limited by its emphasis on the male reaction to oedipal castration anxiety is somewhat startling. Male fears in the model have tended to be reduced to castration anxiety related to the all-powerful father. Some theoretical attention has been paid to the threat of female castration, but little to the boy's subjective sense of female rejection. The boy's sense of genital inadequacy in relation to both mother and father has been inadequately explored. Yet pervasive conscious and unconscious fears of inadequate size are frequently seen in the clinical situation.

The theoretical neglect of the influence of the mother-son interaction at different developmental stages insofar as it impinges on male sexuality seems to me quite strange. In its way, it parallels the male's fantasy solution to his sexual fears. In fantasy, women are available and their nonavailability cannot therefore constitute the problem. In theory as well, the problematic relationship to men is stressed. That females do not figure prominently in the developmental theory which men write about male sexuality is another way of negating the importance of females.

As is well known, both in theory and in life, male psychology dictates a misunderstanding of the female as being the same, neither separate nor different from the male. In fantasy she is lusty, which seems a clear projection of male adolescent sexuality onto the fantasied women and a denial of any sexual distinction. To the extent that such dynamics have influenced our theories, they have obscured a full appreciation of male development. It is not strictly true, as some have claimed, that psychoanalytic theories of sexuality accurately describe male sexuality (even while falling short of elucidating female sexuality). Not just castration anxiety but penis envy is pivotal in the mental life of men. The male insistence on penis envy as a central dynamic in women seems to be partly a projection of men's own feelings toward stronger and more powerful men.

In addition to castration anxiety (fears of the father), men commonly suffer from a sense of inadequacy in relation to the mother and from fear of her as well. The male's fear of the female, of his inability to please her (and his anger at her), stems from different developmental levels: fear of the preoedipal mother who abandons/engulfs; of the anal mother who intrudes/indulges; of the phallic-narcissistic mother who confirms/denigrates masculinity; of the oedipal mother who cannot be fulfilled, rejects, falsely seduces. Maternal identification, stemming from envy or separation anxiety or both, also plays a role in the under-

92

The Omni-Available Woman and Lesbian Sex

lying concerns in male sexuality. It sometimes dictates an attempted transvestite resolution to the oedipal conflict and to its "normal" resolution. Phallic narcissism, reinforced by the male cultural ego ideal of macho sexuality, tends to obscure these underlying dynamics. The fantasies of the omni-available woman and lesbian sex are "windows" on that buried world.

BIBLIOGRAPHY

Bak, R. C. 1968. The phallic woman: The ubiquitous fantasy in perversions. *Psychoanalytic Study of the Child* 23:15–36.
Barclay, A. M. 1973. Sexual fantasies in men and women. *Medical Aspects of Human Sexuality* 7:205–216.
Brunswick, R. M. 1943. The accepted lie. *The Psychoanalytic Quarterly* XII:458–464.
Chasseguet-Smirgel, J. 1985. *Creativity and perversion.* New York: Norton.
Fenichel, O. 1930. The psychology of transvestism. *International Journal of Psycho-Analysis* 11:211–227.
Freud, S. 1920. Beyond the pleasure principle. In *The standard edition of the complete psychological works of Sigmund Freud* 24 vols. (hereafter *S.E.*), ed. J. E. Strachey, vol. 18 (1955), pp. 7–64. London: Hogarth Press, 1953–1974.
——— 1923. The infantile genital organization: An interpolation into the theory of sexuality. *S.E.*, vol. 19 (1961), pp. 141–145.
——— 1924*b*. The dissolution of the oedipus complex. *S.E.*, vol. 19 (1961), pp. 173–179.
——— 1924*a*. The economic problem in masochism. *S.E.*, vol. 19 (1961), pp. 157–170.
Friday, N. 1980. *Men in love: Male sexual fantasies: The triumph of love over rage.* New York: Delacourt Press.
Goldberg, H. 1976. *The hazards of being male: Surviving the myth of masculine privilege.* New York: New American Library.
Horney, K. 1932. The dread of women: Observations on a specific difference in the dread felt by men and women respectively for the opposite sex. *International Journal of Psycho-Analysis* 13:348–360.
Kinsey, A. C., Pomeroy, W. B., Martin, C. E., and Gebhard, P. H. 1948. *Sexual behavior in the human male.* Philadelphia: W. B. Saunders.
———. 1953. *Sexual behavior in the human female.* Philadelphia: W.B. Saunders.
Lukianowicz, N. 1960. Imaginary sexual partner and visual masturbatory fantasies. *Archives of General Psychiatry* 3:429–449.
Mavissakalian, M., Blanchard, E. B., Abel, G. C., and Barlow, D. H. 1975. Responses to complex erotic stimuli in homosexual and heterosexual males. *British Journal of Psychiatry* 126:252–257.
May, R. 1980. *Sex and fantasy: Patterns of male and female development.* New York: Norton.
McDougall, J. 1980. *Plea for a measure of abnormality.* New York: International Universities Press.

Ovesey, L., and Person, E. S. 1973. Gender identity and sexual psychotherapy in men: A psychodynamic analysis of homosexual transsexuality, transvestism. *Journal of the American Academy of Psychoanalysis* 1:53–72.

———— 1976. Transvestism: A disorder of the sense of self. *International Journal of Psychoanalytic Psychotherapy* 5:219–236.

Person, E. S. 1983. Women in therapy: Therapist gender as a variable. *International Review of Psycho-Analysis* 10:193–204.

————. In press. Male sexuality and power. *Psychoanalytic Inquiry.*

Person, E. S., and Ovesey, L. 1978. Transvestism: New perspectives. *Journal of the American Academy of Psychoanalysis* 6:301–323.

Person, E. S., et al. N.D. Gender differences in sexual behaviors and sexual fantasies in a college population. Manuscript.

Thorne, E. 1971. *Your erotic fantasies.* New York: Ballantine.

Zilbergeld, B. 1978. *Male sexuality.* New York: Bantam.

4

Men Who Struggle
Against Sentimentality

ROY SCHAFER

Introduction

Sentimentality often turns out to be a key word in the analysis of men. And when it does, it is likely to come up in the context of a struggle against sentimentality. Those men who engage in this struggle regard sentimentality as a serious fault to be corrected or a great danger to be avoided, and so they give it a prominent place in their analyses. Typically, they do not value for their potentially adaptive uses and consequences the phenomena they subsume under the heading "sentimentality." It is my aim in this presentation to outline a neutral, balanced analytic view of this struggle. To prepare some of the ground for my project, I must first spend a bit of time on the idea of key words in the analytic process.

A large part of every analysis may be described as working out the meanings that the analysand has unconsciously assigned to key words. Sentimentality does not, of course, stand alone as *the* key word in anyone's analysis. Other key words on the manifestly positive side are genuineness, individuality, freedom, integrity, spontaneity, and rationality; on the manifestly negative side are such words as rejection, humiliation, emptiness, dependency, and helplessness. And, of course, much time is always spent on the key words masculinity and femininity.

All of these are key words in that they and the images in which they are embodied refer in large part to major values or ideals. It is with reference to them that analysands try to regulate what they think, feel, or otherwise do in their daily lives and in their analytic sessions. Because these values or ideals are based on infantile prototypes and so are used in an absolute and severe judgmental manner, they are instrumental in shaping and limiting what will be contemplated consciously, disclosed, and explored in the analysis. Also, analysts approach all of these key words with the assumption that they are imbued with closely interrelated basic conflictual issues. Far from floating around as a set of isolated terms and associated images, they are strands in a web of significance.

There are good grounds for the analyst's sustaining an interest, often only implicitly, in the uses and implications of these key words, their imagistic representations in dreams, daydreams, and memories, and their interconnectedness. An emphasis on this aspect of technique is intimately associated with the rise of ego psychology and the psychology of preconscious mental processes (see, e.g., Kris 1952). Because these developments in psychoanalysis expose the arbitrary either/or dichotomization of analytic work into "deep" and "shallow," they allow the analyst greater flexibility in both attentiveness and intervention. From the technical point of view, paying close attention to key words is not necessarily an intellectualized way of working, for typically this aspect of analysis is strenuously and artfully resisted by the analysand. What is in question is the analysand's basic way of making sense, assigning value, and establishing a secure defensive position. The analysand, wanting this source of meaning, value, and safety to be taken as self-evident, presents it as a matter of common sense, that is, as a condition for dialogue rather than as a subject for investigation. It is felt to be too dangerous to do otherwise. The coherence and continuity of ego activity seem to depend on this condition. Nor is the analyst's paying attention to these key words necessarily a superficial way of working, for it confronts the cognitive component of the analysand's disruptive compulsion to repeat. On this account it facilitates the analysis of transference. And looking at the matter of language most broadly, one must say that analytic work is in the nature of dialogue; we work with words, though not with words alone, and some words matter more than others.

I return now to the key word sentimentality and to the theme of this chapter, which is the struggle some men in analysis put up against their own sentimentality and often against the sentimentality of others. Sometimes this struggle is noisy and sometimes it is conducted with quiet desperation. It is well known that many men in our society present themselves as strongly set against being sentimental. I am referring particularly to men who present themselves as aridly obsessional, icily narcissistic, lovelessly depressive, brutally phallic, or psychopathically superficial —in other words, more than a few men, though by no means all or all to the same extent.

Analysts cannot fail to appreciate the fact that these men have grown up in a context of parents and others who have extreme and conflictual values of their own with respect to sentimentality and who, in one way or another, have tried to pass these values on. Nevertheless, analysts cannot view the antisentimentalists' self-presentations simply as a matter of social conditioning and intrafamilial conformity. For psychoanalytic purposes, purposes that are geared to facilitating personal change, analysts cannot view the child simply as a blank page to be written on by a set of like-minded authors. Analysts consider it more important to develop an understanding of how antisentimentality has figured in the child's attempt to resolve conflictual issues centered on sexuality and aggression and comprehended in the terms of the fantasies of early childhood. Antisentimentality is an action, not a static result. Usually, analyzing the struggle against sentimentality helps open the gate to a wide variety of repudiated but developmentally significant and even valuable strivings on the child's part. It is on this basis that successful analysis of large-scale versions of this struggle leads in the long run to greater clarity about, and tolerance of, issues of gender identity, more intense and stable relationships with others, a fuller subjective sense of being alive in a social world and in a worthwhile way, and a more continuous, inclusive, unembarrassed grasp of one's own complex life history as a boy and man. In contrast, analytic impasses may develop when the analyst neglects to look into the lifelong activities that have gone into an analysand's conspicuous antisentimentality, or when the analyst fails, despite the best of efforts, to make analytic headway against it.

For these reasons, an analytic discussion of men who struggle against sentimentality has implications not only for the general psychology of men, in which respect, for example, it will bear on what often seem to be their deficiencies of empathy and their fears of self-disclosure, dependency, and intimacy; this discussion will also have important technical implications concerning both the analysis of resisting and transference and the analysis of diverse aspects of emotional experience in general (Schafer 1964). Additionally, certain significant countertransference issues may come to the fore in the course of analyzing this struggle, and I shall turn to these issues in the concluding section of this chapter.

General Conceptions of Sentimentality

Tastes and mores vary among individuals and social groups, and they change over time and with changing circumstances or contexts. Consequently, the conceptual boundaries of sentimentality are not clear or stable, and the common attitude toward sentimentality is not always predominantly or exclusively positive or negative. It seems that there can be no single, simple, satisfactory definition of the word, no definition that is timeless and value-free.

We cannot be satisfied with the dictionary that defines sentimentality as "excessive emotionality": we must ask: Who decides what is excessive and why or according to which values and ideals and in which circumstances? Or consider, for example, Wallace Stevens's apparently opposite characterization of sentimentality as "a failure of feeling." We must question this judgment in two respects at least—what sort of feeling was Stevens, as a certain kind of man, valuing as successful or true, and to what extent was he reacting specifically against certain kinds of poetry and trying to do what poets have always tended to do, and that is to establish an aesthetic for whatever is new or problematic in their own poetry? Or take Gilbert and Sullivan's poking fun, in their play *Patience,* at Bunthorne, the sentimental young man with his flowers. Weren't they, among other things, using comedy to criticize the affectations of sensitivity that flourished in some quarters during the heyday of nineteenth-century Romanticism? And with respect to Thomas Carlyle's pronouncement, "The barrenest of all mortals is the sentimentalist," we must take into account the fact that he was writing in the post-Rousseauean era when sentimentalism was an ideology which, among other things, was being directed against the ideology of rationalism. Today sentimentalism is under ideological attack by feminists, at least insofar as the social seduction of women into being sentimentalists plays a part in their being exploitable by men as well as by other women, notably their mothers. And it is regularly under attack by serious critics of the fine arts; in a taken-for-granted way, they praise any avoidance of sentimentality in the works they are considering.

This brief survey indicates more than the ambiguity of the term. It also indicates the extent to which sentimentality has been and continues to be compared invidiously to autonomy, power, genuineness, and rationality. Sentimentality tends to be linked to childishness, weakness, irrationality, victimization, insincerity, and womanishness. Consequently, it should come as no surprise that the struggle against sentimentality often occupies a strategic position in the clinical analysis of men.

Subjective Referents of Sentimentality

To which features of emotional responsiveness do male analysands allude when they appear to be setting themselves against
being sentimental? Commonly, these men subsume under sentimentality (or some key word or image equivalent to it) being
tearful, nostalgic, enthusiastic, thrilled, awed, or infatuated; also,
yearning or pining for someone or being playful in an exuberant
or silly way. They say of an experience of this sort that it is not
rational or that they themselves have no reason to feel that way.
They wish to avoid any suggestion that they are naive or immature; they dread being labeled maudlin or self-indulgent; they
cringe before the possibility of acting inappropriately or fool-
ishly. Embarrassed or ashamed, they cover up, minimize, or attempt to dispel any incipient feelings and expressive behavior of
these sorts. They fall silent; they speak with heavy irony or
self-mockery; they become irritable, listless, or circumstantial.
Alternatively, they quickly profess a hopeless attitude when
faced with their own sensitivity; one representative member of
this group lamented, "What good does it do?" before he continued in an increasingly anxious manner to convey a fear of
falling apart and a suspicion that he was being seduced by the
analyst into a weakened position.

Bear in mind, however, that in individual cases it may be only
selected areas of sentimentality that are proscribed. For example,
it may be that sentimentality is tolerated with respect to women
but not men or with respect to sadness but not exuberance. It is,
of course, important to analyze the principles of selection being
employed by the analysand in each instance.

Regressive Aspects of Sentimentality

Speaking analytically and broadly, the struggle against sentimentality may be characterized as a struggle against regression. More
exactly, it is a struggle against what amounts to regression for

each of the male analysands in question, for regression is a term that covers many processes and phenomena. Its application should always be based on an individualized decision. Also, although the handful of these processes and phenomena that I shall take up next cannot be neatly distinguished from one another, they can be discussed under separate headings, and it does seem to be useful to do so in order to sort out the threatening aspects of sentimentality. The processes and phenomena I shall single out are daydreaming, being a baby, identification with one's mother, anality, and latency-age boyishness.

DAYDREAMING

Daydreaming is a complex process that analysts understand as a compromise formation. It is more than a means of erotic and egoistic wish fulfillment as Freud (1908) tended to describe it, for, to one degree or another, it must be viewed in its defensive, moralistic, and adaptive aspects too. In other words, it may be adequately understood only in terms of the principle of multiple function (Waelder 1930). But whatever the relative weight of these various components may be, however pleasant or unpleasant the daydream, and however manifest or latent its essential features, it tends to have a decidedly sentimental aspect. It is sentimental in the way it depends on simplifications and idealizations and in the naive, even melodramatic emotionality that accompanies its renditions of success and failure, good and evil, safety and danger, and gratification and deprivation. Daydreamers are not hard-nosed; they are not engaged in cool and complex appraisals of self and others or of past, present, and future situations. Their daydreams feature illusions, and they imply being asocial or withdrawn. Their daydreaming does not represent the highest level of adaptive functioning of which they are capable. Daydreamers have taken a holiday from external reality, or they have beaten a hasty retreat from it. They are approaching life sentimentally.

For example, the analysand who pines for the analyst over the weekend is engaged in sentimental and idealizing daydreaming. This is so because analytic life with the analyst is often disagreeable in various ways, and, upon analysis, the analyst's physical absence is typically experienced in a complex and highly ambivalent fashion. Similarly, daydream idealizations are implied by nostalgic longings for the family of one's childhood, when in one's cooler moments one recognizes this family to have been a source of much suffering. The case is the same when one is thrilled by the praise of a superior whom one fears, scorns, or mistrusts and when one weeps over a kind word said by a friend who, one realizes upon sober reflection, doesn't really understand that well or care that much.

Analysands who struggle against sentimentality are wary of what they regard as the undermining effects of daydream idealizations. In their eyes, the simplifications of daydreaming undo the unrelenting realism or irony and the absolute autonomy they have worked hard to achieve and on which their invulnerability and worthwhileness seem to depend. They fear and condemn their regressive daydreaming and the illusion-filled emotionality that their daydreams manifest. Because their negative attitude may have had significant adaptive consequences in their development, they may use this fact to buttress the maladaptively defensive aspects of their current antisentimentality.

BEING A BABY

Very often, men imagine sentimentality to be a shift of functioning in the direction of being a baby. As a baby, one is vulnerable to merging into others or, a bit later and analogously, melting mindlessly into symbols such as the home or the flag. In this context, sentimentality means being passive, helpless, yielding, or surrendering. These men fear that they will lose touch with reality and expose themselves in naked emotionality to derision and abandonment. The orality of this regressive move is suggested by the common link between sentimentality and being a sucker and swallowing things whole or, in other words, lacking refined taste. These analysands find it frightening to seek comfort or to accept it when it is offered, no matter how painful or terrifying reality may seem to them at the time. In their daily lives, they may deny their wives and children any chance to mother them, and in their analyses they repeatedly rebuff the analyst as a real or imagined mothering figure.

IDENTIFICATION

For men who struggle against sentimentality, its regressiveness usually involves increased emphasis on intolerable identifications with their mothers. In their sentimental moments they feel womanish or perhaps girlish. On this basis they sense that a threat of homosexual responsiveness lurks behind their image of the sentimentalist. They sometimes claim to document this connection by referring to the blatant sentimentality that characterizes certain aspects of the gay community (e.g., certain figures in the entertainment world). The regressively intensified identification with mother may pertain to any one of a number of developmental phases: it may pertain to the mother as witch or smothering breast, though conspicuously it is likely to center on the sick, suffering, raped, or castrated mother of the primal scene as envisioned by the phallic-oedipal boy.

It should always be kept in mind that, in one of its aspects, a desperately increased emphasis on this sentimentalized identification serves as a defensive regressive move. It is designed to mask signs of identification with the primal father. The primal father is the indomitable, castrating phallic force. He is a man who is in no way womanish or babyish. He is the early awesome ideal figure that Freud (1921) described, the figure whose heights one can never hope to reach and with respect to whom, both fearfully and wishfully, one is always something of a softy, a soft touch, a pushover, even a willing slave, in effect a castrate and sexual partner.

In another of its aspects, this shift of emphasis toward maternal identification may accomplish a hostile and anxiety-relieving caricature of the mother whose emotionality, whatever its nature, stands for both her castratedness and her frightening castrating tendencies. And in a third aspect this shift implies a return to a dyadic relation with mother from which father and siblings are excluded.

The analyst sees in this regressive shift to sentimentality wish fulfillment as well as defense. This doubleness is characteristic of all defensive shifts. What is lacking in these instances is the male analysand's recognition, tolerance, and moderated integration of the androgynous implications of a freer emotionality. What is present is his attempted compromise of what he views as irreconcilable extremes, and because he knows that this compromise cannot be stable or satisfying, he must reject it as dangerous. Thus the analyst confronts a complex layering of wishful and defensive postures, with antisentimentalism on top, the primal father at the base, and the maternal identification in the middle. And all of this gender emphasis may prove in certain cases to serve mainly as a screen for significant pregenital issues. I have already mentioned orality; anality is another such major pregenital issue.

ANALITY

Analytic work also shows that anal ambivalence plays a particularly important role in men's struggles against sentimentality. It has long been known how vividly people construe emotionality in terms of anal fantasy (see, e.g., Brierley 1951, chap. 2). In this regard, people deal with emotions as with fecal matter, that is, both as dangerously sadistic expulsions or explosions and as shameful, dirty, messy incontinence. Although fantasies of this sort are encountered in especially clear form in obsessional settings, they manifest what appears to be a universal equation of affect and feces (and secondarily urine, as when mirth and tears are in question). We need not depend on analytic observation to recognize the ubiquity of this equation, for we encounter it in jokes, colloquial sayings and metaphors, insults, rituals, myths, and fables of every kind.

Thus, being well defended against sentimentality is like having a clean diaper, while unrestrained sentimentality is like "crapping all over the place." "Crapping all over the place" is likely to express as much vigorous and torturing defiance as passive, erotic letting go and opening up. The "tight-assed" person is not sentimental, while the sentimentalist is a sentimental slob. In this context one encounters the well-known unconscious links between conventional femininity and passive anality; for example, to be masculine is to be impeccably toilet-trained, as clean as an astronaut, as controlled as a drill sergeant. As one male analysand put it, when reflecting on the anal fantasy implied in his antisentimentality, "It's like denying I have an asshole."

For these men, it is women who are the sentimental "assholes." It is, by the way, not unusual for women to share this unconscious stereotype and, on this basis, to feel masculine once they stop being "assholes" and dare to maintain their dignity against all the seductions and assaults that are conducive to their behaving otherwise.

In the analytic relationship, a man's antisentimentality is likely to involve not only his enacting sadistically defiant constipation and his fearfully contemplating the possibility that analysis will reveal that his true sexual interest is in passive anal homosexuality. It may involve as well his attempt to seduce the analyst into performing symbolic rape in the form of pressing confrontations and interpretations of his defensive dealings with emotionality; perhaps he can seduce the analyst to make direct demands on him for emotional output.

Consequently, it is more than likely that working out the anal meanings or uses of antisentimentality in the here and now of the analysis will render the entire realm of emotional experience more accessible to expression and understanding. Here I include such potentially adaptive phenomena as the release of strangulated grief, the spilling out of exhilarated exhibitionism, playfulness and tenderness, and the bursting out of proscribed temper tantrums and competitiveness.

BOYISHNESS

Boyishness plays a significant role in men's sentimentality and their struggle against it. I refer particularly to the emotionality of latency-age and prepubertal boys and to their play and playfulness. Boys in this phase of development are passionately serious and passionately playful, often simultaneously so or in rapid alternation. Under good developmental conditions, they are not unduly threatened by latent homosexual and other such aspects of their functioning in this emotional way, as they are resilient when they have gone to extremes or when their experiments have turned out to be too much for them.

The man who struggles against sentimentality defensively introduces significant discontinuity into the life history available to him. He does this by trying to renounce whatever limited boyishness he once enjoyed or suffered, as the case may be. He gives the appearance of having bypassed earlier phases of development. He presents himself as being unable to play or as too vigorously segregating work from play. For him there is no play in work, and there is strenuous work in play. He participates in analysis in the same way. It is unthinkable to be simply playful before the analyst or with him. He would never entice the analyst into playful interaction. Those playful interactions that can and do take place are not tolerated well. He tends to be stodgy and humorless. A shared laugh is something to be coped with, and it may be used to discredit the analyst. At best, he substitutes telling jokes dryly for having open-ended fun. He has no heroes, just as he has no chum or buddy to comfort him or share experiences with him. He is set against the boy he has remained in his psychic reality, just as he is set against the woman, the toddler, and the baby.

Life Historical Background

What, now, is the likely life historical background of this revolt against boyishness and all the other variables I have just mentioned? One family drama seems to have contributed to the development of vigorous antisentimentality on the part of certain male analysands. I cannot say, however, that this drama is sufficient to explain this particular outcome. In broad outline, it seems that, as boys, these men have had to cope with a disappointingly unresponsive and uncomforting mother, a woman who seems to have been depressed and also embittered and rivalrous in her relations with men and boys alike; and further, they may have had to cope with an obsessionally rigid or narcissistically aloof, competitive father who regularly debunked his young sons' enthusiasms and identificatory strivings for both closeness and autonomy. One analysand would imagine his father's voice saying "schmuck" or "good boy," depending on the waxing and waning of sentimental responses. And in a recent paper on tearfulness, Wood and Wood (1984) present an account of a man's struggle against tearfulness that includes some of these features of development as well as current phenomena of the sort I described earlier. One is reminded of Kohut's (1977) emphasis on the damaging effects on healthy narcissism of unappreciative mothers and of fathers who do not tolerate well their being idealized and taken as models by their sons.

One of the functions that gets disrupted under these conditions is what Hartmann (1956) discussed in another context as the testing of inner reality. Hartmann emphasized that it is misguided to equate rationality only with the testing of external reality. He argued that, from the analytic point of view, inner reality, with all its archaic, irrational, volatile, and otherwise extreme features, is as important a part of reality as whatever is of moment in the surrounding world. Here lies the response to the analysand's defensively despondent question, "What good does it do?" The good it does is to increase the analysand's readiness to consciously recognize, participate in, and empathize with his inner reality, and on this basis to achieve what growth and mastery he can where that is needed. Viewed in this light, inner reality is neither a horror to be avoided nor a disease to be cured; it is a world to be transformed in its most shaky and disruptive aspects and to be enjoyed as well as coped with. To this consideration one might add another: unconsciously, "inner reality," along with whatever else is "inner," tends to be equated with femininity and filth. To turn away from inner reality may itself imply a central struggle over negative views of maternal identification, anality, and one's own ideals and aspirations.

Countertransference

I come finally to countertransferences that may arise in the course of analyzing men who struggle against sentimentality. It should be obvious that analysts who are waging battles of their own either on behalf of sentimentality or against it will be more prone to countertransference responses to this struggle. They will identify too much or too little with one side or the other of their analysands' positions or affective experiences. Subtly or obviously, they will try to rid the analysands of their "diseased" sentimentality or antisentimentality rather than understand why these positions have been adopted. They may use the analysands' emotional experiences to immerse themselves vicariously and more comfortably than they could otherwise in experiencing the feelings they have difficulty tolerating and enjoying in their own lives. Alternatively, and with the help of projection, they may combat their own sentimental tendencies by a rigorously skeptical analytic approach to their analysands' sentimentality; on this basis they may neglect the developmental potential and relevance of sentimental responsiveness and thereby limit their own analytic effectiveness.

These departures from the neutral analytic attitude may be characterized metaphorically in terms of some of the psychosexual issues that were mentioned earlier. For example, orally, the analysand may be put on starvation rations or drowned in chicken soup. Anally, the analyst may be constipatedly clean or diarrheic with empathy. The countertransference may be homosexually seductive or castrating in a this-is-our-song atmosphere or in an atmosphere of macho imperviousness, rationalized as advocacy of the reality principle. And so on. In these respects it is well to recall the Scylla and Charybdis of analytic work sketched by Fenichel (1941)—too much need on the analyst's part for volatile affect or too little tolerance of it.

The neutral analyst, the analyst who maintains the analytic attitude, will be enough at peace with his or her own sentimental tendencies to be able to participate through trial identifications in both the regressive features of the analysand's sentimentality and his struggle against it. The analyst will not participate in this empathic way in order to implement or enforce any particular personal value or outcome. His or her guiding value is the health value of knowing reality inside out, as it were, for it is this kind of knowledge that helps the analysand work out less costly and painful solutions or compromises than those with which he came into analysis. In other words, the analyst's technical ideal is neither to conduct an analysis sentimentally nor to turn analysands into sentimentalists. The technical ideal is to find ways to provide for sentimentality a better understood and less threatening place in the analysand's range of responsiveness and awareness. The ideal is an even-handedness in this realm as in all others (Schafer 1983).

Concluding Remarks

Of the many subtopics I could have addressed but did not I should like to mention two. One is the sadistic potential of the struggle against sentimentality—that component of it that may be used to block empathy with others and to deny them their own emotional intensity and scope. The other is the problems that may come up when an antisentimental male works with a female analyst—such problems as the transference conviction that one is being infantilized, effeminized, or incestuously seduced as soon as that analyst pays the least bit of attention to the analysand's emotional experience.

I do hope that in exploring some of the major meanings attributed unconsciously to sentimentality by those men who struggle against it I have made it clear why it is not analytically helpful to attempt to define sentimentality precisely. Sentimentality is such an individual matter that it is best taken as a key word to explore rather than as a fixed, universal phenomenon to capture in a few general words.

BIBLIOGRAPHY

Brierley, M. 1951. *Trends in psycho-analysis.* London: Hogarth Press.

Fenichel, O. 1941. *Problems of psychoanalytic technique.* New York: Psychoanalytic Quarterly.

Freud, S. 1908. Creative writers and day-dreaming. In *The standard edition of the complete psychological works of Sigmund Freud,* 24 vols. (hereafter *S.E.*), ed. J. E. Strachey, vol. 9 (1959), pp. 141–153. London: Hogarth Press, 1953–1974.

———. 1921. Group psychology and the analysis of the ego. *S.E.,* vol. 18 (1955), pp. 67–143.

Kohut, H. 1977. *The restoration of the self.* New York: International Universities Press.

Kris, E. 1952. *Psychoanalytic explorations in art.* New York: International Universities Press.

Hartmann, H. 1956. Notes on the reality principle. *Psychoanalytic Study of the Child* 11:31–53.

Schafer, R. 1964. The clinical analysis of affect. *Journal of the American Psychoanalytic Association* 12:275–299.

———. 1983. *The analytic attitude.* New York: Basic Books.

Waelder, R. 1930. The principle of multiple function. *Psychoanalytic Quarterly* 15:45–62. English translation, 1936.

Wood, E., and Wood, C. D. 1984. Tearfulness: A psychoanalytic interpretation. *Journal of the American Psychoanalytic Association* 32:117–136.

II

*What Men Fear:
Male Vulnerabilities
and Solutions*

5

What Men Fear:
The Façade of
Castration Anxiety

ARNOLD M. COOPER

Introduction

The simplest answer to the problem in my title is that all men fear some things and some men fear everything.

George Stade (1984) has discussed the American fantasy that the achievement of manhood requires liberation from apron strings, a process which is never finally completed. As a result, "all men will remain boys trying to become men" (p. 22), and real men are those who are immune to the control of women even in the form of love. At least a major portion of this feeling is innately consequential to the fact that all men have spent a significant formative part of their lives totally in the care of women who wiped their bottoms, fed their mouths and their egos, and held their hands whenever there was danger or difficulty. The prevalence of forms of macho behavior can be generally understood as counteracting the inner fear of reversion to this earlier state.

Rather than attempting to sort out fears that are culturally induced from fears that are inevitable, either as a consequence of the anatomical distinction between the sexes or of the fantasies of infancy, I will discuss, briefly, male fears as they appear in the psychoanalytic setting.

Brief Review of Literature

Depending on how it is defined, with few exceptions, psychoanalysts are agreed that castration anxiety is ubiquitous, although there are sharp differences of opinion about whether it is central. In discussing Little Hans, Freud (1923) said, "Anyone who, in analyzing adults, has become convinced of the invariable presence of the castration complex, will of course find difficulty in ascribing its origin to a chance threat—of a kind which is not, after all, of such universal occurrence; he will be driven to assume that children construct this danger for themselves out of the slightest hints, which will never be wanting" (p. 8). Rado (1956) and Kardiner (1939) seemed to be among the exceptions, adopting the view that significant amounts of castration anxiety arose only in those cultures where there was specific threat of castration or severe prohibition on infantile genital play.

It is generally accepted today that although castration anxiety may appear ubiquitously, the underlying meanings and origins of the phenomenon vary greatly. When we examine castration anxiety closely in the clinical situation, we find that sometimes it is just that, but that often it is a less fearful disguise for other kinds of fear. What are these other fears? A significant portion of the history of psychoanalysis may be viewed as a reordering of the sources of fear, and I will review some of these dismal lists. Freud, in his earliest version of psychoanalysis in *Studies in Hysteria* referred to a broad range of unacceptable thoughts and feelings that aroused anxiety or shame. As he developed his system he suggested that inhibited or unacceptable specifically sexual wishes aroused anxiety. In 1926 he reformulated his theory of the nature of anxiety, and described a developmental sequence of fears: fear of the loss of the mother or the mother's breast, fear of loss of the mother's love, fear of the loss of the penis, fear of the loss of the superego's love. These were the universal fears. Castration anxiety, although only one in this sequence, and not the ultimate fear, nonetheless was given special place as the heir to the boy's oedipal strivings and the motive for the consolidation of the superego.

Starcke (1973) elaborated this sequence into the idea that each individual learns to fear the loss of what he loves. The experience of weaning, the experiencing of the loss of exclusive possession of the mother, the loss of feces, the loss of baby teeth, are the templates for the imagined loss of the penis.

Melanie Klein (1957), using her object-relational model of infant development, wrote of the very early paranoid fear of the mother's hostile destructiveness, followed by the depressive fears of the loss of the mother. These were the elementary affective states out of which all other fears, as well as other affects, differentiated in the course of development. Other authors have given special emphasis to the fears of the anal phase, as determining for development.

Using a somewhat different early object-relational model and interested primarily in the "basic neurosis" of psychic masochism, Edmund Bergler (1952) later described a septet of baby fears ranging from earliest oral fears to later anal and phallic fears. It was his view that these fears represented the combination of misinterpreted ordinary experiences of infancy and the need for esteem-saving explanations to help avoid the full recognition of infantile helplessness. His septet included the fear of starvation, of being poisoned, of being choked, of being chopped to pieces, of being drained, of being trampled, and finally of castration. It was his view that everyone experiences each of these fears more or less sequentially, in varying degrees. These fears arise out of the narcissistic need to attribute to the fantasied malevolence of the mother the narcissistic injuries inevitably sustained as a result of the discrepancy between infantile omnipotent fantasy and relatively passive reality. While the genetic explanations of Klein and Bergler are, of course, speculative, there is little difficulty identifying adult versions of these fears, and one can view them as derivatives of these early universal experiences.

Psychoanalysts, all impressed by the primitive nature of fears that can be uncovered in adult patients, have continued the attempt to adduce the early experiences that would account for these unconscious contents. Recently Joyce McDougall (1984), a French psychoanalyst speaking from the point of view of object-relations theory, described the three great critical and frightening events of infantile life as the discovery of otherness, the discovery of the sexual difference, and the discovery of mortality, each of these an occasion for terror and trauma. Chasseguet-Smirgel (1984), also of the French school, added to these the discovery of the frightening difference between the generations with their attendant differences in size and power. In her view, the little boy's conviction that his penis is too small to service his mother is a severe trauma to his developing self-esteem.

Heinz Kohut (1984) has described the core fear of annihilation anxiety—the fear of the dissolution of the sense of self or the experience of self-fragmentation. He stated that all later fears, including castration anxiety, are disintegration products arising secondary to the indescribable core annihilation fear. The need to maintain a cohesive and developing self is the organism's essential innate program, and interference with this inherent push toward self-realization sets in motion all fears and rages. Kohut, who saw development in terms of optimal, empathic experiences, nonetheless was explicit in stating that structure building through transmuting internalizations occurs only in the presence of optimal frustration, and that frustration carries with it the threat—that is, the fear—of the loss of a necessary self-object.

Roiphe and Galenson (1981) have suggested that there is an early pregenital stage at about a year and a half when the anatomical sexual difference is noted and when castration anxiety becomes manifest in both sexes. For example, male children at this time, in their view, normally engage in denials of the frightening sexual difference as shown by hyperactivity, increased holding and play with the penis, and a slowed development of fantasy play and body-image integration. Roiphe and Galenson describe that some children are significantly traumatized during this period, and pathological castration anxiety may begin pregenitally, showing later pathological manifestations appropriate to later developmental stages.

One could continue to add to this list of fears. Incidentally, I find it an interesting footnote that Kinsey and associates' study (1948) of male sexual behavior contains no reference to castration anxiety. I chalk that up to midwestern optimism. The variety of pregenital terrors that have been described by different authors, each claiming primacy for the fear described, is, I believe, testimony to the pervasiveness of primitive, fantastic terror that is present in the unconscious life of adults and, therefore, by implication in the developmental life of the child. Clearly, no existing data will support one theory over another, nor are these theories necessarily contradictory rather than complementary. They reflect the theoretical predilections of the theorists and the psychoanalytic need to postulate an early version of unconscious phenomena.

With the possible exception of Bowlby's (1969), every significant psychoanalytic theory has assumed that disappointment, frustration, fear, and rage are inevitable and necessary, at least in some degree, if the baby is to separate, individuate, and develop psychic structure. Fear and rage, the inevitable accompaniments of frustration, are significant motivators for all growth processes, and the infant's frustration is an inevitable consequence of being alive. The central role of anxiety as the guide for adaptation was, of course, the theme of Freud's "Inhibitions, Symptoms, and Anxiety" (1926) and is built into the core of analytic theory.

A Newer View of Castration Anxiety

While psychoanalytic researchers have differed in their view of what is the basic fear or the sequence of fears, there has been almost no disagreement concerning the special significance of castration fear and the castration complex in shaping male behavior. It is now a very long time since Freud proclaimed as a shibboleth of psychoanalysis that the Oedipus complex was the nucleus of neurosis, and today the focus of much of our analytic literature is on preoedipal phases and their fateful outcome in later life. There has been a profound shift by many psychoanalysts in their clinical work, from listening primarily for the cues to oedipal conflicts to picking up the nuances of earlier events and their reverberations in the analytic situation. Under the circumstances of our current knowledge and interest, what is the appropriate place to assign to castration anxiety as an organizing fear for the formation of psychic structure, a central fear of the male? Freud (1937), in "Analysis Terminable and Interminable," concluded that the basic fear for men is the fear of passivity toward another male, a form of castration anxiety. At this late point in Freud's work, it was, I think, no longer clear whether he regarded castration anxiety as primarily an oedipal event or the final form of expression of the earlier losses and fears.

That castration anxiety occupies a special place, at least in conscious thinking, is as evident to any clinician as it is to the man in the street and is illustrated by endless clinical and anecdotal data. Bomber crews in World War II reported that when antiaircraft flack became particularly terrifying, some crew members would remove their flack vests, obviously intended to protect the vital organs, and place the vests over their genitals—what the crew members perceived to be their vital organ. Many men report that frightening stories, or looking at a gory wound, lead to sensations in the groin, sometimes accompanied by tightening of the scrotum and shriveling of the penis. The vernacular is replete with expressions of castration.

It is my emphasis in this chapter that castration anxiety so close to consciousness is so because it is, in some respects, the *least* feared of the baby fears, representing the compromise formations arising out of earlier fears and hiding within it the earlier fears, which are far more threatening. As our knowledge of the significance of earlier object-relational and interpersonal events in early development has increased during the past two decades, it is desirable to try to specify the manifestations of castration anxiety in terms of the developmental events to which they refer. Earlier literature already refers to anal and oral castration. We may wish to refer to castration anxieties secondary to failures of body-image integration or secondary to empathic failures of one or the other parent, or secondary to faulty identifications with one or the other parent, or secondary to difficulties in separation-individuation. In this light, we might look upon castration anxiety as a manifestation of the defensive compromises achieved in the effort to resolve past crises and as a significant indicator of the nature of those crises for the particular patient.

Referring to the phallic phase, Fenichel (1945) said:

> The boy at the phallic phase has identified himself with his penis. The high narcissistic evaluation of the organ can be explained by the fact that just at this period it becomes so rich in sensations, and distinct tendencies actively to pierce with it come in the foreground. . . . The fear that something might happen to this sensitive and prized organ is called castration anxiety. This fear, to which such a significant role for the total development of the boy is ascribed, represents a *result* and not a cause of this high narcissistic evaluation. Only the high narcissistic cathexis of the penis at this period explains the efficacy of castration anxiety; its forerunners in oral and anal anxieties over loss of breast or feces lack the dynamic force characteristic of phallic castration anxiety. (P. 77)

It is my view that our current views of narcissism are far more object relational than libidinal, and we might well consider that it is precisely the anxieties over the loss of the breast or of the love of the mother that can provide quite sufficient dynamic force to propel the individual toward the creation of defensive compromises. Terrifying as it is, the loss of the penis is still only a loss of a part of oneself, a relatively small loss compared with the still-active fears of pre-oedipal total annihilation. What is observed later as castration anxiety is often a desperate attempt to "escape forward," as it were, to more advanced levels of representation, escaping from the more primitive and frightening versions of narcissistic threat.

As I have tried to indicate, no one has conceived of development without the emergence of some hierarchy of fears. Clinically, disentangling those portions of the individual's personality organization that have been constructed for the specific purpose of avoiding fantasied fears, or for the purpose of actualizing masochistically sought fearful fantasies, assumes a major portion of our therapeutic effort. Defense against the disorganizing qualities of these primitive fears as they emerge toward consciousness is a matter of highest psychic priority. If the defenses are successful, what were originally defenses against fears often achieve secondary autonomy and are experienced as if they were wishes of the most powerful sort, the patient being totally unaware of the underlying or originating fears. It is important to recognize that these defenses against fears may themselves be fears, although fears at a higher level of organization, less frightening and tolerable in consciousness, and at times not consciously acknowledged as fears. It is my thesis that castration anxiety, terrifying as it may be, is one of those higher-level fears, organized at a time when structuralization through verbalization and cognition is more advanced, and that therefore it may serve as a defense against more primitive, cognitively chaotic, and disorganizing infantile terrors. Castration anxiety, conscious or close to consciousness and therefore allowing real or symbolic preventive actions to be undertaken, affecting a body part rather than the whole self, is defensive against those earlier, more fantastic fears.

I will next present a brief clinical vignette of a patient I treated some years ago, illustrating the complex intertwining of castration anxiety with other fears.

Clinical Vignette

HISTORY

A forty-year-old researcher, Mr. A., presented for treatment stating that he was suicidally depressed. He felt this was largely a consequence of his increasing conviction that he was a hopeless failure. The patient was a highly intelligent, cultured man of unremarkable appearance, who had been married since age thirty-one to a woman he liked but who seemed even less interested in sex than he. They had had a few wonderful sexual experiences before marriage and had then settled into being good friends.

He described himself as having been a fearful child, unathletic, afraid of bodily injury, especially disturbed at his having to wear glasses, for which he was teased. His father was an affable man, pleasant and passive at home, and physically powerful and athletic. He was friendly to the patient but took no special interest in him or in his academic achievements.

His mother was a powerful figure, self-important, fashionable, seductive, contemptuous of her husband's relative lack of success. She was quite paranoid and talked often of how neighbors were trying to pry into the household secrets. Though without real interest in what her son's talents might be, she regarded him as special and different from other children since he belonged to her. She insisted that he be well dressed, learn how to eat properly in restaurants, and be as ostentatiously bourgeois as she tried to be.

The patient's paternal grandmother was a significant figure who visited a number of times a year, lived with his family during his fourth year, and was lively, loving, and unself-conscious. His most vivid childhood memory was of jumping into his grandmother's bed in the morning and having a tickling session with her, with both of them laughing as hard as they could. This was in dramatic contrast to the mother who, the patient insisted, literally never touched, fondled, or played with him, and attempted to interfere with any of his spontaneous pleasures.

The patient recalls being attracted to the girls in his class in grade school, high school, and college but having no idea how to go about making any contact, convinced he lacked any qualities that would attract a woman. In short, he was a well-integrated, severely narcissistic character, convinced that he was a psychopath, which he was not, and without borderline features. At the time he entered treatment he maintained the firm belief that were he ever to attempt intercourse with a woman other than his wife, who was as sexually frightened as he, she would treat him with such contempt and scorn that he would be crushed for life. He had a significant success phobia, certain that in any comparison with another man, he would be found wanting and would be humiliated. At the same time, he was secretly scornful of everyone, including me.

COURSE OF TREATMENT

For the sake of brevity, I will mention only a few significant foci of Mr. A.'s preoccupations in sessions early in the fourth year of his analysis and will recount a series of dreams that relate to the nature of his complicated anxieties.

In extended associations the patient described himself as made of shit. Napoleon's description of Talleyrand as "shit in a silk stocking" accurately described his self-image. He perceived his body as a soft shit phallus, constantly endangered by women or stronger men. At the start of treatment he spoke of his penis as too small, soft, and unattractive but at the time of the dreams I will relate he felt his penis was at least adequate, and perhaps even beautiful, especially if erect. At this time in the analysis there had been a profound change in his capacity for healthy assertiveness and he seemed to have overcome his fear of success.

He remained terrified of women, their bodies, their parts, their "cutting" behaviors, their fantasied humiliation of him. Female genitalia seemed "spooky" to him, and he mildly depersonalized if he tried to look at his wife's genitals. He remained literally terrified of the idea of being in bed with a woman other than his wife, whom he regarded as nonsexual.

Despite giving vivid descriptions of his mother's insensitivity and somewhat bizarre behavior, several years of treatment passed before he began to be aware of his feelings that she had not always been a good mother, and he was angry at her.

It was late in the treatment before he could acknowledge the beginnings of any sense of relationship and possible attachment to me. He preferred to view me as a technician with a job to do. Underlying this was the certainty that I could have no interest in someone made of shit. This view also served to ward off regressive and frightening preoedipal transferences in which I would emerge as the terrifying mother of infantile fantasy.

The dreams I will report occurred during a two-week period in the fourth year of treatment, after the following changes had taken place in the treatment and in his life. His relationship within the transference had become distinctly more positive. He felt an identification with my kindness toward him and began to see himself as basically a kind person. He resumed a hobby that he had always loved but never pursued because his mother ridiculed it when he was a boy. He found himself hugely attracted to a woman he met at work. During the two weeks prior to the dreams I will report, he had a number of dreams affirming his fantasy that his body substance consisted of shitty fluids from his mother, as part of his anal birth.

Three Dreams

DREAM 1

"I've read of a new procedure for curing cross-eyes. You make three surgical cuts around the eye, two on the outside of the eye and one on the inside. It releases lots of fluid. It works. No one knows why. I feel that I've lagged behind in my knowledge. I must do it. It's simple and rapid. I'm in an operating room. There are parts of equipment that I've never investigated, and I don't know how to handle them. I become unsterile, I touch something. I'm too embarrassed to tell anyone. A doctor there, a man older than me, knows all the parts of the machine."

DREAM 2

"There's a woman in a grave somewheres buried. The woman is a distant relative. They couldn't embalm her properly. We had to be sure she was totally embalmed. I asked, "So what if she's only half embalmed?" They say, "Cockroaches will eat her body. It's a state law to prevent that." There are photographs around the grave. I think it must have a personal meaning for the family.

ASSOCIATIONS

"I know I'm afraid of exploring a woman's body. I know you think that the eye has something to do with female genitalia. I always feel so unappetizing. I can't see how anyone can be attracted to me as a sexual object. Seeing my mother in the bathroom always scared me. I remember the first time my wife had a vaginal discharge. It was a creamy, fetid fluid like spoiled rotten milk. It was a milky discharge, maybe poisonous milk. I've always had a fantasy of being preoccupied with fluids building up in cavities of my body and having to be released. I had the notion that if women can't give milk with their breast the pressure has to be released and it comes out as a discharge through the sexual orifice. I really believed that. I'm not sure that I still don't. I always had the feeling that the buildup of fluid requires an immediate release. Like feces. If I have to go I have to go right on the spot. If I have an urge to ejaculate, I have to do it. The thing about the eye, I was reading in the newspaper about a new cure for some eye disease where they put in botulinus toxin to paralyze the muscle of the eye. It poisons the muscles and temporarily cures the disease. In the dream it seemed terribly important that you didn't have to cut muscles. You'll probably say I'm afraid of anything to do with cutting because I'm not sure that my penis is firmly attached."

"I don't know what the cockroaches are about. I'm comfortable in disgusting situations. As a child, I would think of disgusting things coming out of my mother's bottom. I saw rust stains on towels and assumed it must be something from her that was very disgusting. I think of vaginas as a disgusting sort of place. If I have to put my penis into it, I want to get it out fast. I remember as a child seeing my mother's breasts. I called them fat bellies. She got very angry. I didn't know that breasts made milk. I really thought it was milk coming out of my wife's vagina the first time I saw that milky discharge. As a child, it never occurred to me that

124

milk came out of breasts. Breasts were always frightening, and they were always hidden. I was absolutely astounded by the idea of children being fed by breasts. My mother never told me anything about women. I remember my baby sister's pussy was pretty. It was pink and hairless. Women's parts are bizarre like moon creatures. I hate pussies with lots of hair. I remember looking at pictures of female anatomy once and looking at the cervix. I loved the picture of the cervix. It seemed like a cute button, maybe a little mouth, an end to the passageway or a little nose. I remember thinking that it is the mouth to the uterus and sad that it was covered with all that milky stuff."

The patient continued to discuss these dreams with a powerful sense of sadness interlaced with an even more unusual optimism that he need not continue to maintain such distorted and self-destructive fantasies.

Two days later he had the interesting experience of suddenly recalling several satisfactory sexual affairs that had taken place during his early twenties. Mr. A. said, "I'd completely forgotten these. I'm amazed to remember them. It's hard for me to believe that I put my penis into the womb." He was unaware that he had said womb for vagina. He then went on to speak of how seductive his mother was. "She wore beautiful black dresses with her breasts exposed. She had huge breasts. Like my mother, I look best in black."

He reported the following dream the next session.

DREAM 3

"I'm in the kitchen of our apartment with my wife. I suddenly see three or four brown, flat snakes on the floor moving very fast like cockroaches. They are brown, the color of earth or bugs or feces. I run into the next room for a bug spray. I am frantic. The bug spray is in a jar labeled with a chemical name. I run back, my wife is frantic too. The snakes have found their nest; a large bloated thing with fur on top of it. It's a dead cat. The white fur is being lifted off the body of the dead cat. It's disgusting. I spray, but I feel I can't kill them. There's a plastic bubble around it. We put it in a garbage bag. The big garbage bag is on the street. I have missed the pickup of the garbage. This ominous-looking bag with the thing in it has to sit in our garbage room, which is painted bright red. I write garbage on the bag so that no one will open it. I notice that garbage is the name of the bag maker. I write "trashe" on the bag. I see that I've misspelled it. I cross out the "e."

ASSOCIATIONS

"I always thought sex was dirty. Taking advantage of poor girls, hypnotizing them, sticking my penis where it didn't belong. From the first time I heard that men put their penis in the vagina, I was repelled. When a kid said that my mother—I mean father—sticks his penis in mother, I was revolted. That whole area is dirty. The dead cat bloated like shit. The snakes rapid as roaches. There was a roach here, there are roaches in my apartment, I was masturbating and saw a roach. The flat snakes wriggling is like a disgusting part of my life, like sudden roaches that panic you. I think the dream is about me as disgusting and rotting. It's odd that I dreamed that I'm disgusting after talking of successful sex with women."

"It's odd, maybe I think that I'm a female. I feel like the image in the dream, distended and round. The snakes are soft brown penises. They have a homing propensity to this large, dead cat. It's a nest in plastic. A large balloon with fur on it. Then I can see that it has feet and paws. The dead cat in the state of decomposition. I always thought the womb was an unhealthy place. It had acrid odors. That the womb sheds its lining means that it's a cavity that rots. The sexual parts of the woman are frightening. You never know what will come out of it: liquid, farts. It's like going into a cavern with stalagmites and stalactites. You could get lost in there."

I will end the report of the clinical material at this point. The patient's fantasies and their elaboration are dense, and I can only give a hint of their character in this presentation. A theoretical proposition cannot be "proved" by the presentation of complex clinical data. I hope only to indicate that the point of view I am putting forth provides interesting new ways of thinking about and integrating the clinical material.

Discussion

It is my suggestion that we can describe multiple intertwining fears in this patient, none of them fully subsumed under each other, giving rise to versions of castration anxiety. There are fears of the female genitalia as a poisonous sewer emitting rotten milk and feces, attended by fantasies of his body and penis as weak and useless by-products of this birth canal, all made of shit. There are fears of the female person as overwhelming, disappointing, castrating, and controlling, accompanied by fears that his penis is small and soft and will be swallowed or bitten off or corroded by the vagina. In fact, he prefers to think of the smaller cervix as the vagina. There are fears of the female breast as a squashing, enormous, unattainable symbol of power, with the anxiety that by comparison his penis is a pitiful object of ridicule to any woman, incapable of creating the fluids that connote sexuality. There are fears of the male as hard, castrating, retaliatory, with the consequent fear of exposing his penis in a murderous competition that he must lose. There are fears that his own body is a derivative of his mother's genitalia, disgusting and unacceptable, and unable to support his ideals and ambitions. Furthermore, there are fears of acknowledging the difference between the sexes —in numerous parapraxes, penises and vaginas switch gender and gender is grossly confused. For example, when describing his first ecstatic sexual encounter with his wife, he said, "It was beautiful. She was very wet. I just slid into her penis." The very existence of the sexual difference implies terrifying consequences —mother can make new babies, steal his penis, swallow him into her huge cavity, and more. This fear-induced confusion leads to defensive wishes to have mother's more powerful breasts and genitalia, or to endow her with a penis, or to shed his penis so she won't be envious and so on. I could expand this list of preoedipal fears and their attendant representations in forms of castration anxiety.

The underlying terrors described are terrifying in their own right, and not primarily because they arouse the fear of loss of the penis; rather they are frightening because they arouse the terror of being overwhelmed, they damage the capacity for activity and awaken the threat of being driven back into helplessness and passivity. The new and strange perceptions of infancy, whether of the strange genitalia or of the primal scene, for examples, shake existing cognitive schemata and threaten to extinguish the reassuring power to anticipate, thereby giving rise to potent new anxieties. The fear of castration, as it appears in the oedipal phase, may be relatively *de novo* in some instances, but in the more usual characterologically disturbed patient it represents the arousal of earlier fears of which the fear of castration is the tolerable close-to-consciousness compromise representation. Giving up a narcissistically endowed part is preferable to giving up the narcissistic self. Castration anxiety may not in itself simply subsume and replace the earlier fears; rather it indicates an attempt to disguise and escape from them. Under the best of circumstances, the earlier infantile sense of inadequacy is revivable and feeds the terror underlying the defense of the penis. In cases such as my patient, where development does not proceed relatively undamaged, a veneer of castration anxiety hides the fact that the patient is only too willing to forgo penis narcissism and concede the inadequacy of his penis, expanded to include his entire self-image, in order to assure himself that his rage and envy at his mother need not elicit retaliation from her and that he still merits her care. Simultaneously, in a bitter irony, he unconsciously demonstrates masochistically what it was that she did to him—destroyed him as a person; castration is only one portion of that.

What Men Fear: The Façade of Castration Anxiety

Summary

Psychoanalysts, following Freud, have generally emphasized that castration anxiety is the central fear, for which preoedipal fears represented an evasion through regression. It is my suggestion that, at least in the patients with character pathology who are seen in analysis today, castration anxiety serves to defend against more primitive preoedipal terrors, still active unconsciously and readily activated in the analytic situation.

I have tried to show, with the aid of a hugely condensed clinical vignette, that the clinical presentation of the castration complex may productively lead to a search for underlying fears. These more elemental fears, threatening the narcissistic integrity of the individual, are often masked by a façade of conspicuous castration fears. In these cases the castration anxiety is best understood as a less frightening defensive compromise in which the individual is willing to imagine the loss of a prized possession, however painful that may be, in order to maintain a semblance of wholeness and the assurance of survival.

BIBLIOGRAPHY

Bergler, E. 1952. *The superego.* New York: Grune & Stratton.
Bowlby, J. 1969. Attachment and loss, vol. 1. *Attachment.* New York: Basic Books.
Chasseguet-Smirgel, J. 1984. *Creativity and perversion,* New York: Norton.
Fenichel, O. 1945. *The psychoanalytic theory of neurosis.* New York: Norton.
Freud, S. 1909. Analysis of a phobia in a five-year-old boy. In *The standard edition of the complete psychological works of Sigmund Freud,* 24 vols. (hereafter *S.E.*), ed. J. E. Strachey, vol. 10 (1955), pp. 3–147. London: Hogarth Press, 1953–1974. Footnote added 1923.
——. 1926. Inhibitions, symptoms, and anxiety. *S.E.,* vol. 20 (1959), pp. 77–172.
——. 1937. Analysis terminable and interminable. *S.E.,* vol. 23 (1964), p. 250.
Kardiner, A. 1939. *The individual and his society.* Westport, CT.: Greenwood.
Kinsey, A. C., Pomeroy, Wardell B. and Clyde E. Martin, 1948. *Sexual behavior and the human male.* Phila., PA.: W. B. Saunders.
Klein, M. 1957. *Envy and gratitude.* London: Tavistock.
Kohut, H. 1984. *How does analysis cure?* Chicago: University of Chicago Press.
McDougall, J. 1984. "The significance of the reconstruction of trauma in clinical work."

Paper presented at the American Psychoanalytic Association Workshop for Mental Health Professionals, New York, November.

Rado, S. 1956. *Psychoanalysis of behavior.* New York: Grune & Stratton.

Roiphe, H., and Galenson, E. 1981. *Infantile origins of sexual identity.* New York: International Universities Press.

Stade, G. 1984. Men, boys and wimps. *New York Times Book Review,* 12 August.

Starke, O. 1973. Castration complex. In *The language of psychoanalysis,* ed. J. LaPlace and J-B. Pontalis, pp. 56–60. New York: Norton.

6

The Genital Envy Complex:
A Case of a Man with
A Fantasied Vulva

FREDERICK M. LANE

Introduction

Since Freud first discussed the female's envy of the male genital, the concept of penis envy has become firmly established. It contributes to an understanding of female development and psychopathology. More recently, however, this has been challenged as a male chauvinistic formulation denigrating to women. Women's envy of men and their phalluses emerges as a clinical observation often enough in psychoanalysis, though it is not by any means found universally in adult females. It is, however, seen universally in two- to three-year-old girls as a phase of their normal development (Galenson and Roiphe 1976). Penis envy has been seen as an "organizing metaphor" giving shape to the female character and shaping their object relations to some degree (Grossman and Stewart 1976).

In this chapter I will present a case of a man with a fairly typical obsessional character neurosis who, without perversion or severe narcissistic character pathology, had an unconscious fantasy of being possessed of a vulvovaginal opening. He openly envied women, especially his wife, and demonstrated *vulvar* envy in essentially the same manner that penis envy emerges in the analysis of women. I will consider the possibility that little boys may indeed experience envy of the female external genital as the correlate of penis envy in girls as part of their normal development in response to the discovery of the anatomical difference between sexes and that in some cases it may be seen in adult males. Through the case presented I will explore the manifold integrative and defensive functions served by such a vulvar fantasy and will propose a general complex of thought and affect that centers around envy of the genital of the opposite sex, penis envy and vulvar envy.

Anatomy, Destiny, and Envy

When Freud (1905) first wrote of the psychological differences between males and females, he began with the acceptance of the idea of bisexuality. He said:

> [W]ithout taking bisexuality into account I think it would scarcely be possible to arrive at an understanding of the sexual manifestations that are actually to be observed in men and women. . . .[I]n human beings pure masculinity or femininity is not to be found either in a psychological or a biological sense. Every individual on the contrary displays a mixture of the character-traits belonging to his own and to the opposite sex. . . . (P. 220)

Yet in his contemplation of the infant coming into genital awareness at three and one-half years or so, he characterized both genders as being psychologically male. "The assumption that all human beings have the same (male) form of genital is the first of the many remarkable and momentous sexual theories of children" (1905, p. 195).

The Genital Envy Complex

Not only did both sexes feel that they possessed a penis, but Freud felt both boys and girls remained oblivious to the existence of the female sexual orifice—the vulvovaginal opening. He therefore named the developmental phase of coming into genital awareness the phallic phase. He said of the phallic phase, "[I]t knows only one kind of genital: the male one" (1905, p. 200).

But this illusion was to be shortlived, and what was destined to destroy the myth of the ubiquitous penis was the momentous discovery by the little boy and little girl of the anatomical genital differences between them. This discovery, so artfully described by Freud (1925), leads to a permanent divergence from their original bisexual nature. From this point on the two sexes' view of themselves and of each other would take preordained developmental paths, as would their sexuality. This divergence had an inevitability. As Freud (1924) put it, "Anatomy is destiny" (p. 178).

Thus Freud presented what Schafer (1974) critically calls a "shock theory" of sexual development in the phallic stage. It is the sight of the genital of the opposite sex—that of a parent or sibling in the usual family setting—which determines the diverging responses. On seeing the female genital, the boy responds with the emergence of castration anxiety around the notion that the little girl once had a penis but lost it. Castration anxiety was based on previous experiences of loss, as Freud saw it, of the breast and later of the feces. The female genital is seen as a bodily mutilation—an open wound (Jones 1933). It is this castration complex in males that dominates the movement in the little boy to resolve the Oedipus complex, to give up the incestuous aim to phallically penetrate the mother, and propels him to identify strongly with the father.

The reactive equivalent of castration anxiety in the little boy was the little girl's envy of the penis. Penis envy led to the girl's resentment and devaluation of herself and mother as castrated, to yearnings to repossess the penis, to giving up the mother as primary object, and led her to enter into the oedipal phase with fantasies of having a baby (as a compromise penile substitute) by the father. Penis envy was seen to be basic and a core of early feminine development.

Thus the net result of this gender divergence is castration anxiety in the male and penis envy in the female, an anxiety and an envy that will shape their sexuality, their character, and their sense of self.

However, the boy is not spared the painful attitude of envy. Male envy of the penis size of other men is commonplace, and envy of the father's penis by his little boy is universal. Many analysts have also noted, in boys and adult men, residuals of envy of *women*. There is in many men an envy of the nurturant capacity of the woman as mother—often noted as breast envy (Greenacre 1950; Kleeman 1965; Yazmajian 1966). There is envy of the gestational ability of the woman in the form of uterus envy or womb envy—of the magic of maternal productivity (Boehm 1930; Greenacre 1960; Jacobson 1950; Jaffe 1968; Van der Leeuw 1958; Van Leeuwen 1966). The fantasy of the mother with penis was pointed out by Freud (1905) as part of the boy's initial view of the mother as powerful and not castrated. Jones (1933) saw the phallic woman fantasy as reparative of the vulva-as-wound fantasy that is so arousing of castration anxiety. Bak (1968) sees the envy of the woman-with-phallus as defensive against castration and a pivotal dynamic in all perversions, with.fetishism as the central template of all perversions (see also Sperling 1964). Finally, several authors have noted envy of the vagina itself. Bettelheim (1954) explores a neglected psychological layer in boys, which he states is "a complex of desires and emotions in boys which, for want of a better term, might be called the 'vagina envy' of boys. The phenomenon is much more complex than the term indicates, including, in addition envy of and fascination with female breasts and lactation, with pregnancy and child bearing"(p. 50). Rangell (1953) speaks of penis-vagina interchangeability in fantasy. Zilboorg (1944) points to the powerful overall envy of women by men and feels these manifestations of envy have been obscured by theorists and clinicians who have thrown an "androcentric veil" over psychological data. Tyson (1982) says, "Boys usually make it very clear; they want the penis and the ability to have a baby" (p. 69). In any event, male envy of the female, while it has been noted, appears to play a relatively minor part in male development compared to the female's envy of the male. Its role

The Genital Envy Complex

in the development of paternal feelings in men has been pointed to by Ross (1975).

In considering the case of vulvar envy to be presented, attend to those same bits of clinical evidence that orient us toward penis envy as we listen to female patients. These include genital representation and symbols in dreams, language usage implying fantasied possession of the opposite sex's genitals, traits and attitudes ordinarily ascribed to the other gender (gender dystonic). In addition, look for fantasied body representations of the genital organs of the other sex as well as negative attitudes toward the patient's own. Of course, the presence and persistence of envy itself will be noted, as will the unconscious imitations such envy may lead to.

THE PATIENT

Louis G. entered analysis at the age of thirty-three because of chronic unhappiness and dissatisfaction with his career, his marriage, and especially himself. The only discrete persistent symptom he suffered was chronic mild depression, which was at its deepest on Monday mornings when he returned to work. The depression would slowly lift and weekends would be pleasant. He called this his "Blue Monday" syndrome.

He was deeply troubled in many areas. His career as a young attorney was not faring well. He had had great difficulty getting through law school due to severe examination anxiety and marked procrastination in handing in reports and studying for examinations. Despite a professed ambition to "make it" as a lawyer, his oppositional trends were expressed in resentment of authority and work inhibition. He married at the beginning of law school and relied heavily on his wife's pushing and cajoling to mobilize him to work. He was resentful of his professors, feeling constantly inferior to and judged by them. His greatest fear was reciting in class before his peers, and he experienced much anticipatory panic. Yet he longed to be admired and appreciated by his colleagues. Following graduation he worked for a public service legal organization at low income, and considered himself a failure and a loser.

His marriage seemed to him rather flat, though he saw his wife as devoted to him. Though his sexual adjustment in the marriage was satisfactory, he had had occasional episodes of premature ejaculation. These were quite rare, however, and his sexual functioning was otherwise intact.

His background was unusual. His family consisted of both parents still living, three older brothers, and three older sisters, the patient being the youngest of seven sibs. The family had lived in Europe during World War II and had lived through bombings, shellfire, invasion, and threats of being shot. The father was described as a passive coldly intellectual man who was largely ineffectual as father, provider, and protector during the war. The family survived intact largely due to the protection of the patient's mother who was a resourceful woman whom the patient saw as both highly protective and frighteningly powerful. She was always able to find food, fuel, and lodging. After the war the family emigrated intact to the United States. Here the patient attended high school and went on to college where he experienced the beginnings of his work problems. He was drafted and became a squad leader in the peacetime army for two years. While in service he developed a friendship with a young man whom he felt had an undue influence upon him. This man inspired Louis to go on to law school. He was uneasy about the intensity of this attachment, feeling inferior and submissive to the friend. Louis occasionally wondered about whether this closeness meant a homosexual attachment, although he was not aware of sexual feelings toward his friend.

In our initial session Louis related two memories from childhood that he felt had strongly contributed to his difficulties.

One incident occurred at age four. His sisters had dressed him in one of his mother's gowns, and his father entered and derisively said, "What kind of girl are you with a pickle [penis]?" Louis remembered embarrassment, humiliation, and perplexity at his father's remark, not quite understanding its implication. The persistent sense of inadequacy and doubt about his manhood seemed to him to date from that event.

The other memory, laden with severe guilt and shame, was of sexual arousal while lying in bed next to his mother one night during their migration across Europe. He was nine or ten and remembered trying to put his penis into her from behind. However, he abruptly became frightened and moved away from her.

At the time he began analysis, the patient was living in a small house with his wife and three children, socializing mainly with a close-knit group of Europeans, of which his wife was a member as well. He had just left his public service job and joined a private firm. He spoke English fluently with just a trace of an accent, though in his social community and at home he most frequently spoke in his native tongue. He expressed marked conflict over his push to be assimilated into the American culture. Though conflicted about his religious beliefs, he continued to attend Mass, his mother being an especially devout and ascetic Catholic who had furnished her family with a Catholic education at home.

Thus he began analysis, at the age of thirty-three, unhappy with himself, his marriage, his background, and his career.

THE ANALYSIS

Louis's initial reaction to being on the couch was immediate humiliation. He felt degraded by the supine position. In terms of his yet-undiscovered vulvar fantasy and intense envy of women, one might suppose that the position on the couch somehow tapped this fantasy and pressed this feminine aspect of self toward awareness. Early associations were filled with memories of mortification and embarrassment. He recalled a year's outbreak of nocturnal enuresis at age thirteen, for which he was ridiculed by his sisters. Could this have been an unconscious imitation of his sisters' menses? There was no confirmatory evidence of this, however. He recalled his father being berated by an official on the street and having his beard pulled by the man while Louis stood by, mortified for his father and himself. A contemporary encounter with a man who was blocking his driveway ended shamefully for Louis: he behaved meekly and apologetically instead of showing manly assertion. Finally he recalled his father remarking about his recurrent difficulty in getting out of bed in the morning as a young teenager, that the cause of such laziness must be Louis's masturbating. He indeed had been masturbating at that age and had been ashamed of his masturbation ever since. In fact as he occasionally still did this while looking at "girlie" magazines, he regarded this practice as a perversion. As it later emerged, the guilt-provoking effect of looking at explicit female genital poses was related to his envious vulvar fantasy.

In the first week of the analysis he presented his first dream. "It was filled with emotion-danger. It was like a spy movie—*The Fugitive,* no, not that—the *Counterfeit Traitor.* I woke up with a sad song in my head—about a girl who is sad because her mother is forbidding her to kiss boys."

There was no visual accompaniment to the dream, but the atmosphere was that of danger and had the paranoid flavor of jeopardy which pervaded the early transference. What was striking in the dream was the double reversal in the title—a traitor is a turncoat, but a counterfeit one; therefore a loyal adherent. What was the treason, and why was it false? No associations clarified the question. The translation of this "undercover" disguise later emerged as being in part a reference to his own androgyny.

During this initial phase of the analysis, paranoid mechanisms emerged, and he saw me as eagerly awaiting revelations of his weakness and immaturity so that I could feel superior to him. At the same time he wished to be taken care of by me and for me to care about him. However, what threatened to become an alarming paranoid resistance, where I was seen as a sneering and ridiculing tormentor, was quickly modified, to my great surprise, with little interpretive effort, when the patient had a dream in which I, the analyst, occupied a bed next to his. He said the dream indicated to him that he was taking me into his family—we were sharing a bedroom as he had done with his brothers. This modification of his early paranoid stance was unexpected, and as the paranoid resistance reduced abruptly, the therapeutic alliance was established quickly. The homoerotic elements in this dream were not associated to at this point and the patient saw the dream as a reflection of his determination to become close to the analyst and to figuratively take me into his home. Thinking retrospectively about this facile abandoning of paranoid mechanisms, this "taking me in" rather than projectively expelling me was facilitated by the androgynous fantasy. Despite this easing that strengthened the working alliance, projective mechanisms recurred, but never with the intensity of the initial weeks of the analysis. Prison dreams led the patient to express feeling trapped in his new job with a private law firm. Here, much more was expected of him in the way of professional performance, an equivalent of masculine strength, as he saw it. He likewise felt trapped in the analysis with its inherent dangers of exposure and humiliation. At work he made many self-sabotaging parapraxes. He would schedule a meeting with two different clients at the same time. He would mistake deadlines in briefs and be embarrassingly unprepared. We both saw this self-humiliating acting out as auto-castrative, as he called it.

In the transference he would swing wildly between activity and passivity. At his most passive he would lie on the couch waiting to be "spoonfed" by me—and he felt this was in emulation of his cold, emotionless, and almost inert father who, he said, did nothing all day but read the Bible and go for walks.

He said, "I want to be active and vigorous—this passiveness and unresponsiveness is a copy of my father—I hate this!"

Despite his father's passivity, he recalled that his father was often ridiculing of him. He envied his sisters for his father's attitude toward the girls in the family—he was much warmer toward and accepting of them. Louis recalled as a boy being ridiculed by his father when he tried to work a hand pump at a well and was unable to draw water. His father snickered at this, and he recalled recently working a hand pump and being amazed that he could get the water to flow freely. This imagery was notable in terms of his father's denigration of Louis's phallic-urethral adequacy.

Near the end of his first analytic year he had the following dream:

"It was in Europe—someone was investigating—trying to find someone else—I think a friend of mine. The investigator was my double —it reminds me of analysis. The idea was not to disclose ourselves. Then I was lying down next to my wife (this is the first time I have ever dreamt of my wife). The investigator had a gun and shot me in the side as a warning."

He pointed to his left side. Louis feared that I, the analyst, would find him out. I would find out how weak he was. I was the man with the gun. Louis was the man with the hole in his side. The bullethole, a recurrent dream image, was not clearly seen as a vulvovaginal representation at the time. Instead it seemed a general representation of defect or woundedness, perhaps castratedness—a "phallocentric" obtuseness in the countertransference. The bulletholes appeared in many dreams and were primarily a vaginal representation. Louis related how he idealized certain men, saw them as powerful, and then when they failed him and showed weakness, he felt profoundly disappointed. He said his father should have been a powerful protector, but instead he was a weak and passive man.

Phallic concerns continued in his boyhood recollections. He recalled finding a rusty pistol in a field. His father would not let him keep it and wrestled it from Louis's hand and threw it in the river. His mother had only mild objection to his keeping it. He drew analogies to the penis in this and was aware of its allusion to his manhood.

Phallic conflicts over exhibitionistic situations emerged. Louis was terrified to make presentations to his colleagues and was terrified of having to do litigation in court. He said, "The worst thing you can do is to show off in a group. I react when someone shows off—even you don't like my showing off. When I see someone showing off I want to slap him down. It shows he needs a great big penis—and this is what it will show about me." His exhibitionistic anxieties, which seemed related only to fear of competitive castration, also related to his vulvovaginal envy and dread of its emergence into consciousness. His colleagues would see his "defect."

At the end of the first year he had a dream of people condemned to death being executed by having a small car lowered upon them, crushing them. A prior dream that same night had him wounded in the arm and walking around displaying the wound to various people. He saw this as a punishment dream; he related it to his being punished for his incestuous attempt as a boy and saw the bullet wound as a punishment. He likened his fear of narcissistic mortification and humiliation to being crushed as in the dream. Thinking of the car brought to his mind a joke. "A man was killed in the Ford Motor Plant. How? He tried to tighten the nuts on a Mustang." There was no association to the primal scene, though one could see this dream of the car being lowered crushingly as a metaphor for the parents in intercourse.

In the second year of analysis, negative oedipal themes in which the paternal figure was erotically desired began to emerge. Louis repeatedly expressed wishes he could be closer to me. He felt he was emotionally constricted and often said he wished it were easier to "let me in." He wondered if his liking for me was homosexual, and on more than one occasion he would become frightened on the couch when he felt that I was leaning over toward him from behind—frightened presumably of incipient homosexual attack and, as I clarified, of his own homoerotic wishes.

Vacations caused him to realize how much he needed me. He said after a week's absence:

"I'm glad you are back—I want to be open with you—to accept you —I like you. In a sense you can do whatever you want with me—in a good sense—and I'll do anything for you. I'm afraid you are taking this wrong. It doesn't mean I will dance if you say 'dance.' I'm afraid I will totally embrace your theories. I like you. I must be like you— I would become you."

In this direct quote from an hour at the height of the positive transference we see an expression of erotic and loving attachment accompanied by a fear of passive homosexual submission oscillating with an intense wish to identify to the point of becoming a clone—the very kind of tensions one sees in the positive and negative Oedipus complex. The language is that of powerful wishes to be entered, which was a linguistic reference to his fantasied vulva. He oscillated between a loving submission to father (accompanied by envy of the females in his family who had his father's love) and, on the other hand, a powerful identification with father. At this point a recurrent dream of childhood was remembered. "It is a dream of falling into a big pit—for some reason it is a *woman* falling. I think 'If I'm not afraid of falling, if I just relax, I'll stop falling and start floating up.' That's how I handle the anxiety and fright." Associating to this childhood recurrent nightmare with its relaxation resolution led to an interpretation that the dream represented a wish to regress to a passive state as a solution to the danger—to assume the passivity of a woman would protect him from the danger of injury and castration as a man.

He began to work for a senior aggressive and highly critical female partner in his firm and filled many sessions with portrayals of her castrating criticisms and attacks upon him. He portrayed her as a woman with "a big cock." Here he stated his wish to confront her with her criticalness and aggressiveness, but he sadly noted that he could not. He said, "Women are so protected —they cannot be criticized." His envy of women emerged, clearly. He envied this protectedness of women, their seeming immunity to castrative attack. He envied his wife who had only to care for the children, who seemed to live a life of passive ease, and who did not have to face the dangers of the competitive and dangerous world. Though each weekend he emulated a caricature of this feminine passivity and prerogative to be taken care of (as he saw it), he sadly had to abandon this paradise each Monday, his "Blue Monday" syndrome. Portrayals of women as phallic, powerful, and dangerous alternated with intense envy of feminine prerogatives of passivity and protectedness.

In his third year of analysis, his father fell and sustained a severe injury. He was hospitalized and the patient feared his father might die. At the same time he wished his father *in him*— his passivity and emotional constriction—might die. Two months after his father's crippling injury, the patient accidentally dropped a rotating saw on his foot. It cut through his boot and lacerated his instep. This was by far the most frightening of what before were *symbolic* auto-castrations. Its meaning was understood as such by the patient. It also represented a way of equalizing himself with his injured father. He had to be pressed to go to an emergency room for suturing, as he felt embarrassed about the wound on his foot sustained in such a foolish way. The wound, a slit, and its resemblance to his view of the vulva were in no way connected consciously at this time but were seen as such when the fantasy emerged at the end of the analysis.

The Genital Envy Complex

He related how his mother had encouraged manliness, courage, and a Spartan willingness to endure pain and discomfort. He recalled going to a clinic with her around age ten with a boil on his neck that had to be lanced. She encouraged him to endure the lancing bravely without shouting or crying. He did just that. It was mother, he said, who in her coldly powerful manner taught him to be manly, brave, and to be able to endure pain and discomfort. It was she who, by model and demand, set a powerful masculine ego ideal.

He loved dualities and presented himself as ambivalent in many ways. He likened himself to a donkey in a fable that was hungry but that starved to death standing between two haystacks, unable to decide from which one to feed. The duality involved in his androgynous self-representation was implicit in this.

"I dreamt about you. I came to session with my wife—you preferred me to my wife—that I be a man—my wife is another identity. The feeling was anxious—a kind of rivalry. I think of the pickle episode."

By the end of the third year of analysis there had been marked characterological improvement. Louis had ceased to regress at home, the "Blue Monday" syndrome had become less prominent, his professional work was more effective, his stagefright and procrastination were much diminished. There were no longer any episodes of premature ejaculation. His confidence and feeling of manliness had increased a good deal. In the transference, with working through, his affection for me had become more fraternal in nature, less eroticized. There was little paranoid projection and much less feeling of humiliation and mortification.

At the start of his last year in analysis his father died of complications of his injury. Because of his work in analysis and some resolution of his ambivalence toward his father, Louis was able to proceed with mourning the old man, revising the totally disparaged early paternal image—to include some courage, steadfastness, and even paternal devotion to his family.

A dream revealed more about his masturbatory practices. "I am in Europe with my wife. There are a lot of flies. My wife says, 'I must have opened my legs.' I say, 'That's all right, that's why the French use perfume.' " I reflected that the manifest content derogated the female genital—but the patient, to my surprise, recalled one summer at age eleven or twelve when he was masturbating, he pulled back his foreskin and allowed four or five flies to land on the head of his penis. He then chased them away and continued masturbating. It was a disparagement and denigration of his own penis, and the condensation in the dream was his wife's genital with his own. This resembles Rangell's equation of penis as a vagina turned inside out (1953). He then spoke about a lifelong concern about emitting a body odor and likened the odor to the vaginal smell on his fingers after he made love to his wife—again, an unrecognized reference to a vulvar fantasy.

By this time oral and anal sadomasochistic aspects of the transference had been analyzed as well as a well-formed oedipal-level transference neurosis with both positive and negative oedipal configurations. Termination was discussed and agreed upon a few months hence.

About two months before termination at the end of the fourth analytic year, Louis presented the following dream, which he worked upon for several sessions after reporting it.

"I was lying on a bed in a room. It was like a treatment situation. There was a boy standing in the room. He looked like the son of a client of mine. In the corner of the room there was a break in the floor, a neat opening, where you could fall through. As I am talking to him, I am worrying constantly that he might fall into that hole. There was a constant feeling this might happen, a constant sense of anxiety. The boy knows about the hole but keeps coming dangerously close to the edge."

Associations to this dream came in rich profusion. The hole in the attic was at once a vaginal opening (associated to as "not a vagina"), gaps and imperfections in Louis's knowledge and legal training, a portal through which sexual activity might be viewed, and an opening into his own unconscious which analysis had provided. This hole was also seen as representing his dangerous tendency to "fall into" passive dependent postures with his wife and with me. The hole was one of many in his dreams; open pits, bulletholes abounded in his dream imagery.

The Genital Envy Complex

Other aspects were inferred from the associations related to early wishes to fuse with mother, to penetrate her from behind, to loving erotic oedipal longings. Castration, incompleteness, and penetrability were likewise represented. This and much more became clear approximately one month before termination, when, during a session, the patient reported the following fantasy:

"I just had a fantasy that you stand up from your chair behind me. You are holding a long blackboard pointer—and you point to this area of my abdomen. [He points to the area between his umbilicus and his penis in the midline.]" He recalled that he liked to have this area stroked by his wife during foreplay before intercourse—it was a rather unusual erogenous zone. He recalled that as a young boy he was imitating intercourse with a little girl by lying on top of her and trying to penetrate her in this same area. It became clear to both of us that ever since he was a small boy, Louis had had an unconscious fantasy that below his umbilicus and above his penis there was a female genital—a vulvovaginal opening. He had had an hermaphroditic body image (in the unconscious, similar to the image of the phallic woman). His female genital was superior to his penis—on the lower abdomen, far removed from his anus and from his scrotum as well. It then became clear that his memory of humiliation about being a girl with a pickle was no longer seen by Louis as his father's ridiculing his being dressed as a girl. He was seen instead to be accusing Louis of being a peculiar and defective girl, *because* he had a penis. The penis was, in Louis's projected view of his father's attitude, wrongly tacked onto Louis. It was undesirable and rendered Louis an anomaly.

The dream of the hole in the attic floor foreshadowed the emergence of this unconscious fantasy of Louis's possession of a vulva. This vulvar fantasy expressed his marked envy of his mother and sisters and the advantages of being female. He was indeed a counterfeit traitor—a traitor to his manhood by secretly wishing to be a girl, but only falsely a traitor. His masculine strivings and ego ideal, though ambivalent, were gender syntonic. On the one hand, he really wanted to be as manly as possible. On the other, his feminine strivings were confused with the notions of exemption from others' expectations and invulnerability to castration. His femininity was really limited to a harmless vulvar fantasy tacked like a false beard to his lower abdomen.

Were it not for the emergence into consciousness of this "pointer fantasy," the presence of vulvar envy would not have been formulated. His vaginal dream imagery would have remained symbols of castration to my understanding, and his language imagery—"I want to let you in," "I want to be open to you" —might not have been connected to envy of female capacities. I suspect that much of such data is missed in the analyses of men, though quickly recognized when there are phallic references in the analyses of women. The analyst's phallocentric and androcentric biases may obscure these valuable clues.

The patient returned for one visit a year later and stated proudly that his career had blossomed and the improvements in his marriage, his vocational function, and his feelings about himself had remained stable.

Discussion

This case illustrates clearly the necessity to take into account the multiple factors that determine the final common path to core gender identity, gender role, choice of sexual object, and gender-related aspects of body image and bodily fantasy. This case suggests that envy of the female genital may well be stirred in little boys. Envy in various forms is ubiquitous, though male envy of the vulva may be subject to severe repression and denial.

In the male, bisexual or androgynous self-representations persist (Kubie 1974). On the way to sexual maturity, complex processes and compromises occur throughout early stages of development. Beginning with the primary identification with mother, there is the necessity for completing adequately the separation-individuation process (Mahler 1972) and successfully disidentifying with her (Greenson 1968) in order to establish an unambiguous male core gender identity (Person and Ovesey, 1974 *a, b;* Stoller 1968, 1978). The resolutions in the male of the positive Oedipus complex (maternal-erotic) and of the negative Oedipus complex (paternal-erotic), if successfully resolved, lead to the solidity of a male gender role identity and to the final formation of a superego as a deobjectified psychic structure.

In Louis's case the following can be noted: his core gender identity is unambiguously male and his gender role is largely masculine, despite his doubts about his success in being a man. His sexual object choice is exclusively heterosexual, though he experienced vague and transitory homoerotic feelings in the transference. His ego ideals are largely gender syntonic, typical masculine strivings for strength, assertiveness, activity, stoicism, courage, and so forth. His envy of female prerogatives was powerful. He envied his sisters' place in his father's affections and, as he saw it, their privileges to be passive and exempt from parental expectations of achievement. In addition he saw women as protected from the aggression of others and the consequences of aggression, castration. He envied his mother's strength and coping abilities. She not only embodied elements of a masculine ego ideal but was the source of succor in the family as well. All of these factors converged on his envy of the female and his wish to have a female genital.

The Genital Envy Complex

Various authors have attempted to distinguish the ubiquitous female response of penis envy in the infantile phase of life from the *secondary* appearance of penis envy in adult life neuroses of the so-called phallic woman (Greenacre, 1950; Horney 1924, 1926, 1933). The early narcissistic concerns involved in penis envy in the little girl and the phallic narcissistic investment by the little boy in his penis have been noted in nursery observations by Galenson and Roiphe (1980). These developmental events are to be distinguished from the *adult* complexes of attitudes and symptoms involved in female penis envy and in the envy of the vulva by a male, such as the case under consideration.

I propose that we consider including penis envy and male envy of the female genital in a group of fantasies, feelings, and behaviors that might be termed the *genital envy complex*. This formation may play a central role in certain adult neurotic patterns. The complex consists of the following:

1 There are conscious elements of envy for the character, qualities, and prerogatives that the subject sees as inherent in the opposite sex. This envy may or may not be accompanied by hatred of the opposite sex. There is often an acting out of these envied traits, sometimes to the point of caricature.
2 There is a persistent unconscious wish for and fantasy of being possessed of the genital of the opposite sex. This may be incorporated into the unconscious body image.
3 There is a deprecation of the subject's own genitals.

The complex is itself a compromise formation relating to several areas of conflict and conflict resolution, and serves many dynamic functions. The fantasy genital serves as a symbol of ego ideals, usually embodied in the parent of the opposite sex. In Louis's case the vulva was an incorporated part object representing identification with mother, her power, her courage, and so forth. It served as a defense against castration and bodily injury. Louis could be penisless and yet preserve all the power and survivability of his mother. It was a defense against the aggression that his envy bred toward his powerful mother. It served as a denial of his identification with father, an expression of a wish to be as unlike him as possible. It was a magic talisman for survival, representing the omnipotent preoedipal mother who protected him from the violence of the war around him. It served likewise as a denial of forbidden incestuous wishes; his vulva served to declare he was unequipped for an incestuous penetration of mother. The fantasied genital was a vehicle for the desired negative oedipal union with father; possibly a way to receive father's penis without humiliating anal penetration or disruption of his body integrity. It mitigated to some degree the need for paranoid projection. It represented a fusion with the archaic mother and served as a counterphobic means of accepting the female genital as nondangerous.

The genital envy complex furnishes compromise solutions for conflicts arising in bisexual longings, without disrupting appropriate gender identity, gender role, or choice of sexual object in both the female and the male.

Conclusions

The envied qualities of the opposite sex are often represented as part objects, the external genitals of the other gender, tacked on to one's own body image. Genital envy in the adult is not merely the persistence of the developmental experience of such envy in childhood but represents a complex resolution of many conflicts.

Castration anxiety plays an important role in genital envy formations. This anxiety in males may account for why phallic additions to women's body images are seen so much more frequently clinically than vulvar additions to men.

Although preoedipal issues play an important role, probably the most powerful influence on the formation of a genital envy complex is the negative Oedipus complex with its longing to unite erotically with the parent of the same sex.

Vulvovaginal representations in dreams, fantasies, and language usage in men may be more common than is usually noted. Reasons for this obstruction to observation may be due in part to countertransferential resistance in analysts of both genders. Freud's proposal that the phallic phase was concerned only with the penis, and his naming of that period as "phallic," tends to obscure his important observation that infantile life, sexual development, and the character structure of the mature adult involves elements of bisexuality or androgyny. Such formations as the genital envy complex may appear in men as well as in women and may occupy an important dynamic position in either gender.

BIBLIOGRAPHY

Bak, R. C. 1968. The phallic woman: The ubiquitous fantasy in perversions. *Psychoanalytic Study of the Child* 23: 15–36.

Bettelheim, B. 1954. *Symbolic wounds.* Glencoe, Ill.: Free Press.

Boehm, F. 1930. The femininity complex in men. *International Journal of Psycho-Analysis* 11:444–469.

Freud, S. 1905. Three essays on the theory of sexuality. In *The standard edition of the complete psychological works of Sigmund Freud,* 24 vols. (hereafter *S.E.*), ed. J. E. Strachey, vol. 7 (1953), pp. 125–243. London: Hogarth Press, 1953–1974.

———. 1924. The dissolution of the Oedipus complex. *S.E.,* vol. 19 (1961), pp. 173–179.

———. 1925. Some psychical consequences of the anatomical distinction between the sexes. *S.E.,* vol. 19 (1961), pp. 243–258.

Galenson, E., and Roiphe, H. 1976. Some suggested revisions concerning early female development. *Journal of the American Psychoanalytic Association* 24 (Supplement):29–57.

———. 1980. The pre-oedipal development of the boy. *Journal of the American Psychoanalytic Association* 28:805–827.

Greenacre, P. 1950. Special problems of early female sexual development. *Psychoanalytic Study of the Child* 5:122–126.

———. 1960. Further notes on fetishism. *Psychoanalytic Study of the Child* 15:191–207.

Greenson, R. 1968. Dis-identification from mother: Its special importance for the boy. *International Journal of Psycho-Analysis* 49:370–374.

Grossman, W. I., and Stewart, W. A. 1976. Penis envy: From childhood wish to developmental metaphor. *Journal of the American Psychoanalytic Association* 24 (Supplement):193–212.

Horney, K. 1924. On the genesis of the castration complex in women. *International Journal of Psycho-Analysis* 5:50–65.

———. 1926. The flight from womanhood: The masculinity complex in women, as viewed by men and by women. *International Journal of Psycho-Analysis* 7:324–339.

———. 1933. The denial of the vagina. *International Journal of Psycho-Analysis* 14:57–69.

Jacobson, E. 1950. The development of the wish for a child in boys. *Psychoanalytic Study of the Child* 5:145–152.

Jaffe, D. S. 1968. The masculine envy of woman's procreative function. *Journal of the American Psychoanalytic Association* 16:521–548.

Jones, E. 1933. The phallic phase. *International Journal of Psycho-Analysis* 14:1–33.

Kleeman, J. A. 1965. A boy discovers his penis. *Psychoanalytic Study of the Child* 20:230–266.

Kubie, L. S. 1974. The drive to become both sexes. *Psychoanalytic Quarterly* 43:349–426.

Mahler, M. S. 1972. On the first three subphases of the separation-individuation process. *International Journal of Psycho-Analysis* 53:333–338.

Person, E., and Ovesey, L. 1974a. The transsexual syndrome in males: I. Primary transsexualism. *American Journal of Psychotherapy* 28:4–20.

———. 1974b. The transsexual syndrome in males: II. Secondary transsexualism. *American Journal of Psychotherapy.* 28:174–193.

Rangell, L. 1953. The interchangeability of phallus and female genital. *Journal of the American Psychoanalytic Association* 1:504–509.

Ross, J. M. 1975. The development of paternal identity: A critical review of the literature on nurturance and generativity in boys and men. *Journal of the American Psychoanalytic Association* 23:783–817.

Schafer, R. 1974. Problems in Freud's psychology of women. *Journal of the American Psychoanalytic Association* 22:459–485.

The Genital Envy Complex

Sperling, M. 1964. The analysis of a boy with transvestite tendencies: A contribution to the genesis and dynamics of transvestism. *Psychoanalytic Study of the Child* 29:470–493.

Stoller, R. 1968. *Sex and gender.* New York: Science House.

———. 1978. Boyhood gender aberrations: Treatment issues. *Journal of the American Psychoanalytic Association* 26:541–558.

Tyson, P. 1982. A developmental line of gender identity, gender role, and choice of love object. *Journal of the American Psychoanalytic Association* 30:61–86.

Van der Leeuw, P. J. 1958. The pre-oedipal phase of the male. *Psychoanalytic Study of the Child* 13:352–374.

Van Leeuwen, K. 1966. Pregnancy envy in the male. *International Journal of Psycho-Analysis* 47:319–324.

Yazmajian, R. V. 1966. The testes and body image formation in transvestism. *Journal of the American Psychoanalytic Association* 14:304–312.

Zilboorg, G. 1944. Masculinity and femininity. *Psychiatry* 7:257–265.

7

A Conceptual Model
of Male Perversion

OTTO F. KERNBERG

I concluded in an earlier work (1985) that polymorphous perverse aspects of sexual life, specifically sadistic, masochistic, voyeuristic, exhibitionistic, fetishistic, and homosexual features, are crucial components of normal sexual eroticism and that their absence signals a significant impoverishment of the couple's love life. For this reason, the traditional psychoanalytic definition of normal sexual behavior that limits the role played by polymorphous perverse infantile sexuality to sexual foreplay under the organizing and supraordinate function of genital sexuality is inadequate.

Laplanche and Pontalis (1973) give what seems to me a most elegant and brief definition of perversion:

> Deviation from the "normal" sexual act when this is defined as coitus with a person of the opposite sex directed toward the achievement of orgasm by means of genital penetration.
>
> Perversion is said to be present: where the orgasm is reached with other sexual objects (homosexuality, paedophilia, bestiality, etc.) or through other regions of the body (anal coitus, etc.); where the orgasm is subordinated absolutely to certain extrinsic conditions, which may even be sufficient in themselves to bring about sexual pleasure

A Conceptual Model of Male Perversion

(fetishism, transvestism, voyeurism, exhibitionism, and sado-masochism).

In a more comprehensive sense, "perversion" connotes the whole of the psychosexual behavior that accompanies such atypical means of obtaining sexual pleasure. (P. 306)

In discussing this definition and the history of the concept of perversion in Freud's thinking, Laplanche and Pontalis (1973) ask a central question about genitality:

It is nonetheless reasonable to ask whether it is merely its unifying character—its force as a "totality" as opposed to the "component" instincts—that confers a normative role upon genitality. Numerous perversions, such as fetishism, most forms of homosexuality and even incest when it is actually practised, presuppose an organisation dominated by the genital zone. This surely suggests that the norm should be sought elsewhere than in genital functioning itself. (P. 308)

In practice, psychoanalysts would probably agree in restricting the concept of perversion to "deviations" from the normal sexual act that have a *habitual* and *obligatory* character, which excludes a broad spectrum of behaviors and fantasies characteristic of normal sexuality. At the same time, this restricted definition still presents the problem of the normative nature of any definition of perversion and of "normal" sexuality: Laplanche and Pontalis raise the question of whether Freud, after initially rejecting the descriptive classifications of perversions as not doing justice to the normal functions of polymorphous perverse sexual strivings throughout the individual's psychosexual development, did not end up reinstating the very norm of the abnormality of perversions.

My views regarding this matter, presented in earlier work (1976, 1980) and further elaborated on in this chapter, may be briefly summarized as follows. I believe that "normal" sexual behavior may be more inclusive than the classical definition of normal sexual behavior in psychoanalysis has assumed. I think that the classification of sexual pathology, particularly of the perversions, cannot be based exclusively on the content of sexual behavior per se but must include the nature of the dominant organization of object relations as well. The neglect or underestimation, in the classical psychoanalytic definition, of the functions of polymorphous perverse fantasy and behavior within normal sexual interactions has also led to underestimating the function of perverse features in the idealization that is a normal constituent of the sexual aspects of love relations. In addition, Freud's (1905) assumption that neurosis is the negative of perversion falls short of our contemporary understanding of the complex relations between personality organization, perverse "structure," and pathology of object relations. Intimately linked with these questions is the relation between oedipal and preoedipal determinants of perversion and the extent to which oedipal and preoedipal components enter into certain perverse structures. In what follows, I explore all these issues.

Normal Functions of Polymorphous Perverse Sexuality

One of the most striking, very frequent fantasies of patients with clinical perversions is that their particular solution to their sexual needs provides them with such an intensity of enjoyment or is of such a "sublime" nature that no other type of sexual behavior could possibly match it; the fantasies also contain the idea that the ordinary sexual interests of those who do not experience this perversion can provide them with only a pale reflection of sexual intensity and enjoyment (Lussier 1982). Chasseguet-Smirgel (1984) has pointed to the defensive nature of this idealization of the perversion, a defense usually directed against the analization of all sexual relations that is part of the perversion, a defense that also reinforces the denial of the importance of normal sexual intercourse with its oedipal implications.

Men's idealization of female anatomy, the genitals, breasts, and skin, is part of the sexual excitement linked to falling in love. Thus the idealization of the sexual partner's anatomy—what I am calling erotic idealization—is also a crucial aspect of the normal integration of tender and erotic strivings in heterosexual love relations. In addition, an individual's projection of the ego ideal onto the loved object, which characterizes falling in love, increases the narcissistic gratification provided by the real encounter with this materialized version of the ego ideal, while, simultaneously, the love of the object expresses the gratification of object libidinal strivings. It may appear trivial to state this fact, if it were not that Freud (1921, p. 113; 1914, p. 88) assumed a depletion of narcissistic investment in the state of falling in love. The idealization of the loved object, then, also carries with it the idealization of the genital encounter, of one's own and one's partner's body and genitals, as they touch and merge with each other.

The voyeuristic, exhibitionistic, sadistic, and masochistic fantasies and wishes, the homosexual implications of the identification with the partner's excitement and orgasm on the part of the couple in love, all contribute to the symbolic expression of the crossing of the boundaries of the oedipal situation, the overcoming of the prohibitions against identification with the oedipal figures. These fantasies, wishes, and interactions are also bridges for symbolic fusion or merger of two bodies that express symbiotic longings, a fusion that is enacted in the sense of loss of control in mutual excitement and orgasm. The normal idealization of body parts of the loved object with fetishistic functions also may extend to clothing and other possessions.

These erotic idealizations may inspire artistic and religious pursuits, and while such "perverse" tendencies may also serve the function, in clinical perversions, of creating a "neosexuality" (McDougall 1985), or the evasion of the oedipal situation by idealizing preoedipal sexual precursors, I believe that these types of idealization normally blend with oedipal aspirations and provide to sexual love a transcendental quality, linking it with art and religion.

In contrast to the fantasy of the patient restricted by a clinical perversion that his perversion is the ultimate reach of sexual enjoyment, when polymorphous perverse sexuality is integrated, in the course of successful psychoanalytic treatment, with sexual fantasies and behavior that reflect the resolution of oedipal prohibitions against genital sexuality, the result is a dramatic enrichment of sexual experience.

Erotic idealization thus may serve normal as well as pathological functions. All idealizations may be considered to stem from conflicts around ambivalence, and erotic idealization of polymorphous perverse sexuality is no exception. But the integration of hatred within a love relation in general enriches it and its erotic excitement, whereas idealization of a particular perversion is a secondary defense recruited in the service of denial of castration anxiety and regression to the anal phase.

The male heterosexual idealization of a woman's body creates a sense of mystery and excitement about her body that transcends ordinary aesthetic considerations and, particularly, the conventional limits of aesthetics. This idealization permits the person in love to tolerate the conflict between the wish to incorporate the beloved person and yet acknowledge the ultimate impenetrability of both her body and her mind. This idealization facilitates the tolerance, in other words, of the limits of the capacity for merger, the impenetrable nature of the other, while still maintaining alive the endless desire for such merger. Erotic idealization radiates sexual desire into social life, builds and maintains the interpersonal tensions that signal the activation of oedipal fantasies and scenarios in the social structure.

Erotic idealization also strengthens the permanence of longing and preserves love under conditions of hatred that are a normal part of human ambivalence, heightened in the intensity of the object relation of the couple in love. In other words, a man who is sexually excited by a woman who enrages him illustrates the function of erotic idealization in dealing with ambivalence.

The male homosexual's erotic idealization of his partner's body also reveals, upon analytic exploration, elements of heterosexuality: the fantasied relation between the oedipal mother and the little boy, which Freud first described in his paper "On Narcissism" (1914). The little boy's wish to have his penis admired by mother and thereby overcome the infantile fears over an inadequate penis that could not compete with father's and fulfill the demands of mother's vagina (Chasseguet-Smirgel 1984), the assurance of the possession of a good, loving penis as contrasted to an aggressive, poisonous one, all are satisfied by the excited admiration of the homosexual partner's penis and by the partner's excitement and admiration of the homosexual patient's one.

A Conceptual Model of Male Perversion

The exhibitionistic, voyeuristic, fetishistic, sadistic, and masochistic implications of the erotic idealization of the penis and of homosexual play with it are illustrated in the frequent male fantasies of being sexually excited by manual stimulation without being permitted to achieve orgasm, the wishes for passive stimulation of a man's own penis as well as for aggressive penetration of the sexual partner's body cavities. The narcissistic identification with the partner's sexual excitement and orgasm and with the partner's admiration of the subject's own body are linked to oedipal and preoedipal fantasies that are remarkably alike for homosexual and heterosexual male patients, and again point to the normal, universal function of polymorphous perverse tendencies. Similar considerations, of course, could be made for the functions of homosexual components in women's exhibitionistic fantasies and excitement and in women's excitement in erotic play with the erect penis that responds with excitement and orgasm to her control over it.

In my experience, psychoanalytic exploration regularly demonstrates the pervasive functions of homosexual elements in both sexes in enriching the erotic idealization of heterosexual sexual interactions. The problem, then, becomes one of defining how normal perverse tendencies are transformed into fixation, how the multiplicity of sexual fantasies and behaviors are transformed into a restrictive, obligatory behavior, how the concomitant erotic idealization is transformed into a defense that denies the importance of the dissociated or repressed sexual impulses linked to the forbidden oedipal realization.

A Prototypical Case of Perversion at a Neurotic Level of Personality Organization

I have reported earlier (1985) on a case of male shoe fetishism with a clearly neurotic personality organization. A fictional case stemming from a strikingly relevant work of art, the recent Australian film *Man of Flowers,* directed by Paul Cox, illustrates the central dynamics of male perversion at a high or neurotic level of personality organization so dramatically and in so condensed a way that I am using it to illustrate the corresponding psychodynamic issues.

The film centers around the internal experiences of an attractive, highly cultivated, middle-aged, wealthy art collector who is sexually aroused by flowers and statues of women and who has a voyeuristic perversion. He pays a young model at a local art school to perform a striptease for him every Wednesday and achieves orgasm without undressing or touching her. On one occasion, in fact, the intensity of his sexual excitement is such that he achieves orgasm even before she is completely naked. He cannot touch her, not even when she offers herself to him.

This young woman lives with a sadistic male painter, whose work is distasteful and primitive and whose painting techniques have a quality of diffuse smearing. Even his dog is portrayed as an ugly, revolting animal. This painter is a cocaine addict who exploits the young model financially and takes the money she receives from the voyeuristic art collector. We learn from her that her painter used to have "an interminable erection," which is why she initially loved him, but he is now no longer interested in sex. Her posing as a model in the art school and stripping for our voyeuristic hero illustrates the ease with which she offers her body for observation.

The art collector is in psychotherapy with a therapist who seems intended to represent the "normal" male: he is effective, exploitive, lecherous, and brutish. In contrast, our voyeuristic hero is depicted as refined and artistically sensitive, not only in his exquisite sense for plastic and visual arts but also in his playing the organ in a church while implicitly longing for purity and ethical values.

Frequent flashbacks, carried out with a technique that produces pictures highly reminiscent of Balthus's paintings (a conscious or unconscious linkage between the hero's voyeurism and Balthus's portrayed pedophilia?), reveal the intense sexual excitement our hero experienced as a little boy by his mother's body (particularly her provocatively exhibited breasts), the punishment he received from his father for being sexually excited by and literally reaching out for the amply visible breasts of a seductive aunt during a visit to their home, and the father's punishing him by dragging him by his ear out to the street.

The exhibitionism of the little boy's aunt clearly replicates the sexual provocativeness of the mother, whose physical closeness and seductiveness are a counterpart to the father's distant, awe-inspiring, frightening demeanor. Flashbacks show us how walks to the park with both parents expand and diffuse the little boy's excitement and erotic longing for the mother with the experience of statues and flowers in the park and, later, evolve into the hero's central interest in sculpture and painting.

A homosexual female friend of the young model suggests a menage-à-trois with the wealthy art collector. Eventually the two women introduce themselves to the art collector's house and induce him to suggest to them to touch and kiss each other in his presence in order to learn about himself "from a distance," a confused implication of his excitement in identifying himself with one or both of these women.

The film culminates in a perfect crime. The art collector, after being blackmailed by the model's painter boyfriend (from whom she has finally run away in protest against his mistreatment of her), visits him in his home, where he is supposed to buy a painting or simply give the painter a large amount of money as the price of the painter's silence regarding the art collector's voyeurism and as part of an effort to rescue the model from the painter's exploitive control over her.

The art collector meets the brutish, exploitive, untalented, and promiscuous painter who is already involved sexually with another woman and then, under the pretext of buying a painting, lures him to his own home. The painter arrives while the hero is absent and is killed with a mechanical device constructed with dartlike parts from a sculpture in the garden. This weapon is a slingshotlike contraption, similar to one the hero had used in a symbolic revenge against his father by breaking a window in the room his parents were in after he had been violently expelled from their presence because of his efforts to touch his aunt's breasts.

The art collector plays the organ in the church while the murder is in progress and illustrates, in one stroke, how an extremely inhibited, shy, friendly art lover could become a sly murderer/ avenger.

At the end of the movie, in a Magritte-like scene, the art collector walks toward the top of a hill where he observes the landscape, and while only his outline is seen as a black silhouette against the blue skies crossed by wild birds, the silhouettes of three other men are seen walking toward him, then standing still, surrounding him at some distance. The viewer's initial anxiety regarding whether these men are out to arrest the art collector, punish him for his crime, or kill him gradually changes, as this scene is maintained in absolute silence and almost immobility, into the evocation of a growing feeling that our hero is now standing firm, as one man among other men, firmly planted on the ground while looking into the distance.

The viewer is clearly expected to identify with the art collector throughout the film, including the final uncertainty of whether he will be attacked or will now be joining other men with a sense of mastery and triumph. Finally, there is a humorous quality to the disposal of the painter's body, achieved by our hero with the help of a strange, out-of-this-world art merchant and metal worker whose major interest is to make human-size copper sculptures. With this person's help the art collector seals the body into a copper sculpture that bears the painter's semblance, a sculpture donated by the art collector to the city, in the very park that reminds him of his youth.

Man of Flowers dramatically illustrates the internal world of the art collector, the idealization of women's bodies reflected by his voyeuristic perversion, and the fear of castration defended against by the avoidance of touching a woman, the sexual inhibition, the voyeuristic replacement of penetration, and the devaluation of the castrating, brutal father. The regression to the anal phase, defended against by idealization of painting and art, and the split-off projection of anal dirtiness, messiness, and brutality on the cocaine addict-painter friend of the idealized woman model are underpinned by a humoristic portrayal of the disgusting, almost fecal nature of that painter's dog, a truly disgusting creature.

A Conceptual Model of Male Perversion

Male power is associated with brutality, exploitiveness, crude sensuality, and vulgarity, as illustrated in the image of the painter as well as of the therapist and other casual male figures. The film illustrates our hero's effort to maintain an idealized linkage with his mother and to rescue her from father in the displaced rescue of the young model from the exploitive painter. A dominant, antisexual, castrating female instructor at the art academy where the young model poses illustrates the split between the idealized mother on the one hand and the antisexual, derogative, and cruel mother on the other.

At the end, we are left with the question of whether our hero, with his treacherous, triumphant murder—his symbolic killing of father—will have acquired "realistically" father's powerful penis or, to the contrary, whether he enacted in fantasy the destruction of father without ever, particularly after this murder, being able to identify with a powerful yet loving oedipal father. Are we dealing with the internal world of a pervert who would not be able to break the vicious circle of the pervert structure? The copper encasement and public display of the decaying body of the murdered painter (father) symbolizes at least partially a successful sublimation of anal traits into art; but it does not tell us whether the lonely, intelligent, and sensitive voyeurist art collector will be able to break out of his restricted world.

This film illustrates features typical of male perversion, including: (1) a devaluation of sexual intercourse as a defense against and rationalization of impotence; (2) the idealization of a woman's body in the context of incapacity to penetrate it—this would, of course, apply as well to the idealization of male bodies in the case of homosexual perversion, in contrast to the idealization of breasts, genitals, and other female body parts in heterosexual perversion; (3) art as a sublimatory expression of that idealization; and (4) idealization of aesthetics as a reaction formation against the regression to the anal phase of sexuality, the condensation of father's penis with disgusting vulgarity (and the unconscious equation penis equals feces).

The film illustrates, in addition, the hero's longing for strength and power without having to identify power with a despicable, despised brutality of father. The self experience and portrayal of our hero reveals a man who may lash out secretly against the brutal father but who cannot identify himself with a strong image of man in which power and aggression are contained and controlled by love: this is also typical for male perversion. Finally, a man's longing for a sexually, emotionally, and intellectually mature, attractive, and available woman, without his having to succumb to sexual inhibition in the presence of such a perfect, idealized mother figure, is illustrated by contrast, with the obvious inability of our hero to gratify his sexual longings in the context of an emotional relation with an attractive, available woman.

In the film, the oedipal rebellion is achieved in a subterranean, dishonest way; the film illustrates the frequent fantasy in pervert patients that only by dishonest means, with "as-if" qualities in their behavior, can they identify with father's strength, thus requiring the stratagems of the weak and small against the powerful and big. In the end, robbing father of his power interferes with a real identification with him.

Devoid of its artistic and movingly human features, the personality of our hero appears impotent and as suffering from a devaluation of sexual intercourse. The image of an unavailable, brutal, and distant father is pervasive. The hero dissociates between an idealized but desexualized and a sexualized but emotionally unavailable woman and experiences himself as weak, inhibited, and inferior. In addition, perhaps, at a still deeper level, the hero evinces the need to deny the envy of the powerful and gratifying mother by dissociating the sexual control over a prostitute from the idealization in fantasy of the dead mother.

With all these dynamic features in mind, the psychoanalytic proposal that neurosis is the negative of perversion may now be reexamined. In many cases of clinical perversion in which patients show features remarkably similar to those illustrated by the film, that statement actually holds. To put it differently, there are patients with a habitual, obligatory replacement of ordinary sexual relations by a restricted, partial sexual drive—for example, as in the case we have seen, the voyeuristic component of infantile sexuality. The sexual life of these patients may be restricted to a perversion, but these patients may also show a wealth of sublimatory functioning in their relationship to art, in their capacity for relating in depth to other people, including even stable love relations and a capacity for differentiated understanding of others and of themselves.

In contrast to the hero's actual murder of the oedipal rival in the film, in clinical reality aggression is usually well controlled, and even sadistic perversions at this level have an "as-if" quality, presented as a scenario or the enactment of a play, which is in sharp contrast to more severe, often life-threatening forms of perversions, which I examine later on. We see, in short, a sexual perversion in the context of a neurotic personality organization, with integrated object relations, good identity formation, and the predominance of repression and related, advanced defensive operations.

Here the splitting of the ego between acknowledgment and denial of the differences between the sexes and the generations, typical for perversions (Chasseguet-Smirgel 1984), has the character of a mutual dissociation of two broadly organized, contradictory types of ego integration, rather than the more primitive type of splitting of part object relations with the corresponding inability to integrate total self and total object representations. In these cases with neurotic personality organization, a perversion replaces a sexual inhibition, just as a sexual inhibition may be conceived of as replacing the polymorphous perverse aspects of infantile sexuality linked with the Oedipus complex. And, in all these cases, preoedipal issues are usually in the background or emerge only as defensive regressions from dominantly oedipal conflicts.

Homosexuality in a Neurotic Personality Organization

Male homosexual patients with a neurotic personality organization and the corresponding structural characteristics of their world of object relations typically show the dominance of an unconscious submission to the oedipal father related to guilt over their oedipal longings for mother and to castration anxiety. In other words, they present a defensive structuralization of the negative oedipal complex within the context of a consolidated ego identity, the prevalence of total or integrated object relations, and a predominance of oedipal strivings and of defensive mechanisms centering on repression.

In submitting to the oedipal father, they defensively identify with the mother and often present the narcissistic homosexual object choice described by Freud (1914)—that is, they choose as their love object a man who represents themselves as a child and whom they treat in a motherly way. In fact, there are patients whose homosexual identification is with themselves as the child being loved by mother, while their longings for mother have been displaced onto motherly men who protect them from both the forbidden relation with mother and from the dissociated cruel and sadistic father. The same patient may identify himself alternately, in different homosexual love relations, with the giving mother or the dependent son.

These are patients who typically present an intensification of the erotic idealization of the male body mentioned before, but often they are also capable of idealizing women's bodies as long as the genitals are excluded. They may long for desexualized relations with nonthreatening women, while their relationships with soft, womenly men signals, by the same token, the rejection of aggressive, "brutally" heterosexual men representing the persecutory oedipal father.

In their love relations, they are often able to have stable object relations that include both genital excitement and tenderness toward the same man, illustrating that the concept of perversion does not preclude the capacity for integrating genital and tender feelings in the same object relation. These patients often tolerate polymorphous perverse fantasies and activities, and they may show a broad range of sexual behaviors as long as the obligatory homosexual condition is maintained. The idealization of art as a defense against significant regression and the dissociation of direct anal and oral enjoyment from such split-off idealizations are also typical for these cases.

A Conceptual Model of Male Perversion

What are the boundaries between homosexuality on the level of a neurotic personality organization and the normal homosexual components of male sexuality? From a purely psychoanalytic view, this question might be answered by stating that neurotic homosexuality implies the habitual, obligatory nature of homosexual interests and relations that signal the failure of normal resolution of infantile oedipal conflicts. Normal resolution of these conflicts entails identifying with the oedipal father in a full relation with an adult woman and fully accepting the function of paternity together with that of heterosexual sexuality.

In terms of conventional morality, however, and of prevalent cultural bias, it may well be that this boundary is drawn very differently in different societies and historical periods; the nonconventional exploration of this boundary by psychoanalysis may be hampered by the unavoidable cultural biases infiltrating all social sciences. I shall reexamine this question after exploring more severe levels of organization of homosexuality as well as of male perversions in general. In any case, neurotic homosexuality must also be differentiated from homosexuality at the next level of organization, namely, that of borderline personality organization, and, particularly, from homosexuality rooted in a narcissistic personality structure.

Perversion and Homosexuality at the Borderline Level

The clinical situations we encounter at the level of borderline personality organization are multiple and complex, with differing degrees of organization of perverse structure, differing qualities of narcissistic features, differing qualities of superego integration, and differing intensity of aggressive drive.

We may descriptively differentiate, first of all, those cases of borderline patients who present multiple perverse features in chaotic coexistence with each other, without any clear predominance over genital sexuality, from cases in which a dominant perversion (i.e., a habitual and obligatory restriction of sexual fantasy and behavior) has crystallized. As I have pointed out in earlier work (1985), borderline patients with chaotic, polymorphous perverse sexual fantasies and behaviors but without a consolidated perversion have a better prognosis for treatment than those with either an organized perversion or a general unavailability of sexual eroticism.

It needs to be stressed that this unavailability is not due to repression but to a lack of development or deterioration of the very capacity for erotic excitement and idealization, a characteristic of some of the most severe cases of borderline patients, whose anhedonic quality of life experience still presents us with puzzling clinical and theoretical questions.

In all borderline patients we find a dominance of preoedipal conflicts with pervasive preoedipal aggression infiltrating the oedipal conflicts as well, a characteristic I have explored in earlier work (1984). Here, and only in summary, I wish to stress that we usually find that borderline male patients experience mother as aggressive and potentially dangerous; hatred of mother extends to hatred of both parents, whom the child later experiences as a unit. A contamination of the image of father by aggression originally projected onto mother and then displaced onto him, together with a failure to differentiate the parents from each other, produces in boys an image of a dangerous father/mother that leads the boy to view all sexual relationships as dangerous and aggressively infiltrated. The image of the oedipal father acquires terrifying, overwhelmingly dangerous and destructive characteristics, and castration anxiety is grossly exaggerated and overwhelming.

Under these circumstances, the unconscious prohibitions against sexualized relations with women acquire a savage, primitive quality, manifest in severe masochistic tendencies or in paranoid projections of superego precursors. We may find both idealization of mother in a defensively split-off image of her, contrasting with opposite, dangerous, sadistic mother images, and idealization of father in the negative oedipal relation as a defense against the split-off, dangerous father of the positive oedipal relation. The unrealistic and frail nature of both the idealized and the threatening oedipal objects leads to chaotic interpersonal relations, instability of object relations, and, when secondary narcissistic development is present, to the devaluation of all intense emotional involvements, with a defensive consolidation of a pathological grandiose self structure. The pathological grandiose self replaces ordinary idealizations with a pathological idealization of the sexual object in the form of projection of this grandiose self onto the sexual partner.

At this level of personality organization we find, in short, two dominant types of dynamics, which may be expressed in two types of male homosexuality. First is a consolidated homosexual perversion in a nonnarcissistic borderline patient in which a dominantly preoedipal type of homosexuality usually involves the unconscious wish to submit sexually to father in order to obtain from him the oral gratifications that were denied from the dangerous, frustrating mother. Here the patient's relationship to the idealized partner may rapidly acquire demanding, greedy, eternally dissatisfied qualities that reflect oral needs and frustrations, efforts to omnipotently control the sexual partner, and the tendency to extract by force the oral supplies the partner is suspected of withholding. These patients' sadistic impulses may be immediately projected and appear as a strong potential for activation of paranoid fantasies. Ongoing splitting operations facilitate the devaluation of sexual partners who frustrate the patient's oral needs, the idealization of new partners, and lead to sexual promiscuity in the middle of intense and chaotic clinging demandingness and sadomasochistic interactions.

These patients' idealization of desexualized women may also acquire primitive, dependently clinging features and sometimes lead to revengeful identifications with women in the form of caricaturized, pseudofeminine behavior that expresses the denial of the need of mother by identifying with a depreciated caricature of her. These patients' chaotic interactions, exploitiveness, ruthlessness, and yet desperate clinging illustrate both their capacity for emotional involvement and their lack of capacity for object constancy.

The other alternative at this level of personality organization is, as mentioned before, the consolidation of a narcissistic personality structure with a dominant homosexual identification.

This identification frequently reflects the unconscious fantasy of being both sexes at the same time and, therefore, the denial of the narcissistic lesion of being condemned to belonging to one sex only and to have to long eternally for the other one. The consolidation of a narcissistic personality structure and of homosexuality in this context leads to the search for other men who are idealized replicas of the pathological grandiose self. The relation with these men may be maintained as long as the needs for admiration on the part of the patient himself are gratified by the partner, yet excessive envy is not stirred up, and the partner is not prematurely devalued in the course of defensive operations against envy. In practice, such carefully balanced homosexual relationships are difficult to maintain, and male homosexuals with a narcissistic personality structure usually present either a stable but exploitive relationship with a nonnarcissistic, subservient, masochistic man with by far greater capacity for object investment than they have or a long series of brief, exploitive relationships or casual encounters with equally inclined partners.

The surface functioning of these patients may be much better than that of the type mentioned earlier. Their relationships may be emotionally shallow and exploitive, but they are much less chaotic, and, if sublimatory capabilities are present in other areas and the capacity for object investment in nonsexual areas is better maintained, they may, over the years, gradually devalue their conflict-ridden sexual encounters and end up in a relatively satisfactory, asexual social equilibrium.

I have seen several patients with narcissistic personality and homosexuality who establish such an equilibrium by their early or late forties. They may have occasional sexual encounters or fleeting affairs, but also other friendships with men (often previous lovers) that may develop into socially gratifying and sometimes even close friendships without any further sexual involvement. They may similarly establish somewhat distant but stable relations with women friends; sexual gratifications, in these cases, end up as dissociated and somewhat mechanical engagements, while their mostly asexual life provides them with stability. This is in dramatic contrast to the later life experiences of homosexual men at a neurotic level of personality organization, who are able to maintain stable and gratifying relations with another man throughout many years or even a lifetime.

The most severe cases of male homosexuality are those in patients with narcissistic personality and what I have described as malignant narcissism (1984). Here we find patients with homosexual, paranoid, sadistic, and antisocial tendencies, as is the case quite frequently in male prostitutes and the aggressive type of male transvestism (the "drag queen"). The aggressive infiltration of the pathological grandiose self in malignant narcissism leads to a failure of the defensive function of homosexuality against the direct expression of primitive aggression. In contrast to the function of perverse tendencies under normal circumstances to recruit aggression in the service of sex and love, sex and love are here recruited in the service of aggression. In extreme circumstances this leads to perversity of object relations, that is, ruthless exploitation, symbolic destruction of objects, and actual violence.

A Diagnostic Frame for Male Perversion

I trust it has become clear by now that I think one cannot speak of a perverse structure or integrate all the pathology included under male perversion within one frame or category. There may, for example, be greater differences between male homosexuality on a neurotic level of personality organization and male homosexuality of a borderline or narcissistic type than between neurotic homosexuality and other types of nonhomosexual neurotic character pathology in men.

By the same token, there may be greater differences between nonhomosexual perversions in the context of a neurotic personality organization and similar perversions at the level of a borderline personality organization than between such perversions and other nonperverse neurotic character pathology. It seems to me that, in practice, in terms of indications and contraindications for psychoanalysis and in terms of analyzability and prognosis, these observations have been recognized for a long time. Differences between clinical practice and theoretical outlooks may have been influenced, at least in part, by cultural biases.

In clinical practice, I would suggest the following classification of male perversion, based on levels of severity. The criteria consist of increasing pathology of internalized object relations, superego pathology, dominance of aggression, and primitivization of ego organization.

NORMAL POLYMORPHOUS PERVERSE SEXUALITY

The clinician often neglects the inhibition of polymorphous perverse sexuality that is of significant importance in normal enjoyment of love and sex. Clinically it is of interest that, for example, with patients presenting sexual inhibitions, it is only when polymorphous perverse sexual tendencies are freed in a sexual relationship that a full resolution of oedipally determined sexual conflicts can take place. Or else, as another example, it is at the stage of transition from a borderline personality organization with multiple polymorphous sexual tendencies into a neurotic personality organization, a change that otherwise indicates definite improvement in the patient, that a sexual inhibition may set in, replacing the previously "free" polymorphous perverse sexual trends and requiring renewed analytic work in this area in the context of dominant oedipal conflicts and neurotic symptomatology.

ORGANIZED PERVERSION AT THE LEVEL OF NEUROTIC PERSONALITY ORGANIZATION

In cases of organized perversion at the level of neurotic personality organization, we find the typical perverse syndromes of which neurosis may be considered the negative. These neurotic patients present dominant oedipal features with anal and oral regression, but without a dominance of preoedipal conflicts or aggression, or loss of ego identity, object constancy, or the corresponding capacity for object relations in depth.

A Conceptual Model of Male Perversion

POLYMORPHOUS PERVERSE SEXUALITY AS PART OF BORDERLINE PERSONALITY ORGANIZATION

In patients with polymorphous perverse sexuality as part of borderline personality organization, polymorphous perverse sexual fantasies and behavior are present without an organized perversion, that is, they present the typical sexual chaos, with homosexual, heterosexual, exhibitionistic, voyeuristic, sadistic, masochistic, and fetishistic features of borderline patients. These cases are definitely not perversions in a clinical sense. Focusing on their polymorphous perverse tendencies is of interest only in the sense that it reflects a prognostically favorable development that contrasts with that in borderline cases who present a severe inhibition of all eroticism and of erotic idealizations.

BORDERLINE PERSONALITY WITH A STRUCTURED PERVERSION

Borderline patients with a structured perversion are those with prognostically more severe types of perversion than the neurotic type. They lack identity integration and object constancy, and primitive defensive operations predominate. They do not show idealization, denial, reaction formation, and projection based on repression typical for the neurotic level of personality organization, but rather exhibit a clear predominance of splitting and related operations. These cases of perversion are more difficult to treat and have a more guarded prognosis than ordinary borderline pathology. In this type of personality organization we also find typical cases of hysteroid male patients who present cross-dressing and predominantly passive and effeminate character traits.

NARCISSISTIC PATHOLOGY WITH PERVERSION

Cases of narcissistic pathology with perversion are even more difficult to treat. As mentioned before, the homosexual identity in some of these patients may be intimately integrated into the pathological grandiose self. In this connection, many male homosexual patients with narcissistic personality structure display powerful defenses that rationalize and protect their homosexuality as an ego-syntonic part of the pathological grandiose self. Therefore, they do not wish to be treated, but may even present an ad-hoc "ideology" regarding the superiority of male homosexuality.

This phenomenon is of interest because it illustrates that the extent to which homosexuality is ego-syntonic or ego-alien has no relation to the extent to which the personality structure of the patient is neurotic, borderline, or narcissistic. The homosexuality of a neurotic personality structure may also be ego-syntonic. Many patients with neurotic personality structure and a severe symptomatic neurosis or character pathology request treatment but insist on wanting to maintain their homosexuality in spite of their willingness to undergo psychoanalysis. Yet, with analytic treatment, they may be able to resolve their homosexuality, while such resolution is less likely in narcissistic patients who appear to be equally satisfied with their homosexual orientation.

PERVERSION IN THE CONTEXT OF MALIGNANT NARCISSISM

Among patients who exhibit malignant narcissism are many "drag queens," male homosexuals with antisocial tendencies, and those with severe, life-threatening sadistic homosexual perversions. As is true for all patients with antisocial personality proper, the prognosis for psychotherapeutic treatment of the corresponding subgroup within this category is practically zero.

PERVERSION IN PSYCHOSIS

Organized perversions in patients with psychotic functioning have many features in common with those of malignant narcissism and life-threatening sadism. When sadistic features are prominent, these patients are usually extremely dangerous.

Does it make any sense to use the term "perverse structure" to refer to any of these groups? I believe it does, and would reserve this term for patients with an organized perversion and borderline personality organization. The severity of the pathology, the guardedness of the prognosis, the enormous difficulties in the treatment of these cases all warrant, it seems to me, applying the term "perverse structure" to these subgroups. In contrast, my classification tends to reduce, more than has been true in the past, the diagnostic and prognostic differences between perverse organizations at the neurotic level of personality organization on the one hand and ordinary neuroses and neurotic character pathology on the other. If I am right in assuming that this is a clinically reasonable conceptual shift, it would raise new questions regarding the spectrum of psychoanalytically treatable patients with perversions.

The Boundary Between Male Homosexuality and Normality: A Second Look

We can now return to the question of where to draw the boundary between homosexuality imbedded in a neurotic personality organization and homosexual tendencies that might be considered equivalent to other polymorphous perverse features of normal sexuality. Here we encounter theoretical, clinical, and cultural problems.

Theoretically, within a psychoanalytic frame of reference, one may question whether homosexuality could ever be considered a "normal" variant of sexual life. If overcoming the oedipal constellation means a man must be able to identify with the sexual and paternal functions of the father, then any homosexual orientation would imply a limitation in this regard. If, in clinical practice, we encountered cases that would, indeed, correspond to a homosexual object choice without significant evidence of conflicts involving castration anxiety, fear of a full genital and tender involvement with a woman, fear of competing with the oedipal father in the sexual realm, and fear of an overwhelming, persecutory mother image, the psychoanalytic theory of the crucial importance of infantile sexuality in determining unconscious sexual conflicts and orientation would have to be revised.

One might, of course, cynically assume that, given psychoanalysts' theoretical bias, we might never find what we do not want to see. Against this argument, however, stands the reality of sharply differing opinions regarding these matters in the psychoanalytic field and determined tendencies in some quarters to radically reexamine basic psychoanalytic assumptions in this area. One example is the theoretical views of Morgenthaler (1984), who proposes that polymorphous perverse sexuality reflects basic, objectless sexual drives, while both homosexuality and heterosexuality constitute organized, object-related structures that may be either normal or pathological.

From a clinical viewpoint, the situation is equally complex. If homosexual tendencies simply behaved like other polymorphous perverse trends, we would expect a spectrum of homosexual responses—from a perversion in the sense of a habitual and obligatory restriction, at one extreme, to occasional homosexual impulses, fantasies, and behavior, at the other, into what I have described as the normal homosexual components of polymorphous perverse aspects of heterosexual interaction. However, I can only say, on the basis of my own clinical experience over the years and that of colleagues, that we do not find such a spectrum. I have seen very few cases of occasional homosexual behavior in male patients who otherwise would present no major character pathology and would thus correspond to the spectrum extending from neurotic homosexuality to normality.

By far the large majority of patients encountered who present casual homosexual behavior or a bisexual orientation belong to the borderline spectrum of pathology—that is, they present homosexual behavior as part of polymorphous perverse features in borderline personality organization, or occasional homosexuality as part of a narcissistic personality organization. In other words, casualness or occasional selection of homosexual partners and "bisexuality" in a loose sense are usually found in homosexuality that is more severe than that linked to neurotic personality organization.

Clinically, therefore, we find a definite orientation of sexual behavior toward heterosexuality at a point when the personality organization is not neurotic or, to put it differently, when normal resolution of the Oedipus constellation provides the freedom for an autonomous selection of a dominant sexual orientation. Put simply, we just do not find, except very rarely, male homosexuality without significant character pathology.

In addition, while not all male patients with neurotic personality organization and homosexuality resolve their homosexual orientation in the course of psychoanalytic treatment, those who do so are usually patients who resolve major neurotic character pathology as well. The treatments usually are, however, long and difficult. In contrast, some patients with borderline personality organization and narcissistic personalities find it easier to abandon their homosexual behavior without a major resolution of their character pathology. In other words, some patients with severe pathology of object relations find it easier to switch their overt sexual orientation than do healthier, neurotic patients with homosexual structure who have a deeper investment in object relations.

From a clinical viewpoint, then, there appears to be a discontinuity between neurotic male homosexuality and normality, and the orientation toward one or the other sex does not follow the usual distribution of polymorphous perverse sexuality.

From a cultural viewpoint, this question could be raised: To what extent do strong cultural biases against male homosexuality have something to do with the observed discontinuity? In other words, are there conventional social pressures that discourage male homosexual behavior, even though the disposition to it is more prevalent than actual behavior would indicate? One argument in support of this hypothesis is that we may indeed observe a range of casual homosexual behavior in women that would follow the theoretically expectable range for all polymorphous perverse sexual trends.

This higher frequency of occasional, nonobligatory homosexual interaction in women is illustrated in Bartell's (1971) sociological study of group sex, which suggests that it is relatively easy for ordinarily heterosexual women to engage in homosexual encounters in the context of group sex, in contrast to the enormous reluctance, fear, or revulsion of men without previous homosexual behavior to engage in such encounters.

It may be that men are more concerned or uncertain over their sexual identity than women, which, of course, may be explained in terms of a cultural bias more strongly directed against male than female homosexuality; or it might be explained in terms of different characteristics of early psychosexual development. I am referring to the fact that the first object of both sexes is a woman and that girls but not boys normally have to undergo a change in libidinal object as part of their oedipal development.

Still another explanation of the relation between homosexual behavior and psychosexual development—or rather the hypothesis that homosexuality may develop for reasons other than psychosocial and/or psychodynamic determinants—refers to genetic predispositions. While some recent research would seem to speak in favor of a genetic or prenatal hormonal disposition to homosexual behavior in animals, at this point the evidence as applied to humans is inconclusive (Ehrhardt and Meyer-Bahlburg 1981). Also, from a theoretical viewpoint, it is questionable to what extent one might assume a genetic predisposition to homosexuality that would not be importantly influenced by psychosexual development in early childhood.

It seems to me that the major weight of the clinical impression is that male homosexuality, at least as we can explore it psychoanalytically, presents itself clinically as linked to significant character pathology. From a clinical viewpoint, then, the boundary between male homosexuality and normal polymorphous perverse sexual trends is a sharper one than we would expect theoretically.

Some Technical Problems in the Psychoanalysis of Perversion

I believe it is essential that the analyst who treats patients with well-structured perversions, whether at a neurotic or at a borderline and narcissistic level, maintain an attitude of technical neutrality in terms of the final outcome of the patient's sexual orientation. An attitude of technical neutrality, however, does not mean an analyst must maintain impassive indifference with patients who present, for example, a sadistic perversion that might endanger others or themselves. Technical neutrality always includes concern for the safety of the patient, those with whom he interacts, and the protection of the treatment situation itself.

But it is crucial that the analyst permit the patient to determine his own sexual orientation and object choice. Analysts have to free themselves from a possible conventional bias that might well apply to conditions other than the psychoanalytic situation. The analyst's freedom to experience his or her own polymorphous perverse sexual tendencies in the emotional reactions to the patient's material, to identify with the patient's sexual excitement as well as with that of the patient's objects as part of the ebb and flow of the analyst's countertransference potential, may help to bring to the surface primitive fantasies linked to the preoedipal determinants of polymorphous perverse sexuality that will otherwise remain dissociated, repressed, or even consciously suppressed.

Patients with organized perversions often present a "false incorporation," or pseudoincorporation, of the analyst's interpretation as part of an extremely subtle devaluation of the oedipal father projected onto the analyst (Chasseguet-Smirgel 1984), thereby creating particular difficulties in the treatment. The patient acts "as if" he were incorporating the interpretation, in an unconscious mockery of the analytic process that replicates the unconscious mockery of the power of the oedipal father and the pseudoidentification with him based on an anal regression and secondary idealizing defenses against destructive spoiling of what is received.

This development may take the form, for example, of the patient's asking clarifying questions that would indicate that he has heard the analyst's interpretations "but not quite," and is trying to subtly adjust them for a better understanding of himself. It is as if the patient were "just about" to obtain some understanding; the analyst is frequently left with a vague uneasiness about whether authentic work is carried out. The fact that deep transference regressions may take place under these circumstances and that an authentic change of transference paradigms can be ascertained may reassure the analyst about the authenticity of the interaction, and yet a doubt remains about what is real and what is as if.

This defensive constellation should be differentiated from the unconscious spoiling of interpretations and the greedy incorporation and destruction of them that is typical of narcissistic personalities. In fact, the analyst's awareness that this process, so typical for narcissistic personalities, also obtains with organized perversions in nonnarcissistic patients may alert him or her to the fact that this particular defense is active, and permit its interpretation. Other forms this defensive operation may take is the patient's childlike "boasting" about what he learns in his analysis, his discussion of his analysis with many other people in a subtle ridiculing of the oedipal father—at a symbolic level, we might say, sharing his penis and degrading it in the process.

An important differential diagnosis is involved in the careful exploration of a patient's indifference to or revulsion at the female genitals. The repression of sexual excitement behind such devaluation should be differentiated from the incapacity for erotization of body surfaces in general, which is characteristic of some very severely ill borderline and narcissistic patients. In these latter instances, no change can be expected before a severe regression in the transference develops that permits the reactivation of what may amount to a very early mother-child relationship, the development of a new capacity for tenderness that reinvests skin erotism, the idealization of body parts, and the early roots of polymorphous perverse sexuality in general. In contrast, in the better-functioning patients in whom loathing and disgust of the female body is a regressive defense against extremely severe castration anxiety, the working through of that anxiety, of the fear of and revulsion against a powerful and cruel father, and of the inhibition of the capacity for identification with him usually precede the capacity for tolerating the reemergence of sexual excitement with female genitals.

In perversions as well as in all other cases of severe sexual inhibition, it would seem crucial to explore in great detail the patient's sexual fantasies and activities in masturbation and actual sexual interactions. Frequently, subtle defensive avoidance of such an exploration occurs in the form of the patient's willingness to openly discuss some aspects of his sexual experiences while carefully leaving out other aspects; it sometimes takes many months for the analyst to become aware of the avoided area.

In other cases, the profuse display of chaotic sexual fantasies and activities, the patient's apparently total "freedom" of sexual expression, may be used defensively against the avoidance of central aspects of the transference, particularly primitive types of negative transference dispositions. Here the chaotic sexual life characterizing the patient in all his other interactions is also utilized as a defense against an in-depth object relation involving the analyst, and the task is very different: the analysis of the object relation in the transference has to be highlighted and linked to the defensive "smearing" of the analytic situation with primitive sexual material.

Finally, the analysis of perversion should contribute to highlighting the crucial functions of normal polymorphous perverse sexuality in ordinary neurosis and neurotic character pathology and contribute to deepening our understanding of the corresponding psychopathology as well.

BIBLIOGRAPHY

Bartell, G. D. 1971. *Group sex.* New York: Signet Books.
Chasseguet-Smirgel, J. 1984. *Creativity and perversion.* New York: Norton.
Freud, S. 1905. Three essays on the theory of sexuality. In *The standard edition of the complete psychological works of Sigmund Freud,* 24 vols. (hereafter *S.E.*), ed. J. E. Strachey, vol. 7 (1953), pp. 125–245. London: Hogarth Press, 1953–1974.
———. 1914. On narcissism: An introduction. *S.E.,* vol. 14 (1957), pp. 67–102.
———. 1921. Group psychology and the analysis of the ego. *S.E.,* vol. 18 (1955), pp. 65–143.
Ehrhardt, A., and Meyer-Bahlburg, H. 1981. Effects of prenatal sex hormones on gender-related behavior. *Science* 211:1312.
Kernberg, O. 1976. *Object relations theory and clinical psychoanalysis.* New York: Jason Aronson.
———. 1980. *Internal world and external reality: Object relations theory applied.* New York: Jason Aronson.

————. 1984. *Severe personality disorders: Psychotherapeutic strategies.* New Haven: Yale University Press.

————. 1985. The relation of borderline personality organization to the perversions. In: *Psychiatrie et psychanalyse: Jalons pour une fécondation réciproque.* Quebec: Gaëtan Morin Éditeur. Pp. 99–116.

Laplanche, J., and Pontalis, J. B. 1973. *The language of psychoanalysis.* New York: Norton.

Lussier, A. 1982. Les deviations du desire. Étude sur le fetichisme. Paper presented at the 42nd Congress of French-speaking Psychoanalysts, Montreal.

McDougall, J. 1985. *Theaters of the mind.* New York: Basic Books.

Morgenthaler, F. 1984. *Homosexualitat, heterosexualitat, perversion.* Paris: Qumran.

8

The History of
Male Homosexuality
from Ancient Greece Through
the Renaissance: Implications
for Psychoanalytic Theory

ROBERT S. LIEBERT

Introduction

Homosexuality is a subject rivaled by no other in the psychoanalytic purview as a confusing maze. It is constructed of theoretical propositions, civil libertarian sentiment, gut emotional responses from individual clinicians—who are, after all, children of the culture—and sensitivity to political pressure. Among the number of plausible entrances into this maze, the one I have chosen is historical. I will examine what we have learned from a small group of recent studies, each distinguished in its scholarship, with respect to the history of male homosexuality from ancient Greece through the Renaissance.

I view this historical survey as an opportunity to raise fresh and perplexing questions that have the potential for advancing us toward a more satisfactory conceptualization of homosexuality than currently exists. Our present body of psychoanalytic propositions addressing homosexuality falls far short of an acceptable standard for casual explanation.

Freud's writings on the subject remain the matrix for contemporary thinking.[1] His views are embedded in his theory of character which was, for better or worse, moral as well as scientific.[2] Thus, in his model of human behavior, the achievement of genital heterosexuality and sublimation of homosexuality are essential attributes of a psychologically mature man, regardless of alternatives provided by the culture or subjective satisfaction with these alternative adaptations. Freud himself remained troubled throughout his life by the contradiction between his theory, in which there is no way around viewing homosexuality as a failure in normal psychological development, and his personal acceptance and repeated statements that homosexuality is neither a pathological entity nor immoral, nor is it a reason for personal shame. Thus, in a letter to an American mother, he wrote, "Homosexuality is assuredly no advantage but it is nothing to be ashamed of, no vice, no degradation. It cannot be classified as an illness; we consider it to be a varation of the sexual functions produced by a certain amount of arrest of sexual development" (1937, p. 786).

Freud's theory clearly informs what can be schematically summarized as the four principal current developmental and unconscious psychodynamic explanations for adult male homosexuality. These four determinants are generally viewed as all contributing in varying degrees in any one individual. They are: (1) *phobic avoidance* of women due to the unresolved legacy of the oedipal stage of inordinate castration anxiety and the unconscious conviction that women personify the realization of men's

1. Although reference to and consideration of male homosexuality are extensive in Freud's writing, see particularly *Three Essays on the Theory of Sexuality* (1905) and *Leonardo da Vinci and a Memory of His Childhood* (1910).
2. Philip Reiff (1959) has given a thorough discussion of this issue. Also see Murphy (1983/84) with regard to the more specific question of moral judgment in Freud's concepts of bisexuality and homosexuality.

fears of mutilation; (2) *narcissistic arrest,* with the incapacity to love or erotically desire objects who are other than an idealized mirror of themselves; (3) *poor individuation,* with an unconscious threat of "engulfment" and "loss of boundaries" posed by physical and emotional intimacy with a woman, because she reactivates the failure in the resolution of the separation-individuation stage of early childhood development; and (4) *identification* with an overly invested, seductive, and/or controlling mother in the face of an emotionally absent or inadequate father as model for identification in negotiating the oedipal phase.

I cannot now embark on a comprehensive critique of these explanations.[3] Suffice it to say that all four are generally present as influential psychic forces. Their presence, however, hardly allows for the conclusion that they are the determinants of the specifically homosexual orientation. Moreover, they are the same conceptualizations we invoke in explaining the major character and neurotic pathology we observe clinically in male heterosexual patients.

At a more fundamental level, there is a problem in elevating the psychoanalytic theory of psychosexual development, which applies to and describes most individuals, to the status of a "law" of normal, healthy epigenesis. To do so necessarily relegates all individuals who are exceptions to a category of "not healthy," "not normal," or, in the terms of the model, psychopathological. This value then obtains irrespective of our independent assessment of this person's intrapsychic organization, social adaptation, and subjective sense of satisfaction and pleasure. We risk the possibility, therefore, as a consequence of limitations in our knowledge of sexual and gender identity development at this time, of foreclosing the understanding of unusual lines of development by prematurely endowing the theory with the authority of "laws of behavior." Thus psychoanalytic theory is challenged by the homosexual who is capable of both loving and sustaining a relationship, has pleasure in sexual activity, is reasonably decent, and finds everyday life acceptably enjoyable and fulfilling.[4]

3. See Marmor's (1980) critical discussion of the traditional psychoanalytic position on homosexuality.
4. See Reiss's (1980) review of the studies of psychological tests in homosexuality. He

Our understanding of homosexuality has been facilitated in recent years by the progressive shift toward seeing the subject as the "homosexualities" rather than the more monolithic "homosexuality" (see Bell and Weinberg 1978). This change in outlook has been consistent with the crucial data provided over the past decade by developmental studies that focus on two related issues: (1) conformity to and deviance from *culturally defined* gender role behavior during preschool years through latency; and (2) the *subjective sense* of maleness and femaleness that is the core of an individual's gender identity.[5]

In addition, recent studies of variations in prenatal androgen levels and their effect on the hypothalamus have commanded attention to physiological states that, under certain potentiating childhood social conditions, may contribute to the outcome of sexual preference in one group of homosexuals (e.g., Dörner et al. 1975; also see review of neuroendocrine studies by Tourney 1980).

I have briefly touched on some of the difficulties that I see in the traditional psychoanalytic approach to homosexuality and some of the more promising lines of exploration. I will now turn to the study of the past in the hope that aspects of the problem can be further illuminated.

Historical Perspectives

Over the past seven years, five distinguished books have appeared that when taken together and supplemented by a handful of shorter studies, comprise an unbroken history of male homosexuality from ancient Greece through the Renaissance. The first, *Greek Homosexuality,* is by one of the foremost living Hellenic schol-

firmly concludes "that there are no psychological test techniques which successfully separate homosexual men and women from heterosexual comparisons. . . . [Moreover] the commonly used psychological assessment tools do not show any evidence of greater pathology among homosexual women or men than among heterosexuals" (p. 308).

5. Among the more notable studies in this area are those by Friedman and Stern (1980), Green (1974), Money and Ehrhardt (1972), Person and Ovesey (1983), and Stoller (1976).

ars, Sir Kenneth Dover (1978). Professor Amy Richlin (1983) examines homosexuality in ancient Rome. Professor John Boswell (1980) continues the narrative from the beginning of Christianity through the thirteenth century in his *Christianity, Social Tolerance, and Homosexuality*. This work is extended into the Renaissance by Alan Bray's *Homosexuality in Renaissance England* (1982) and by a study of the same period in Italy by Professor James Saslow (1986).

Let me first convey a sense of the overall flow and dramatic shifts in the history of male homosexuality over these two thousand years; and then, because of the constraints of space, I shall concentrate my discussion on issues raised in examining the patterns in Greece and Rome.

By "homosexuality" I refer to the obtaining of more than incidental sensory pleasure through bodily contact with persons of one's own sex, regardless of whether the individual's interests are exclusively homosexual or actively bisexual. By adhering to this restricted usage, we can begin our discussion with a foundation of relatively clear data upon which to build.[6] Although perhaps strange in a psychoanalytic study, I am not, in this chapter, particularly concerned with fantasies, inasmuch as historical data on this aspect of the problem are tenuous.

Passionate and loyal friendships between men are central in Homeric epic from the eighth century B.C., most notably the friendship between Achilles and Patroclus (*Iliad*, 18:22ff.). There is, however, no allusion to physical expression. Not until two centuries later do we locate the first indications of actual sexual activity. Our knowledge is derived from literally hundreds of surviving Greek vases depicting older males on a continuous scale of intimacy with adolescent males, ranging from conversation, to offering gifts (see figure 1), entreating, titillating or embracing (see figure 2), and, finally, copulating.[7] This visual evidence is

6. My definition of homosexuality stands in contrast to the term "gay," which refers not simply to erotic attraction and fantasies but also to a particular collective life style and aesthetic sensibility and outlook shared by many, although by no means all, homosexuals.

7. Boardman (1980) cautions against regarding vase images "as if they were tracings of photographs of life." Rather they are largely conventional symbols for figures and acts that are portrayed in a stylized manner at a time when realistic art did not exist.

FIGURE 1

Man offering a cockerel to a youth. Red-figure cup by the Euaichme
Painter; c. 470 B.C. Oxford, Ashmolean Museum. PHOTO: Courtesy of
the Ashmolean Museum.

FIGURE 2

Man titillating a youth. Red-figure cup by the Brygos Painter; early
5th century B.C. Oxford, Ashmolean Museum. PHOTO: Courtesy of
the Ashmolean Museum.

integrated with a lengthy transcript of an oration at a trial in 346 B.C., involving homosexuality[8]; poetry spanning several centuries (e.g., the anthology compiled by Meleager, c. 100 B.C.); comedy, particularly that of Aristophanes (c. 445–385 B.C.); and the writings of contemporary philosophers (most notably Plato, c. 427–347 B.C.) and historians (e.g., Thucydides, c. 455–400 B.C.).

It will be helpful to first state some general characteristics. It is highly significant to note that in ancient Greek there were no nouns corresponding to English nouns for "a homosexual" or "a heterosexual," since it was assumed that virtually every male, at different times, expressed love and sexual desire toward both males and females. Greek society accepted the alternation of homosexual and heterosexual behavior in the same individual. Moreover, there is little evidence to suggest that such an alternation or coexistence of sexual activities was perceived as creating untoward conflicts, either for the individual or for society. However, within this arena of acceptance, the forms of homosexual behavior were quite rigidly codified. Indeed, important aspects of this behavior were considered within the purview of Athenian legislation. I shall come back to the very different standards for acceptable sexual behavior on the part of Athenian male citizens in contrast with noncitizen freemen and slaves. For citizens, a homosexual relationship was only to be accepted between a mature man (*erastes*) and a youth between the onset of puberty and the growth of facial hair, let us say age thirteen to sixteen or seventeen (*eromenos*). This relationship was closely tied to a pedagogical ideology, in which the mature man was mentor and model for the youth, not simply in scholastic issues, but about those matters that were the fabric of life in that world, matters that today we ideally think of fathers imparting to sons.

A moment ago I mentioned the rigid codification of the manner

8. In a trial with significant political consequences, a public figure, Timarchos, was prosecuted for having prostituted himself as a young man to another male, which, under the law, would be cause for his being disbarred from political office. A forty-five-page printed transcript of the argument by the prosecutor Aeschines survives. The argument is entirely concerned with homosexual codes and practices. This text (Aeschines i, *Against Timarchos*, 346 B.C.) is, as Dover emphasizes, one that uniquely gives us access to the attitudes that it was prudent to profess in public with regard to the subject of homosexuality during the classical period.

FIGURE 3
Man and youth copulating. Black-figure amphora by the Berlin
Painter; c. 540 B.C. London, British Museum. PHOTO: Courtesy of the
British Museum.

FIGURE 4

Satyr homosexual group (detail). Red-figure cup by the Circle of the Kikosthenes Painter; late 6th century B.C. Berlin, Stiftung Staatliche Kulturbesitz. PHOTO: Courtesy of the Stiftung Staatliche Kulturbesitz.

in which homosexuality was practiced. Some salient characteristics of this code were first, although love for one another exists in both the youth and the mature man, erotic desire and arousal are present *only* in the older partner. Second, moreover, the almost exclusive position and means of copulation was standing, intracrural thrusting by the adult—that is, moving the penis back and forth between the thighs of the other (see figure 3). The youth is passive and unaroused and submits to his *erastes* only after a period of courtship, often marked by gifts. The youth never initiates the sexual activity. Rather, he finally marks his respect and gratitude for his older admirer by granting the erotic favor that is so desired.[9] Third, fellatio, anal sex, and even masturba-

9. In *The Symposium* (c. 415 B.C.), Plato has Socrates pointedly describe how he repudiated the unabashedly seductive advances of the beautiful youth Alcibiades because such a reversal of roles was a violation of the proper order of the *erastes-eromenos* relation-

tion appear virtually exclusively in art and myth as the province of satyrs—the half-man, half-beast representations in Greek mythology of that which is barbaric or unacceptable (see figure 4). Nevertheless, these activities were presumably part of the constellation of desires and could acceptably be engaged in with male prostitutes, foreigners (noncitizens), women, and male slaves with no particular opprobrium (see figure 5). These groups, of course, were the ones excluded from the exercise of political power. Of crucial importance here is the fact that if a citizen of any age yielded orally or anally to another male, or accepted money, he was assumed to have rejected the role of citizen; and, indeed, serious consequences could and *did* result if subsequent to his exercising public functions these past activities came to light.[10] Fourth and finally, erotic friendship between men of the same age, so far as we know, did not exist. Thus there were no "homosexuals," meaning men who were homosexual in the sense that we use the term today, far less a "gay community." Most important, the distinction was forcefully maintained between the acceptable form of homosexual desire and behavior and what was unacceptable—namely, behavior that in Greek culture was considered "female" sexual behavior. If behavior was confined within these prescribed boundaries, there was no apparent conflict between masculine gender identity and being erotically drawn to another male.

Ungaretti (1978) has stressed that the socio-political-educational aspect of the *erastes-eromenos* relationship reflected a system of unequal and hierarchical relationships. The culture prized single victors. This is portrayed in the accounts of glory on the battlefield and in the preparation for the military—the "Games" (Olympic, Pythian, etc.), where there was no equivalent of present-day silver or bronze; only the "victor." It should also be noted in this context that the prebearded youth was not yet of military age. The hierarchical nature of the homoerotic relationships is

---

ship. The inhibition of manifest sexual arousal in the *eromenos* during the act of copulation bears testimony to the degree of early, rigid socialization of sexuality in Greece given what appears to be the low threshold for penile arousal that generally characterizes the male adolescent. Of interest in this connection, Dover observes that in vase painting an athletic youth with a relatively small penis is consistently depicted as the physical ideal.

10. As in the trial of Timarchos (see note 8).

FIGURE 5
Heterosexual group (detail). Red-figure cup by the Brygos Painter;
early 5th century B.C. Florence, Archaeological Museum.
PHOTO: Courtesy of the Archaeological Museum.

underscored by the total absence in Greek mythology of a homosexual relationship between two male gods; rather, such relationships always involve a god and a mortal.

As the preeminence of the Hellenic world evolved into the domination of Western culture by the Roman Empire, bisexuality continued as a normative practice. It was Edward Gibbon's celebrated conclusion that "of the first fifteen emperors Claudius was the only one whose taste in love was entirely correct" (1776–1788, I:78, n. 40), by which Gibbon meant exclusively heterosexual. Although Gibbon's precise estimate of this matter is conjectural, the climate of great tolerance is evident in the public nature of Hadrian's love for the Bythinian youth Antinoüs (see figure 6). Antinoüs died in a drowning accident, after which the bereft emperor renamed cities after him and had statues and memorials erected throughout the Roman empire as shrines for devotion.

The data from ancient Rome are less precise than those from Greece. Scholars, therefore, have less clear agreement about patterns of homosexuality in Rome. In contrast to Greece, exclusive homosexuals and a small "gay" subculture existed, but those individuals were the object of invective, as evidenced in graffiti and satire. Nevertheless, tolerance for homoerotic desire and activity was extensive. Pairings, again, were usually between mature bisexual men and youths, who were often noncitizens. Neither Roman law, until the third century A.D., nor Roman religion drew distinctions between homosexuality and heterosexuality. Rather, social status and power configurations were of more concern than the gender of the sexual object. As in Greece, passive homosexual behavior on the part of the male citizen was condemned, although, again, acceptable in those denigrated in the culture and precluded from the exercise of power.

A fundamental difference between Greece and Rome was that in Greece the *erastes-eromenos* relationship was regarded as a fundamental element in the educational and socializing process, and was idealized in art and literature. In Rome no comparable ideology existed. Rather, homosexuality was simply one means of casual pleasure (see figure 7), with no claim in art, literature, or public proclamation of its being otherwise. Hadrian may be regarded as an easily accepted exception to the general mode.

FIGURE 6

Antinoüs. Marble; Roman, *c.* A.D. 132. Vatican, Museo Laterano.
PHOTO: Courtesy of the Museo Laterano.

FIGURE 7

Homosexual group. Augustan Silver Cup; late 1st century A.D.
Oxford, Ashmolean Museum. PHOTO: Courtesy of the Ashmolean
Museum.

We cannot regard the distinctive homosexual patterns of Rome apart from the context of that culture any more than we can those of Greece. I will address some aspects of this complex issue presently.

The tolerance that marked pre-Christian, Western culture progressively lessened in the three centuries between about A.D. 200 and 500, as society became predominantly rural and totalitarian in government, and life was increasingly influenced by Christian thought, largely embodying the Judaic moral tradition.[11] Thus in the fourth century laws were enacted prohibiting homosexual marriages (thereby implying that such an entity must have existed) and imposing the sentence of death for selling or forcing males into prostitution. Nevertheless, for many centuries the Church assumed a casual attitude toward homosexuality. The only passages in the New Testament that have almost universally been interpreted as prohibiting homosexuality are in Paul's epistles. And even here, Boswell (1980), after considering the meaning of "natural law" at that time and the meaning of the original Greek, argues that what Paul meant was that homosexuality was simply not natural, meaning uncommon, out of the ordinary, not what later came to be regarded as "against nature," that is, the order of God. In other words, Boswell maintains that Paul's original text has been mistranslated and the meaning misinterpreted to serve much later antihomosexual Church attitudes.[12] Moreover, within the Church and monastic orders there is widespread documentation of sympathetic attitudes toward homoerotic desire as well as its actual consummation.

Then, over a brief span of time, the attitude of tolerance shifted to one of pronounced ambivalence, expressed on the one hand by the Emperor Justinian's outlawing homosexuality, with the threat

11. The Jewish attitude toward sex has varied from epoch to epoch (see Bullough 1976). In the post-exilic period (c. 600 B.C.) until the destruction of Jerusalem in A.D. 70 (i.e., the same years as the eminence of Greek culture), sexual pleasures of all kinds were virtually equated with the satanic and a code of extraordinary rigidity was prescribed, including severe condemnation of homosexuality. Bailey (1955) suggests that the increasing antagonism the Jews felt toward homosexuality was engendered by the threat they felt from Greek culture as a source of influence and the pull toward assimilation.

12. Many scholars remain unpersuaded by Boswell's analysis and conclusions about the passages condemning homosexuality in Paul's epistles (e.g., Crompton 1981; Moore 1981; and Thomas 1980).

of the death penalty, in A.D. 533 in Constantinople. On the other hand, passionate same-sex friendships appear to have continued among the clergy, albeit more quietly. In marked contrast with both earlier and later periods, there is virtually no surviving literature expressing homoerotic sentiments and practices dating from the sixth to the middle of the eleventh century. Moreover, we have essentially no idea of the place homosexuality had in the thought or lives of the nonclerical military, peasant, and aristocratic sectors of society. Moral theologians were by and large silent on the subject and in most parts of Europe antihomosexual laws were rarely acted upon.

During the course of the eleventh century there was a dramatic shift from rural economy and family-oriented rural ethics to an urban economy and diversified city life. In addition, literacy spread outside of the clergy and interest rose in the heritage of classical and early Christian learning. This shift was accompanied by the reappearance of a genre of homoerotic literature in Latin from the male communities of the abbeys and cathedrals that was highly conventional in form (in addition to Boswell 1980, see Stehling 1984). Furthermore, homosexuals were accepted in prominent positions in both the secular and religious levels of society. Present-day examination of contemporary poems, letters, and other documents, however, often leaves unclear what was overtly homosexual and what was simply passionate friendship. In sum, during the medieval period, homosexuality was not particularly hidden from public view, and opposition to it, when expressed, seemed based more, although not entirely, on individual preference rather than on formulated moral grounds.

Then, almost unaccountably, in the second half of the twelfth century, rabid hostility to homosexuality appeared in the popular literature, which was shortly followed by vociferous condemnation in theological and legal writings. Although part of a more general fabric of theological erotophobia, homosexuality was no longer regarded as a matter of personal preference of a respected minority. Rather it was unequivocally treated as a morally sinful, socially dangerous aberration. Official disapproval by the Church was decreed by the Lateran Council of 1179, and this radical change in position was given its theological justification in the subsequent arguments of Thomas Aquinas (*Summa Theologica*, 1266–73). Thereafter, until two centuries later, men engaging in homosexual acts were considered heretics and persecuted and executed. Such men were the objects of a crusade, which also sought to eradicate Jews and other non-Christians from most parts of Europe, and to stamp out witchcraft and sorcery, with which homosexuality was associated (see also Goodich 1979).

With respect to the broad historical course I have presented, there are minor debates among scholars about details. Of greater importance, historians are far from being in agreement about the causal factors that account for the radical shifts in the position of homosexuality from epoch to epoch. In fact, I think it fair to say that no one has, as yet, offered a persuasive comprehensive explanation.

To return to our historical narrative, the two centuries of violent condemnation and persecution rather abruptly reversed themselves following the Black Plague in the middle of the fourteenth century. In Italy there was a return to the earlier tolerance of homosexuality, accompanying the rise of capitalism, beginning forms of democracy, and serious attempts to wed Church teachings with classical writings in a new philosophical humanism.

The new philosophical humanism came to be called Neoplatonism. Its center was at the Accademia Platonica in Florence under the patronage of the Medicis. The movement received great impetus during the mid-fourteenth-century pontificates of two great popes, Nicholas V (1447–1455) and Pius II (1458–1464). Both pontiffs were eager to reconcile Church dogma with the new learning from antique sources, and employed hundreds of scholars and copyists in this pursuit. Whereas Aristotelian thought had been important to Thomastic theology, in the new approach to antiquity the writings of Plato were to be reconciled and integrated with traditional Christianity.[13] The Neoplatonists consid-

13. The central thinker in this school was Marsilio Ficino (1433–1499), who was the first to translate all of Plato's works into a Western language. (The complete works were published in 1484.) The Neoplatonists conceived of man as basically good, but fallen as a result of Original Sin. The path to redemption was largely through intellectual discipline. Ficino affirmed the concept of "Platonic love" from Plato's *Symposium* and viewed pleasures of the flesh as antithetical to the ascension of the soul. Saslow has discussed in his study of the Humanist Courts in Italy during this period that while abstinence from pleasures of the flesh was the philosophic ideal, many in the courts faltered in its pursuit.

ered the task of human existence to be an inner process wherein the soul strove to ascend to higher and higher degrees of knowledge and love, leading ultimately to a sense of communion with God. The Neoplatonic concept of the purity of love profoundly influenced the poetry and literature of the sixteenth century. In this intellectual and religious climate, the form that homosexuality assumed was largely modeled after that of ancient Greece, and the classical myth of Zeus' abduction of the beautiful Trojan youth Ganymede became the organizing metaphor.

In exchange for serving as cup bearer and bed companion to the God, Ganymede is given immortality. This motif was represented literally hundreds of times in Renaissance art (see Saslow 1986), as exemplified by Correggio's *Abduction of Ganymede* (c. 1530, see figure 8). Thus within the conceptual vocabulary of Neoplatonism, in which Ganymede represents the more spiritual realm of the Christian soul—the mind—leaving behind earthly and corporeal elements, to ascend to a state of ecstatic contemplation, homosexuality became acceptable again as part of an idealizing relationship between, once again, a mature man and a youth. The ideal was the fusion of the erotic and the spiritual. As in the past, the same opprobrium surrounded prostitution and assuming the passive sexual role, although it must be stated that we know little about what men actually did together in bed. And again, there is virtually no record of same-age lovers. Another cautionary note is that, as with previous periods, we have knowledge of the ideologies and sexual practices in intellectual, artistic, and aristocratic circles, but not of the common man.

The manner by which the popular currents of Neoplatonism could be utilized as the manifest expression of more private communication is exemplified by Michelangelo Buonarroti (1475–1564). Michelangelo, at age fifty-seven, gave a presentation drawing of the *Abduction of Ganymede* (figure 9) to his beloved twenty-three-year-old Roman nobleman, Tommaso de' Cavalieri, toward whom the artist felt an unprecedented experience of passion.[14]

14. Tommaso remained a close and loyal friend of Michelangelo's for thirty-two years, until the artist's death. Although scholars are divided with respect to the question whether Michelangelo engaged in overtly homosexual relationships with young men during his adult life, there seems to be uniform agreement that the relationship between the artist and Tommaso was never sexually consummated (see Liebert 1983).

FIGURE 8

Correggio, *Abduction of Ganymede,* oil on canvas; *c.* 1530. Vienna,
Kunsthistorisches Museum. PHOTO: Courtesy of the Kunsthistorisches
Museum.

FIGURE 9

Copy after drawing by Michelangelo, *The Rape of Ganymede,* black chalk; 1532 (?). Windsor, Windsor Castle. PHOTO: Courtesy of Windsor Castle. Copyright reserved.

Michelangelo's Ganymede, with eyes closed and his right arm limply draped over the eagle's wing, is enraptured as the eagle spreads his legs and buttocks. The figure of this athletic youth is a masterful rendering of the ecstasy of passive yielding to anal eroticism in the embrace of a more powerful being.

The degree to which homosexuality was easily tolerated during the Renaissance in Italy is not only supported by the data that suggests that a number of the major artistic and intellectual figures of the period were actively bisexual, but also particularly well illustrated in the instance of the artist Giovanni Antonio Bazzi (c. 1477–1549). In Rome Giovanni became known as "Il

Sodoma." This contemporary of Michelangelo was described by Vasari (1568) as having come by his nickname "as he always had boys and beardless youths about him of whom he was inordinately fond" (vol. 3, p. 285). Despite his predilection, Sodoma was renowned in Siena, Milan, and Florence, and received papal commissions at the Vatican Palace and an honorary title from Pope Leo X.

What is perhaps the most striking aspect of the pattern I have just described is that in keeping with the general duality of ethics and life in the Renaissance, there was unequivocal ecclesiastical and secular official condemnation of homosexuality, particularly when minors were involved. Moreover, there were laws that could be called upon to back up these "official" positions. In this respect, Renaissance Italy differed from ancient Greece.

In contrast to the picture in Italy, in England during the late Renaissance we encounter the first publicly open homosexual subculture, similar to aspects of "gay" culture today—in the "molly houses" of London. These were taverns in which exclusive homosexuals gathered to drink, sing, and dance with each other. The molly houses would be well tolerated for several years, after which there would be raids, trials, and frequent executions. Then, after a silent period, they would reopen and be tolerated for several more years, only to become once again the objects of savage persecution. Alan Bray (1982) persuasively argues that this cycle of toleration and persecution served society's purposes by concentrating the group by seeming to sanction them, and then constraining them with periodic violence.

Discussion

My greatly condensed survey of this two-thousand-year history of homosexuality suggests many more questions than are resolved. This material does, however, have important implications for the direction of further inquiry.

To begin, it has become axiomatic to regard the origins of any individual's sexuality as the complex outgrowth of biological, social, and intrapsychic forces. It may be further stated that in different periods of history and in different cultures, what I conclude to be a universal homosexual potential is coded and expressed throughout a range of behavioral enactment, fantasized possibilities, and repressed and unconscious thoughts. Thus at any time and in any place, what is behavior, what is fantasy, and what is repressed are highly inconstant and variable in relation to definitions of deviance, whether on a moral basis or that of psychopathology.[15] Therefore, no theory that purports to account for this mode of sexual behavior can command respect unless it takes into account the matrix of social structure in which the individual is placed. As Hartmann, Kris, and Loewenstein (1951) articulated the problems some years ago, in each environment certain predominant pathways of discharge and sublimation of drives and their derivatives are more or less acceptable and accessible. Therefore, in a given society, some patterns of resolution of conflict and behavior will be facilitated and others impeded.

The evidence from ancient Greece and Rome strongly suggests that all men have a strong potential for arousal by and pleasure in erotic activities with both male and female partners. History, thus, strongly supports Freud's general postulates with respect to the bisexual nature of man.[16] The similarities between what we mean by homosexuality in our time and what was meant in ancient times are, however, overshadowed by the differences.

15. The sociologist's view of deviance has been succinctly expressed by Kai Erikson (1964): "Deviance is not a property inherent in certain forms of behavior: it is the property conferred upon those forms by the audience which directly or indirectly witnesses them" (pp. 10–11).

16. Freud early stated his view of bisexuality in *Three Essays* (1905), "I have regarded it [bisexuality] as the decisive factor and without taking bisexuality into account I think it would scarcely be possible to arrive at an understanding of the sexual manifestations that are to be observed in men and women" (p. 220). Then, as late as 1937, in *Analysis Terminable and Interminable,* he stated "that every human being is bisexual" in the sense of having the capacity to distribute his libido "either in a manifest or latent fashion, over objects of both sexes . . . without the one trend interfering with the other" (p. 244). At times, Freud used the concept of bisexuality to connote that which we now consider the constellation of masculine and feminine identifications that constitute the integrated (or, when failures in development have occurred, not so integrated) representation of self.

While it can be asserted that in Greece and Rome adult homosexuality in certain forms was acceptable, it can be equally asserted that homosexuals were not.

Among Greek citizens—and the distinction is crucial between citizen and noncitizen, inasmuch as citizenship was one of the most powerful organizing principles of values and social attitudes —homosexual behavior was acceptable as a part of one's total sexuality, which was also to include sexual relations with women, marriage, and family (see Dover 1978 and Hoffman 1980). And even within these limits only certain homosexual activities were acceptable. What was acceptable varied dramatically in accord with the role expectations for each of the stages in the unfolding from adolescence into married manhood.[17] At all stages, oral and anal receptive activities were reserved to a denigrated class—that is, noncitizens. Yet the male adult citizen could participate as the active partner with a noncitizen, who played the passive role associated with women.

The study of homosexuality over the course of centuries seems to me to compel recognition of the interrelationship between individual and collective psychology. If we accept the proposition that the homosexual component in male sexuality is universal, it would seem that different social orders have found different ways of *both* permitting and forbidding overt forms of homosexuality, through the selective use of the label "deviant." Thus a balance is achieved between the need to provide an enduring fabric to the society, usually in the form of reproductive nuclear families, and also to permit the expression of homosexuality, however vicarious or shaped by reaction formation.

Thus in the late medieval period, when collective reaction formation reached murderous proportions, men had to be found who were having sex with other men in order to provide reality to this psychic scenario. If men practicing homosexuality could not be found, Inquisitors decided that certain men were doing so

17. Lewis (1982/83) gives an interesting reading of the great lyric poet Pindar's (c. 518–c. 438 B.C.) view of elements in the Greek life cycle in the relationship between the god Poseidon and his *eromenos* Pelops. When Pelops comes of age he asks Poseidon for help in winning his bride. Thus, having granted homosexual favors for the god in his youth, Pelops feels entitled to call upon Poseidon for affirmation of his heterosexuality in manhood.

anyway, since if they declared them heretics, therefore possessed by the devil, it followed that they must also be homosexual. Such was the fate of the large and important Order of the Knights Templars (see Bullough 1976, pp. 395 ff; cf. Legman 1966).

This enactment at the societal level of intrapsychic splitting and conflict would also appear to be borne out by the pattern in England during the Renaissance, with the cycles of homosexuality seeming to be sanctioned as long as contained in the molly houses, then periodically being persecuted.

Despite the extraordinary range over time in degrees of toleration, all of the social orders I have considered have, so to speak, found it necessary to extinguish, suppress, and carefully socialize the forms of the manifest expression of the homosexual potential. Although the exception is generally allowed in some denigrated or disenfranchised class of males, or magically and ritualistically invested in figures such as the transvestic shaman in many primitive cultures, one "iron law of history" has been that males must conform to male gender roles and not to those of females.[18]

The issue of why so strong a prohibition exists against males playing female roles has, most appropriately, been the subject of extensive inquiry by psychoanalysts. Two related considerations have been proposed to account for the prohibition. One validly addresses the unconscious concerns with castration and oedipally related issues. The other, which I would emphasize, involves the struggle men wage their entire lives to resist the pull of their infantile and early childhood identifications and yearnings for reunion with mothers and their female surrogates. To yield, however, to that ever-present temptation is also to invite dissolution of the sustaining integrated structures of thought, affect, and defensive organization that form the stable sense of self. It is to risk the emergence of primordial anxiety.

Psychoanalysis, uniquely, *can* yield substantial clarification as to why any particular individual, regardless of the prevailing cultural climate, develops in the sexual manner that is distinc-

18. Of importance in this context is Ford and Beach's (1951) classic study of sexual patterns in seventy-six primitive societies. They found: (1) homosexuality was present in virtually every society; (2) it was never the predominant type of adult sexual activity; and (3) in forty-nine of the seventy-six societies (64 percent) some homosexual activity was regarded as normal or socially acceptable for certain members of the community.

tively his or hers. The study of homosexuality over the centuries suggests caution, however, to psychoanalysts about regarding homoerotic behavior as sufficiently explained by pointing simply to the nature of or problems in the mother-son dyad. Greek and Roman patterns indicate that homosexuality satisfied needs not otherwise adequately satisfied in those societies. When I say not "sufficiently explained," it is not to say that the childrearing practices and role of mother in a particular society are not crucial factors. Rather, it is more complex. As Kardiner (1945) and others have elaborated, specific childrearing practices shape character and behavior in ways that are functional for the needs and goals of each culture.

In this spirit, we can consider aspects of Greek family life that probably contributed to the picture I have drawn. But, as you will see, these specific characteristics are not unique in the history of family structures. We must therefore go further and look to other functions that the Greek form of homosexuality might have served. I present the following more as a means of orienting ourselves, not as "the explanation." In the Greek family, the mother, as woman, was politically powerless and confined to running the home and overseeing the raising of her children, with, characteristically, little shared intimacy with her husband and few other meaningful outlets. This situation with mothers has led some to suggest their strong and vicarious, and also highly ambivalent investment in their sons. This mothering, coupled with the apparent absence of fathers from a vital role in the early years of male children, must be heavily weighted as formative in shaping the sexuality of the Greek male. Indeed, one wonders whether the frankly erotized relationship between mature married men and youth, within a pedagogical ideology, fulfilled needs for both parties that were aroused, but unmet and unresolved, in the early father-son relationship and resolution of the oedipal stage.[19] We think, in this connection, of The Odyssey, and the power of one of the principal lines of the narrative—of

19. For a picture of Athenian family life, the role of women, and some of the possible impact of these on psychological development, see Pomeroy (1975), who focuses particularly on women; see Simon (1978) for a scholarly traditional psychoanalytic exploration of the interrelationship of Greek life, thought, and literature; and see Slater (1968) for a full but quite naive use of psychoanalytic theory in this area.

the son Telemachus, who patiently waits from birth for twenty years for the return of his father, Odysseus.

But if this family structure is not unique in history, how can it be linked to extrafamilial forces in Greek life that further shaped male sexuality? Let me give one example. Greece was a constantly warring state, and perhaps homosexuality cannot be separated from its military function, given the distinctive organization of their armies. Specifically, older and younger pairs of warriors would do battle together, each loyal and inspiring to the other. The legendary, near-invincible Band of Thebes exemplified this arrangement. Warfare, by the time of the ascendancy of Rome, differed from that of Greece in giving less emphasis to camaraderie and more to coordinated organization within and between legions.

This exploration of the past sensitizes us to current change. And, indeed, over the last fifteen years we have been witnessing a dramatic increase in social tolerance for homosexuality. Inextricably linked to this has been marked increase in individual self-esteem in homosexuals and in cohesiveness of an emergent gay subculture (see Liebert 1971). These changes have spurred a stormy reconsideration of the designation of "disorder" by mental health professionals.

We are aware that individual identities change and community socialization takes place in response to current and prospective historical circumstances. The processes and mechanisms by which the intrapsychic changes are effected, nevertheless, remain to be understood.[20]

For example, it is increasingly apparent that rigorous population control is necessary if we are to avoid ecological disaster. Is not one of the new ideologies generated by this grave awareness the idea that women need not consider it their primary function to bear and raise children, and thereby perpetuate the species? In fact, the perpetuation of our species now demands the opposite. In parallel, there is diminished necessity to socialize all males into

20. The study of the complementarity of individual intrapsychic processes and historical conditions has become subsumed under the term "psychohistory." The two figures whose scholarship in this difficult interdisciplinary area have been the most illuminating are Erik Erikson (e.g., 1958, 1969) and Robert J. Lifton (e.g., 1968, 1979).

being reproductive heterosexuals. Thus the social forces suppressing homosexuality in developing males are less punitive, resulting, among other things, in heterosexuals who are more comfortable expressing their androgyne.

With this change, we see in analysis male homosexuals whose goal now is not to effect change in orientation but to resolve the neurotic and characterological conflicts that prevent them from achieving deeper and lasting homosexual relationships, and to dissolve some of the psychic scar tissue that inevitably results from growing up in a family with traditional values, knowing that one's fantasies are homosexual and that one is expected to take one's place in a manifestly heterosexual culture.

In our clinical work with individual homosexual patients we address their unique developmental histories and particular constellations of disturbances in psychic structure, controlling fantasies, and unpleasurable affect. But we should approach our task informed by the realization that history is quixotic and that we exist on a small point in the arc of time.

BIBLIOGRAPHY

Aeschines. (346 B.C.). Against Timarchus. In *The Speeches of Aeschines*, i, trans. C. D. Adams. Cambridge, Mass.: Harvard University Press, 1948.
Aquinas, T. (1266–73). *Summa theologica*. New York: Benziner, 1947.
Bailey, D. S. 1955. *Homosexuality and the western Christian tradition*. London: Longmans, Green.
Bell, A. P., and Weinberg, M. S. 1978. *Homosexualities: A study of diversity among men and women*. New York: Simon and Schuster.
Boardman, J. 1980. Review of K. J. Dover's *Greek Homosexuality*. *Journal of Hellenic Studies* 100: 244–245.
Boswell, J. 1980. *Christianity, social tolerance, and homosexuality: Gay people in Western Europe from the beginning of the Christian era to the fourteenth century*. Chicago: University of Chicago Press.
Bray, A. 1982. *Homosexuality in renaissance England*. London: Gay Men's Press.
Bullough, V. 1976. *Sexual variance in society and history*. Chicago: University of Chicago Press.
Crompton, L. 1981. The roots of condemnation: Review of J. Boswell's *Christianity, social tolerance, and homosexuality*. *Commonweal* 108: 338–340.
Dörner, G., et al. 1975. A neuroendocrine predisposition for homosexuality in men. *Archives of Sexual Behavior* 4:1–8.

The History of Male Homosexuality

Dover, K. J. 1978. *Greek homosexuality.* Cambridge, Mass.: Harvard University Press.

Erikson, E. H. 1958. *Young man Luther: A study in psychoanalysis and history.* New York: Norton.

———. 1969. *Gandhi's truth: On the origins of militant nonviolence.* New York: Norton.

Erikson, K. 1964. Notes on the sociology of deviance. In *The other side: Perspectives on deviance,* ed. H. Becker, pp. 9–21. New York: Free Press.

Ford, C. S., and Beach, F. A. 1951. *Patterns of sexual behavior.* New York: Harper.

Freud, S. 1905. Three essays on the theory of sexuality, in *The standard edition of the complete psychological works of Sigmund Freud,* 24 vols. (hereafter *S.E.*), ed. J. E. Strachey, vol. 7 (1953), pp. 125–243. London: Hogarth Press, 1953–1974.

———. 1910. Leonardo da Vinci and a memory of his childhood. In *S.E.,* vol. 11 (1965), pp. 59–137.

———. 1937. Analysis terminable and interminable. In *S.E.,* vol. 23 (1964), pp. 209–253.

———. 1937. Letter to an American mother. *American Journal of Psychiatry* 57:786.

Friedman, R. C., and Stern, L. 1980. Juvenile aggressivity and sissiness in homosexual and heterosexual males. *Journal of the American Academy of Psychoanalysis* 8:427–440.

Gibbon, E. 1776–88. *The Decline and Fall of the Roman Empire.* 6 vols. New York: E. P. Dutton, 1957–62.

Goodich, M. 1979. *The unmentionable vice: Homosexuality in the late medieval period.* Oxford: Clio Press.

Green, R. 1974. *Sexual identity conflict in children and adults.* New York: Basic Books.

Hartmann, H., Kris, E., and Loewenstein, R. M. 1951. Some psychoanalytic comments on culture and personality. In *Psychoanalysis and Culture,* ed. G. B. Wilbur and W. Muensterburger, pp. 3–31. New York: International Universities Press.

Hoffman, R. J. 1980. Some cultural aspects of Greek male homosexuality. *Journal of Homosexuality* 5:217–226.

Kardiner, A., et al. 1945. *The psychological frontiers of society.* New York: Columbia University Press.

Legman, G. 1966. *The guilt of the Templars.* New York: Basic Books.

Lewis, T.S.W. 1982/83. Brothers of Ganymede. *Salmagundi* 58–59:147–165.

Liebert, R. S. 1971. The gay student movement: A psychopolitical view. *Change* 3: 38–44.

———. 1983. *Michelangelo: A psychoanalytic study of the man and his images.* New Haven: Yale University Press.

Lifton, R. J. 1968. *Death in life: Survivors of Hiroshima.* New York: Basic Books, 1982.

———. 1979. *The broken connection: On death and the continuity of life.* New York: Basic Books, 1983.

Marmor, J. 1980. Homosexuality and the issue of mental illness. In *Homosexual behavior: A modern reappraisal,* ed. J. Marmor, pp. 391–401. New York: Basic Books.

Meleager. c. 100 B.C. *The poems of Meleager,* trans. P. Whigham. Berkeley, Calif.: University of California Press, 1976.

Money, J., and Ehrhardt, A. A. 1972. *Man and woman, boy and girl: Differentiation and dimorphism of gender identity from conception to maturity.* Baltimore: Johns Hopkins University Press.

Moore, J. C. 1981. Review of J. Boswell's *Christianity, social tolerance, and homosexuality. American Historical Review* 86:381–382.

Murphy, T. F. 1983/84. Freud reconsidered: Bisexuality, homosexuality and moral judgment. *Journal of Homosexuality* 9:65–77.

Person, E. S., and Ovesey, L. 1983. Psychoanalytic theories of gender identity. *Journal of the American Academy of Psychoanalysis* 11:203–226.

Plato. c. 415 B.C. ? *Phaedrus,* trans. W. Hamilton. Harmondsworth: Penguin, 1973.

———. c. 415 B.C. ? *The symposium,* trans. W. Hamilton. Harmondsworth: Penguin, 1951.

Pomeroy, S. B. 1975. *Goddesses, whores, wives, and slaves: Women in classical antiquity.* New York: Schocken Books.

Reiff, P. 1959. *Freud: The mind of the moralist.* New York: Viking.

Reiss, B. F. 1980. Psychological tests in homosexuality. In *Homosexual behavior: A modern reappraisal,* ed. J. Marmor, pp. 296–311. New York: Basic Books.

Richlin, A. 1983. *The garden of Priapus: Sexuality and aggression in Roman humor.* New Haven: Yale University Press.

Saslow, J. M. 1986 *Ganymede in the Renaissance: Homosexuality in art and society.* New Haven: Yale University Press.

Simon, B. 1978. *Mind and madness in ancient Greece: The classical roots of modern psychiatry.* Ithaca, N.Y.: Cornell University Press.

Slater, P. E. 1968. *The glory of Hera: Greek mythology and the Greek family.* Boston: Beacon Press.

Stehling, T. 1984. To love a medieval boy. *Journal of Homosexuality* 8:151–169.

Stoller, R. 1976. *Sex and gender.* New York: Science House.

Thomas, K. 1980. Rescuing homosexual history. *New York Review of Books* 27: 26–29.

Thucydides. c. 411 B.C. *The Peloponnesian war,* trans. R. Warner. Harmondsworth: Penguin, 1954.

Tourney, G. 1980. Hormones and homosexuality. In *Homosexual behavior: A modern reappraisal,* ed. J. Marmor, pp. 41–58. New York: Basic Books.

Ungaretti, J. 1978. Pederasty, heroism, and the family in classical Greece. *Journal of Homosexuality* 3:291–300.

Vasari, G. 1568. *The lives of the painters, sculptors, and architects,* 4 vols., trans. A. B. Hinds. New York: E. P. Dutton, 1927.

III

Men Growing Up:

Developmental Epochs

9

Reciprocal Effects of Fathering on Parent and Child

PETER B. NEUBAUER

Instead of speaking about the reciprocal effects of fathering, I suppose it would be more correct if the title of this chapter were "On Being a Father." This would emphasize the inner experience of fatherhood. But this presentation is quite limited, for it does not follow the role of fathers through the developmental stages. It is, to say the least, most difficult to predict the effect of early parental interactions on further development.

The new interest in fathers has many roots: there is the women's liberation movement and its demands for new definitions, the increased divorce rate, the ever-accelerating number of fathers who have custody of their children, and the shared care-giving that occurs because mothers are working. But, in addition, studies focusing on preoedipal development have led to a new assessment of parental roles.

I am concerned that the role of the father is being studied in the way that has too often been used to explore mother-child relationships. As long as we maintain the notion that development proceeds from the dyadic to a triadic relationship, we maintain a position that is no longer tenable. There are those authors who assign to fathers who care for their young children the role of mother-substitute. Yet when we examine father-child relationships, we have to emphasize from the child's side (1) the father as the only caregiver, (2) the father as a participant caregiver, and (3) the child's capacity to respond to multiple caregivers. From the father's side we have to examine the effect of the caregiving function on his identity and psychosexual organization.

Historical Review

Early psychoanalytic propositions viewed preoedipal development solely in the context of mother-child interaction, with fathers not gaining significance until the oedipal phase. Thus object-self organization and separation-individuation were formulated primarily as mother-child interaction experiences. Whenever other objects appeared in the child's life, they were seen as being secondary to the primary role of mother. Furthermore, it was assumed that the mother's continuity of care provides the trust and security that form the cornerstone of the infant's capacity to delay gratification, to tame the drives, and thereby to widen the power of the ego. From this position it appeared logical that any interruption or intervening relationships between mother and child could either dilute or disrupt these essential elements which build the appropriate representational world.

Until recently, this focus has contributed to the exclusive study of mother-child relationships and, in doing so, confirmed its role as a primary, organizing experience. However, we have now begun to study the earliest father-child relationships with the same interest. But, as I shall propose later, even such widening of the field of observation may be insufficient if we are to consider the whole range of relationships from infancy through childhood, particularly the processes of differentiation of object-self, of objects and self, and the internalization of different object relationships. Many workers have made substantial contributions over the last few years concerning the influence of fathers on infant development. Some stress the differences between father and mother in their actions with the child (e.g., the mother's comforting attitude versus the father's action-stimulation and the potential consequences of these differences on early development). Others are impressed by the similarities in the child's responses to either mother or father, dependent as usual on the caregiving quality. Nevertheless, I have not as yet found any longitudinal studies that clearly establish the consequences when the father is also a primary caregiver or the only one, nor are there any systematic studies by analysts or reports of the analysis of adults when the father was an early or sole caregiver.

We can assume that either the boy or the girl's dependency on father must have an impact on the child's gender identification, on the progressive-regressive pulls, and therefore on the phallic-oedipal conflict constellation. These surely are the classic considerations when outlining the normal developmental dynamic sequences. These formulations are based primarily on the position that both boys and girls are first dependent on mother and only later shift toward a triadic relationship. Much has been written about the fine-tuning between mother and infant—the cognitive-affective stimulation and the dyadic orchestration that provides the child with the ability for self and object differentiation.

I stress this point because it implies that the infant establishes a single relationship first, and only when this is securely achieved is the child able to expand object relations and progress into the phallic-oedipal phase. For instance, many studies address themselves to rivalry, jealousy, and envy as part of this oedipal triadic interaction, but only lately have these feelings been seen during earlier phases. Indeed, over the years psychoanalytic treatment confirmed the assumption of first the early dyadic and, only later, the triadic constellation; thus genetic data and reconstruction, as well as many forms of pathology, have been seen to be connected with the absence or inappropriateness of mother's capacity during the preoedipal period.

At a time when the fathers were not asked by the mothers, family, or cultural tradition to take part in the early child care, a number of assumptions were made:

1 That the woman is primarily a nurturing person, while the father is a providing person. I suppose this notion was transmitted to boys and girls over generations. The father came "into play" only as the children became older.

2 Psychological studies seem to indicate that when the fathers do indeed participate in early caregiving, their attitudes are substantially different from those of mothers. Whether these differences will have an impact on further development and whether they are somewhat inappropriate to the infant's needs are questions that remain to be answered.

3 The child will "select" the parent according to his or her psychosexual stage of development.

Fortunately, we now have *Father and Child* by Cath, Gurwitt, and Ross (1982), a book that brings together the significant studies done over the past decade. Numerous observations document the capability of the infant for earlier bonding and attachment to father. Some chapters focus on the child's gender development when the father is a primary caregiver. We have long been aware of the differences and difficulties in outlining the sexual development of girls compared with those of boys. Some reasons for these were associated with the position regarding the mother—that is, boys start in the heterosexual position, while girls have a different road to take to make the shift of their affections to father. If we accept this formulation, it will be most important to pursue the inquiry into the psychosexual development of boys when the father is the primary early caregiver or a participant caregiver.

All in all, these formulations confirm the importance of the early father-child relationship. Nevertheless, they place too much emphasis on the dyadic aspect, on the comparison between mother-child and father-child interactions. This emphasis is primarily a by-product of the field of observation and the research design rather than due to the child's developmental demands. Even so, as long as we limit the child's life to mother-child or father-child components, we still exclude many other relationships that have or will gain significance: the grandparents, the nurse, the siblings, and others. With each, new qualities of relationships are formed. Each may at times reach a priority based on the child's alternating needs.

Reciprocal Effects of Fathering on Parent and Child

Lamb (1978) studied the attachment of the child to mother *and* father and concluded that they are the same, except for the difference in quality. Lamb found that the infant at age eight to twelve months reacted to father's play with more interest. Father's stimulation or activation seemed to be more intense; mother's seemed more comforting. Of course, we should be extremely cautious in interpreting either attachment as more positive in its effect on further development, for it depends on factors such as timing, dosing of stimulation, the infant's disposition, the tolerance, the gender, and most of all the infant's search for both parents.

Lamb's investigations concern the interaction of the infant to both parents and to others. Some of these are done under laboratory conditions. They are finally freeing us from the restriction of the exclusive mother-child field of observations.

In early family histories, before the advent of nuclear families and then of single-parent ones, the infant was exposed to many different family members interchangeably. There were older siblings, grandparents, caregivers; those who could afford it employed others to help in or take over child care duties. Our present focus on single exclusive relationships may be more an expression of present-day family life than the average experience of children through the ages. As I shall discuss later, this does not modify our assumption of the primacy of the parental objects. Nor does it modify our proposition of the significance of primary objects in life. What it does say is that these primary objects should not be viewed in the context of dyadic, but rather as multiple object relationships, and that these relationships may contribute to the emergence of the primary interplay with the mother.

The New Role of Fathers

The fathers, in their new roles, will have gained a true participation in the transgenerational continuities. As they share in child care, they have access to reliving their own preoedipal world, to connect with their childhood images of their parents. Their own past preferences, jealousies, and rivalries do not wait to be reactivated only during the oedipal phase of their children. The infant's demand for an empathic responsiveness beyond the physical and cognitive stimulation can open for the father avenues of recognition of defenses and repressions.

Mahler's (1975) steps of separation-individuation, differentiation practicing, rapprochement subphase, and so forth, must also be studied in the context of the triangularity of multiple early relationships. Object constancy described in a system of a dyadic relationship to mother must be investigated regarding multiple object internalizations. Similarly, the role of transitional objects must be extended. When there are many objects available to whom the child can turn for gratification, does this then alter the need for the transitional object? An investigation of this question may clarify the issue of whether transitional objects are required primarily because of relationship deficiencies or because of the child's inner disposition.

The role of the father in psychoanalytic theory has very often been seen in the context of the phallic phase, that is to say, in relation to castration anxiety. The anticipated punitive aspect of father, it is assumed, contributes to the disengagement from mother and reinforces a positive identification with him; while at the same time the wish for his elimination prepares the basis for the oedipal complex.

It will be important to see to what degree there will be a modification of these sequences when the father is a primary caregiving person. Will the need for rescue from the symbiotic tie be negotiated at an earlier phase, and will the struggle between the longing for the possession of mother and for the turning against father be negotiated differently? What has been outlined mostly in connection with the development of the boy must then also be carried to the course of development of the girl, when the father is an early primary object. All of this, in some way, may influence the steps of separation-individuation and what are discussed later as aspects of the primacy of the object during the oedipal phase.

The infant's faculty to attach himself is often tested by his

Reciprocal Effects of Fathering on Parent and Child

response to separation. Thus separation from father, when father takes part in child care, has been studied. Kotelchuck (1972) observed infants from the age of six to twenty-one months as having equal separation reactions to father and mother, but not to strangers. Others have extended these studies. Spelke (1981) has found that one-year-old infants with fathers who are intensively involved in their care have *less* separation reaction (and when left alone with a stranger, they show less distress). These findings deserve replication and explanation. Those reasons offered indicate that babies who have both parents available are less distressed on separation. How this affects separation and individuation and the establishment of self-object representations still needs further investigation.

I am in agreement with Abelin's (1975) investigations, his assumption that there is an early triangularity and that when the infant is six months old father becomes most interesting to him. His concept of a "double mirror" explains the infant's capacity to differentiate early objects, which in turn affects self-object differentiation. Thus, during the beginning preoedipal phases, the child's interaction with father leads to an alternate experience from that with mother and contributes to a distribution of libidinal ties with a lowering of the dependency on mother. Father in this sense assists in the lowering of the symbiotic tie to mother. Father becomes a libidinal, ego-enhancing object, before aggression and conflicts emerge during the phallic and oedipal phase.

Abelin's formulation of a triangularity from the first few months of life has been questioned by those who propose that a differentiation of various objects and a polarization can only occur later. If we change the term "early triangularity" to "the capacity for early multiple relationships," Abelin's general propositions may become more acceptable, and then we can explore the role of fathers in this context.

Clinical Studies

The Child Development Center studies of infants in a mental health daycare center, primarily infants with an unmarried mother, indicate how successfully infants and toddlers are able to lean on those available to them and to form multiple relationships.* It is significant that these infants form strong relationships to the caregivers. These relationships may at times be a substitute for the absent relationship with their mother or may exist side by side with an appropriate maternal contact. Often it increases the child's wish to form a similar close relationship to mother, which gains increasing importance. Such observations and others alert us to the need to study children not only in the context with parents but in a broader spectrum of interchangeable relationships. The child's capacity to extract from each adult what he needs is impressive; the differentiated interrelationship may contribute to an internal differentiated object representational world. At the Child Development Center my coworkers and I came to the following conclusions:

1 In the presence of multiple caregivers, the search for mother is maintained or, when she previously was absent, can begin to assert itself.
2 Normally endowed infants explore the available human environment to extract the needed stimulation and gratification.
3 Continuity of care does not necessarily imply exclusive continuity of care by one person. What appears to be important is the continuity of relationships.
4 The infants' individual dispositions to form relationships vary greatly, dependent on drive and ego characteristics. Some infants actively engage in interactions, while others react only to environmental stimulation. Thus the "reading" of the infant, the dosing of the stimulation, becomes an essential part of the attempt to repair the deficiency syndrome resulting from the unevenness of stimulation so that the child's capacity to form object relations is set in motion once again.
5 The matching of the caregivers' capacities and the infant's needs

*The Child Development Center, a division of the Jewish Board of Family and Children's Resources, is located in New York City.

is most important. The child's selection of the caregiving person, when there is a choice, gives us important clues about the infant's special requirements at given times.

6 Since mothers are not always able to match all their children's demands equally, the availability of others gains significance, not only as a choice but as a complement to eliciting the full potential of children with various dispositions.

7 While in our group of children it was difficult to decide who, at various times, was an infant's primary caregiver, mother maintained or gained an increasingly important position.

In the past we were more impressed by the dilution of the attachment to objects when mother was not fully available and when there were multiple caregivers. But under these circumstances the child may have suffered from the inappropriateness of the caregiving qualities and, therefore, from the inability to form attachments, rather than from the availability of multiple objects. Thus continuity of care in the affective, cognitive, and perceptual senses becomes more related to the one-to-one relationship between mother and infant. Such a formulation excludes the continuity and reliability of care by many adults who seemed to provide the child with a nurturing environment that supported development.

What is striking is not only the child's capacity to respond to different caregivers and the contribution they make to development, but that the child, in spite of it—or, one may have to say, because of it—chooses the mother increasingly as the primary object, as if the innate striving toward a single object maintains significance. What these findings stress is the ability of the infant to draw, from a variety of sources, gratification and stimulation, and that the infant does not find a dilution of attachment or an interference with it. The past literature on this subject seems to be based on the reaction of infants to conditions in which they were unable to form any attachment and thus they moved from one to another interchangeably without achieving the necessary steps toward imitation, incorporation, and identification.

How do we explain the fact that fathers gain equal importance to mothers during the phallic-oedipal phase in spite of father's past nonparticipation in the infant's care during the preoedipal phase, a phase considered so crucial for the achievement of object permanence and, later, object constancy? Psychoanalytic propositions assume that there are innate, built-in phase sequences that demand psychosexual phase organization—that is, that children at this stage search for triadic fulfillment. Nevertheless, the achievement of some degree of object constancy as a prerequisite for separation-individuation does not seem to parallel the child's relationship to father. Does father object constancy occur only during the phallic-oedipal phase? If so, how do we explain this?

The study of one-parent children (Neubauer 1960) when father is absent or when he is a nonparticipant in caregiving indicates the child's evolving longing for father, which is at times described as either "father hunger" (Abelin 1975) or "father thirst" (Herzog 1980). My own study has indicated that the child responds to father's absence by forming an idealized image of him and thereby creating a father image that will fulfill the child's own changing needs through the developmental phases. This search for father is surely influenced by mother's attitude. Furthermore, it can be assumed that when mother is absent, one would be able to observe in the child a longing and thirst for mother with equal longing for the absent parent.

An investigation into early sibling relationships (Neubauer 1983, Solnit 1983) further leads me to emphasize again that pre-oedipal triangularities exist among mother, sibling, and child. In these triangularities rivalry and envy become intense experiences, experiences that often increase the longing for the object. These experiences are then carried into the phallic-oedipal constellation. Thus these findings reconfirm the disposition toward phase organization that organizes the multiple object representations toward an increasing triadic position. In this connection, I have (1985) suggested speaking about primary objects—mother, father —in the context of multiple relationships and referring to object primacy when the parents gain the exclusive significance during the phallic-oedipal phase. Studies must be extended beyond mere infant observations to learn about the steps of differentiation, of object and self, of those that lead to gender identity and those that lead to the oedipal child in the context of triangularity. If we follow Peter Blos (1967), we have to consider here the notion that only during the adolescent period will we find the solution of the various oedipal constellations. The second individuation—the negative oedipal position—will allow for a reorganization that will decide the outcome of preoedipal and oedipal conflicts.

Vignettes

So far I have addressed myself to the child and his relationship to parents. Now I shall turn to some aspects of the fathers' responses to the children. In the following vignettes, I consider some of my male patients and their relationships to their young children. The vignettes focus on the family interaction and father's function and do not address many pathological conditions for which the fathers come for treatment. While three vignettes cannot lead to generalizations, they may lead to the formulations of certain issues, at least for a subgroup of fathers.

VIGNETTE 1

This patient came from a family characterized by a marked poverty in overt reactions. His father was distant, work-oriented; the mother engaged in carrying out the social functions of a woman of society. She did this with pleasure and she gave it great importance. The older sister withdrew early into reading. She was unapproachable, and this made it impossible for my patient to act on his feelings of rivalry or to establish a playful companionship with her, for she treated him in a most intolerable way, mainly as though he did not exist. The children were given over to nurses and housekeepers who frequently changed. My patient became inept in social intercourse and, later in life, while very active in many social functions, he felt detached and reserved, an attitude he carried over to the analysis. Expressions of either anger or pleasure were kept to a minimum. When his daughter was born, a well-endowed, engaging child, she made a most significant contribution to her father's life. While I as analyst feared that he would carry over his relationship to his sister to his daughter, he threw himself fully into the relationship. He spoke about his pleasure in her in an affectionate and, for him, unusually loose way, he enjoyed the expression of her lustfulness and he was empathic with her pain. He took part in early child care, spent much of his nonprofessional time with the family and, with such intensity toward his daughter, that his wife felt, for a short time, excluded. Through the child he relived the various stages of his own development. Thus in contrast to his past experience, his family became the central focus of his interest, and this stimulated the recovery of repressed emotions, which furthered the psychoanalytic treatment.

VIGNETTE 2

This patient remembered that from early childhood he felt different from the other members of his family; that he was more talented, more sensitive and intelligent than they were. He was embarrassed by their behavior and through the years he sought status in social and religious groups different from those to which his family belonged. His relationship with women before he married was limited. He was self-oriented and his priority in life was his professional advancement. He finally married a much younger woman and they had two children, to whom he paid little attention. He came for treatment because the marriage broke up.

At the time of his marital separation, a complete change occurred in him. Suddenly there was nothing more important to him than his children, who lived with their mother. He made himself fully available to them, seeing them every morning, evenings, over weekends; he cooked for them and took care of them with an intensity that made any other aspect of his life unimportant, to a degree that he neglected his professional career. He fought for the right to be with his children and to have shared custody. Now he used his contact with them to fulfill his need for a family life and to regain his wife. He was aware that in the past he had assigned to his wife the role of housekeeper and mother, while he maintained the role of provider and kept a geographic and emotional distance. The crisis in his marriage changed this. He was empathetic with the loneliness of his children, and thereby his narcissistic isolation broke down. Since he had never had a family life, he now struggled to save it. The mother, who was always a "good mother"—I do not know whether she was a "good enough mother"—took care of her children in an easier, nonstructured way, compared with the father's attitude. She seemed to have longed for a protective relationship and she understood her children's attachment to their father, but she did not further it, for she was involved in disengaging herself from her husband.

For the first time the patient allowed himself a painful attachment based on many fears from his own childhood; the attachment was furthered by his children's enthusiastic response to his availability.

VIGNETTE 3

This patient had been married for ten years and had three young children. He was an ambitious person, who, out of fears on many developmental levels, asserted full control at home and in business. He supervised the children's activities, the older children's schoolwork, and the household. His wife liked to live unburdened by conflicts, simply and without searching for recognition or achievements. She took the children as they were. Their problems did not arouse concern or the need for intervention. She resented, therefore, her husband's overinvolvement and concern, which she experienced as intervention demanding submission. This patient responded to his own family with shame and the wish to disengage himself from it. His mother conducted the family activities; his father invariably accepted her decisions. From adolescence, he had affiliated himself with a group that was religiously, economically, and socially different from his own. He craved acceptance from this new world but always felt as an outsider. In spite of his professional success, his fears of living in a hostile world continued, affecting his social and sexual life.

From the very beginning of the marriage, he focused on his children's welfare and made himself available to them. This was furthered by moving his offices to his house. He regulated his children's activities, and they became attached to him and turned to him for comfort and stimulation. He would stop at nothing to offer them security, for his home became his only safe dominion. The protection of his children served his self-protection; his love for them gave him hope for a future for them that he could not secure for himself.

Discussion

These vignettes document five points.

To these patients, caring for a very young child was never a threat to their masculinity. It would be too simple to assume that their professional success shielded them from a threat to their gender identity. Furthermore, their paternal function differed from that of their fathers. Their role in child care did not press them into a dyadic role with their children, but rather they wished to include their wives in their affectionate relationship. This is a most interesting finding.

Second, their participation in early child care evoked an empathic mobilization that helped them to overcome their personal reserves and resistance. Thus "the regression under the auspices of caring" for their children was one from which they drew for their own comfort and by enacting fantasies of wish fulfillment reaching deep into their own childhood.

This finding contradicts that of those authors who understand early triangularity as taking place between both parent (mother) and child with the assumption that the mother transfers her own relationship to the father via her own feeling for him.

The role of the wife was different in each of these vignettes. Whether she resented the husband's interest in taking part in or taking over child-care functions, these fathers acted on their need for closeness to their children, independent of her position.

In one additional case not summarized, divorce activated a paternal attitude that until then was not exercised.

It is clear that I have simplified the complex psychic function

Reciprocal Effects of Fathering on Parent and Child

in order to stay within the limits of this topic. At the same time, I am aware that these investigations need to examine further the reasons why these patients were able to care without anxiety and regression and threat to their often conflicted phallic-oedipal organization.

Summary

I have pointed to a number of aspects that determine father-child interaction and its potential affect on both father and child. More than this, I have suggested that the studies of father-child interaction should not replicate the studies of mother and child. Rather, they should be undertaken within the family interaction and in connection with significant object relationships.

Instead of a model that suggests the development from a dyadic to a triadic object world, we should think of one that outlines a broad multiple object choice within which the primary object ties occur and which lead to the oedipal primacy of the parents.

The new role of fathers opens new questions about early development. It may be self-evident that with the participation of fathers in child care, the exclusive role of mothers in early development has changed. Our model of early dyadic object relationship has to be readjusted. The consequences of this on preoedipal, oedipal, and adolescent development have yet to be studied.

BIBLIOGRAPHY

Abelin, E. 1975. Some further observations and comments on the role of the father. International Journal of Psycho-Analysis 56:293–302.
Blos, P. 1967. The second individuation process of adolescence. Psychoanalytic Study of the Child 22:162–186.
Cath, S. H., Gurwitt, A. R., and Ross, J. M. 1982. Father and child: Developmental and clinical perspectives. Boston: Little, Brown.

Herzog, J. M. 1980. Sleep disturbance and father hunger in 18- to 28-month-old boys. *Psychoanalytic Study of the Child* 35:230.

Kotelchuck, M. 1972. The nature of the child's tie to his father. Ph.D. diss., Harvard University.

Lamb, M. E. 1978. The father's role in the infant's social world. In *Mother/child, father/child relationships,* ed., J. H. Stevens and M. Matthews, pp. 245. Washington, D.C.: National Association for the Education of Young Children.

Mahler, M. S. 1975. *The psychological birth of the human infant.* New York: Basic Books.

Neubauer, P. B. 1960. The one-parent child and his oedipal development. *Psychoanalytic Study of the Child* 15:286–309.

———. 1983. The importance of the sibling experience. *Psychoanalytic Study of the Child* 38:337–351.

———. 1985. Preoedipal objects and object primacy. *Psychoanalytic Study of the Child* 40 (in press).

Solnit, A. J. 1983. The sibling experience: Introduction. *Psychoanalytic Study of the Child* 38:281–284.

Spelke, E. 1981. Perceptual aspects of social knowing. In *Infant social cognition,* ed. M. Lamb and L. Sherrod, p. 341. Hillsdale, N.J.: Lawrence Erlbaum Associates.

10

The Contribution of Adolescence
to Male Psychology

EUGENE MAHON

Introduction

If society begins with the *renunciation* of instinct, one could argue that psychoanalysis begins with the *recognition* of instinct. A study of the psychology of the male is therefore a study of instinct and its vicissitudes in one gender. If the relationship between instinct and gender is the general focus of this book, the particular topic of this chapter deals with the marriage of the two concepts in adolescence.

From an etymological point of view, instinct and gender seem devoid of chauvinistic distinction. "Instinct" seems to mean what moves us and "gender" seems to mean where we came from. The psyche, however, more than the sum of its words, seems to have placed great emphasis on the anatomical sexual difference. And this therefore is also a focus of this chapter.

If becoming a man means crossing the river of childhood to enter the land of maturity, adolescence can be thought of as the search for the proper vessel to set sail in and complete the journey. The vessel is of course no more or less than a metaphor for the components of the conflicts in the psyche of the young male, who, developmentally incomplete at the outset, hopes by the end of adolescence to have aligned the inner structures of his mind with the outer structures of reality and society in a manner that can be called "mature." This remarkable journey has been called an identity crisis, a trial mourning, a second birth, a second individuation, a psychological moratorium, and probably many other things, as investigators have attempted to put names on its multifaceted surfaces. Adolescence could be also thought of, perhaps, as a great thaw: in Ferenczi's fanciful mind latency was seen as a recapitulation of the ice age; similarly, adolescence can be viewed as puberty's creation of an inexorable thaw, the icy ego structures of latency melting in the heat of hormonal awakening and anatomical expansion.

If adolescence can be thought of as the new representational world that puberty insists on after its demolition of latency, this new representational world can be compared and contrasted to the old world of infantile imagos that have now to be deconstructed and reconstructed, so to speak. The incestuous stables have to be irrevocably cleaned by the young Hercules, a task or series of developmental tasks that confront each developing member of the dramatis personae of the human condition.

If the developmental tasks of the first five years of life are the attainment of object constancy and the development of the infantile neurosis, and if the developmental tasks of latency can be summarized as the maintenance of the repression barrier of infantile amnesia so that the ego structure of latency (Sarnoff 1976) can ensure an education and the transmission of the cultural heritage, how could we summarize the developmental tasks of adolescence? When hormones and anatomical growth make a young male as sexual and as tall and as strong as his parents, incestuous desire and taboo clash with such force that the mind is almost torn asunder.

Society has opted for the same resolution of this conflict for millennia: young Oedipus should leave Thebes. The young adolescent male, after a rebellion that clamors for independence (symbolized by the wish to stay out as late as he chooses) using mainly dependent weapons (anal messiness symbolized in the refusal to keep his room clean), should develop the psychic maturity to leave the home of incestuous objects and earn a living for himself and his new objects beyond the hearth of origin.

Although boys discover their penises in the latter half of the first year of life (Kleeman 1965), and there appears to be an early genital phase at eighteen months of age (Galenson and Roiphe 1971), the "maleness" of boys is most exuberant in the phallic phase (approximately age four). The castration complex and the Oedipus complex do of course temper the exuberance with neurotic deceptions. The animistic preoperational thought processes of the three- to six-year-old turn the anatomical sexual difference, curiosity about sexual intercourse, procreation, and nighttime separation from parents into a primal scene of utter distortion: in the eyes of children sexual intercourse is an act in which sadistic parents abandon their wards and then dismember each other in the privacy of their own room. Things that go bump in the night are not understood as projections of infantile rage; the anatomical sexual difference is not seen as biological necessity but rather as a consequence of castration, loss, crime, and punishment. The infantile criminal will not be released from the prison of neurosis until the experience of adolescence provides the key. The psychology of the male, the sense of growth or immaturity, the level of normality or pathology, will depend on the search for and acquisition of the keys of maturity. In this chapter I emphasize that part of the search that takes place in adolescence, a most significant part in the opinion of most observers of the human condition.

Adolescent Development

In *The Universal Experience of Adolescence,* Norman Kiell (1964) suggests that there is a basic uniformity of adolescent development in all societies and illustrates this thesis with over two hundred personal documents ranging from antiquity to the present and representing many cultures. Kiell quotes Ernest Jones—"[the adolescent] recapitulates and expands in the second decennium of life the development he passed through during the first five years of life, just as he recapitulates during these first five years the experiences of thousands of years in his ancestry and during the pre-natal period of those millions of years" (p. 11)—and then Kiell gives many examples of individual authors' struggle with this recapitulation, which, while it may be a universal experience, is also a uniquely existential individual phenomenon. Of the many examples that he cites, two stand out to me as brilliant, eloquent statements of the adolescent male mind trying to plumb the depths of the psychological revisions and recapitulations that are altering irrevocably the coordinates of the psyche. In his autobiography Thomas De Quincey (1889) wrestles with the idea of the transition from the childish mind to a mature consciousness: "But when, by what test, by what indication does manhood commence? Physically, by one criterion, legally by another, morally by a third, intellectually by a fourth—and all indefinite . . . ?" (p. 855). De Quincey goes on to compare childhood and maturity to two tropics with an *intertropical* region between them so that it is impossible to define exactly where the line of bisection is. However, De Quincey pushes himself further and further to distill from the compound elements of his adolescence the moment of truth that ushered in his manhood:

> . . . [H]ow . . . shall we seize upon any characteristic feature . . . which belongs to conscious maturity? One such criterion, and one only, as I believe, there is—all others are variable and uncertain. It lies in the reverential feeling, sometimes suddenly developed, towards woman, and the idea of woman. From that moment when women cease to be regarded with carelessness, and when the idea of womanhood, in its total pomp of loveliness and purity, dawns like some vast aurora upon the mind, boyhood has ended; childish thoughts and inclinations have passed away for ever; and the gravity of manhood, with the self-respecting views of manhood, have commenced. (P. 857)

It is instructive to compare De Quincey's romantic definition of the moment of manhood with what might be considered a more philosophical depiction. John A. Rice (1942), the founder of Black Mountain College, in North Carolina, describes the beginning of manhood in his autobiography, *I Came Out of the Eighteenth Century*, in existential terms.

> While he was an infant he absorbed knowledge, taking it in through his tissues, with thought or care. Then, in boyhood, he became a collector, of birds' eggs, stamps, tobacco tags, baseball averages, dates —anything that can be arranged in series. But if he is to become a man —some do—he grows tired of counting and collecting, and a terrifying thing happens: he ceases to be a scientist, he begins to ask, "What does it mean?" and with the coming of this question there comes the first step into manhood. To know is not enough. (P. 869)

If in his excerpt De Quincey anticipates Freud, Rice seems to have studied Piaget. Their observations can certainly serve to introduce in literary language what psychoanalysts have struggled to depict in developmental instinctual structural parlance or what Piaget has attempted to articulate in genetic-epistemological terms.

The psychoanalytic literature beginning with Freud has recognized that the "transformations of puberty" are complicated physiological, hormonal, anatomical, and, of course, psychological revisions of earlier conflicts. Revision seems too passive a description for a process that reworks the past into a new organic metamorphosis: if a chrysalis is not a butterfly in strict *biological* terms, this contrast can be emphasized even more forcefully from a developmental point of view in a discussion of the chrysalis of the mind.

Freud's theories of infantile sexuality changed with the vicissitudes of the intuitions that shook his remarkable mind. Whereas at first he believed that the infantile psyche would have to wait until puberty for early issues to be sexualized, gradually he came to realize that sexuality began in the first five years of life. This revolutionary discovery made it necessary to see adolescence not as the *prima volta* of sexuality but as Act II of an earlier drama. If the adolescent was capable of orgasm, it became clear to Freud that the first five years could be pictured as an elaborate form of foreplay. "The child is father to the man" began to be more sexually literal than figurative for Freud as compared to Wordsworth. As analysis began to reflect ego psychological and preoedipal emphases, theories of adolescence began to shift and change accordingly. Whereas Helene Deutsch and the early disciples of Freud might have viewed adolescence as a recapitulation of the Oedipus complex, later theorists stressed the psychological components they felt were neglected in early formulations. Erikson and Anna Freud, receiving the baton of ego psychology that Sigmund Freud offered in "The Ego and The Id" (1923), recognized adolescence as a watershed of the mind, a time for risorgimento, psychosocial moratorium, object removal. Erikson (1959) felt that a moratorium in adolescence allowed the mind an oasis in which identifications that were "imprinted," so to speak, in childhood could be revised and reworked until a "final" identity could be arrived at when the crucible of adolescent experience was through with its experiment. Anna Freud saw the ego's task in adolescence as one of *object removal:* to wean the infantile mind from incestuous imagos that would shackle it to neurosis forever if the ego was not summoned by the dictates of reality to spread its wings and leave the nest.

If Erikson stresses identity formation and psychosocial moratorium, Peter Blos (1979) stresses "passage" as in *rite de passage,* suggesting the thrust of the developmental momentum that sweeps the adolescent psyche toward maturity. Blos has described adolescence as a "second individuation," comparing the risorgimento of the teenager to the earlier processes of individuation described by Margaret Mahler (1967). He has given considerable attention to the structural changes that follow the wake of the adolescent passage leading to a new consolidation of psychic structures by the end of adolescence. Blos has emphasized in particular the development of the male ego ideal, a structure that he believes is the heir of the negative Oedipus complex. Ideals that are magical in midadolescence and bear the imprint of primitive symbiotic grandiosity become tempered with experience in the normal course of development so that, at the end of adolescence, a male is able to see his father not as the disappointing fallen idol but as a man in his own right. The importance of this developmental sequence in normal male development can hardly be stressed too forcefully in the context of our topic.

Jean Piaget places his emphasis on the nature of the intellectual

234

endowment of the adolescent. When the teenager develops the capacity for formal thought, which Piaget also calls hypothetico-deductive reasoning, the worldview immediately changes (Flavell 1963). As Rice has so eloquently articulated in the preceding quotation, "to know is not enough." Meaning becomes the issue. For Piaget the human being has to overcome egocentrism at each phase of development, must accomplish the "art of decentering," as he might have phrased it. Consequently, the adolescent at first uses the capacity for formal thinking to think about himself, so to speak, which explains the abundance of narcissism and intellectualism that is so typical of adolescent adaptation. Gradually the adolescent learns to "decenter" and to use the elegance of formal thought to explore the full complexity of reality and not only the anguish of Narcissus.

Daniel

I like to think of adolescence as a voyage that begins on the shores of latency and ends in the land of adulthood. It is common for the fledgling sailor to have cold feet initially, to consider mutiny halfway through the voyage, but there is no way to become an able-bodied seaman without being at sea. The following brief case histories present examples from various stages of the voyage.

As a young child Daniel was a live wire of oral-aggression masquerading as phallic despotism. His mother was depressed and unable to nourish him emotionally. His father saw him only as an oedipal rival, a situation comparable to his own experience with his father, and was unable to meet any of his preoedipal needs. To complicate matters, a housekeeper who seemed to be meeting those needs and had assumed the function of a primary caretaker left abruptly when Daniel was three and one-half, saying she would return, a promise that was not kept. An analysis that began in prelatency and ended in midlatency helped Daniel to identify his grief and return his developmental lines to normal. However, when adolescence began he had a dream that suggested that development was still a major conflict for him. "I am running in the woods. Snakes appear. They come close to my face. I run and run. There are other children younger than me playing nearby. I try to make the snakes go in their direction."

At the time of this dream Daniel was thirteen years old and beginning to be able to free associate to material such as this. He was able to understand my interpretation of the unconscious wish in the dream, that the emerging sexuality of his developing penis (snake) be disavowed and relegated to others younger than himself. To my interpretation he responded: "My sister [2 years older] didn't get her period until she was thirteen. I've had wet dreams and erections since eleven. It's not fair." It seemed clear that Daniel was inclined to see development as a deprivation, something that was thrust upon him sooner than his sibling and other rivals had to contend with, a tragic precocity that would force him to say farewell to childhood (Kaplan 1984) before he was prepared. There was a poignant irony in his dilemma: having used a cocky phallic stance from the age of three to thirteen, when adolescence confronted him with his maturing anatomy he was at a loss to know how to use it. While he may have used a penis for defense, so to speak (phallic character armor), for many years, he was not prepared for the "real thing" when it arrived. It seems clear that childhood machismo does not prepare one for the male role one should assume in adolescence. I am reminded of Michel Leiris's book, *Manhood: From Childhood to the Fierce Order of Virility* (1984), a work of self-revelation that depicts graphically how an excess of fear and aggression in childhood can color one's definition and experience of manhood forever after. Leiris is not the only author who comes to mind in this context: Hemingway could be added immediately to a list that would probably expand rapidly enough with a little thought. But to return to our young hero who dreams that adolescence would leave him alone and bother someone else: at age seven, with a little help from his analyst, he had built a boat out of wood, which he called the "catch-up." It was a play on words—a pursuit of the lost ketchup of childhood, a wish to catch up with his older sibling, an attempt to recover the lost housekeeper and retrieve the even earlier emotional loss of the mother and many other overdetermined strands of meaning. And yet as time caught up with him in the form of adolescent development, he seemed to be saying "I can only catch up with my future after I've taken hold of my past."

If young teenagers like Daniel do not exactly welcome the transformations of puberty, the existential forces of physiology and time do not wait for a timid psyche to be ready for them: the adolescent finds himself at sea like it or not, sink or swim. Clinical experience, as reflected in psychiatric nosology, suggests that while discrete groups of "sinkers" as opposed to "swimmers" could be defined statistically and categorically, the "sinkers" swim occasionally and the "swimmers" sink and it is perhaps wiser to use a developmental macroscope when studying the fauna of adolescence rather than the too-narrow focus of a nosological microscope. Precision is one thing. A kind of diagnostic prejudice is another. Let us take a look at a midadolescent struggling adaptively, sinking but mostly swimming, it would seem, in the waters of development.

Billy

Billy, a sixteen-year-old high school student, was looking forward to a date he had arranged with a prospective girlfriend. The girl's mother intervened and interrupted the tryst for some reason. Billy was irate, as a subsequent fantasy and dream bore witness to. While in a museum with the girl sometime later he had a fantasy that Dracula was playing the organ and wreaking destruction on his audience at the same time. Billy had little trouble recognizing the hidden intent of the fantasy: to destroy the authority figure that had come between him and his mate. A dream took the issue even further. Dracula was playing the organ again in the dream but the plot was more elaborate. Billy was with his friend Hermann. As Dracula played, a hydra, a snake, and a dragon confront the two young heroes. They struggle but eventually slay the beasts. Billy's associations to this dream went in a variety of directions. Dracula's organ and orchestra could be a disguised wish to return to his previous school, where he was a member of the orchestra. The snake could be the oboe he was unable to play, not having enough wind. In the previous school he had academic troubles as well as musical ones, and the dream was an attempt at remediation of past humiliations. There was an elaborate series of associations to hydras, snakes, and dragons, through which means Billy demonstrated his extraordinary knowledge of the evolution of all species from sea squirts and segmented worms. An adopted child, Billy's interest in evolution was a multidetermined matter, but one dominant meaning was to learn all there was to know about life and procreation and master a biological trauma that was beyond his control by intellectual prowess. Jilted by biological parents in the past, or slighted by the mother of a girlfriend in the present, Billy seemed to be marshalling all the forces of primary and secondary processes that phantasy, dream, and intellect could muster to ensure victory over neurosis. As a young male struggling with traumas from the past and instincts of the moment, Billy seemed destined to become a swimmer rather than a sinker.

If getting on the ship can be difficult, as the example of Daniel suggests, getting off the ship after a successful voyage may not be uneventful either. By choosing teenagers who have difficulties getting on and off the imaginary boat of development, I mean to imply not that adolescence is always an impossibly turbulent voyage that almost takes the life of the navigator but rather that all share the conflicts; resolutions come easily to some and defy the best efforts of others.

Jason

A nineteen-year-old college student who sought treatment when his success with object relationships could not match his academic achievements will illustrate a central thesis of this chapter: disembarkation from the imaginary ship of adolescence can be severely compromised by the high seas of neurosis. Jason's conflicts interfered with his ability to experience heterosexuality as other than a state of emergency, each step a perilous induction into "the fierce order of virility." Like Leiris, Jason too was carrying traumatic baggage from childhood, and his psychological journeys were weighted down with neurotic legacies: a mildly dyslexic child, he found himself in the shadow of a superior sibling and an ambitious father. A grand-scale infantile neurosis full of aggression and passion was not so much resolved as shelved and was ready to make its presence felt all too often in latency and adolescence. Jason unashamedly vowed to be an academic success, amass a greater fortune than his father, and end with an oedipal triumph to make up for all past humiliations. Jason could not see how this burning ambition in one psychological sphere might be interfering with adaptive performance in another. Though he wore his Oedipus complex on his sleeve, he could not see its implications in day-to-day human relations. For instance, one summer an encounter in the photocopying room with a young woman he had designs on troubled him greatly. The room was a quiet spot in an otherwise busy office, teeming with peers and rivals. As he approached the woman to announce his interest in her, he became speechless and felt that his face was about to crumble into pieces. Naturally he withdrew, his love undeclared and obviously unrequited. He was bewildered by his cowardice and was full of self-hatred. A frankly oedipal dream did little to enlighten him, its contents experienced like psychological foreign bodies rather than fragments of his mind that could help him to understand himself. In the dream his mother appeared in a dark corridor and a man's hand was reaching up under her dress. That the hand could be his own filled him with horror, not to mention equal amounts of contempt for such preposterous Freudian notions. A dream about a steel butterfly was easier for him to swallow. He sensed that the metaphor of a steel butterfly described him well: a Clint Eastwood façade surrounding an interior that was more frivolous and tender. He sensed that intimacy with a woman would involve getting used to affects that he had always considered effeminate at best, infantile at worst.

His caricature of man as made of steel was a reflection of his distorted readings of the human condition. Sexual intercourse—indeed all social intercourse—was a kind of primal scene in which the vulnerable might get trampled upon and devoured. This led to splitting mechanisms that compromised reality testing: in the transference the analyst was often surrounded with light, "like a deity," as were the women Jason fell in love with. This projection of power on the analyst and lovers made it virtually impossible for the hidden, weaker side of Jason to approach the god or goddess without fears of disintegration. It seems clear that he was attempting to join "the fierce order of virility" and that the analytic task lay in opening his eyes to the tender compromise of love and hate that is the hallmark of the human condition.

Conclusion

My focus in this chapter has been to elucidate the contributions of adolescence to the development of male psychology, normal and pathological. If De Quincey's definition of manhood is acceptable to a modern reader, the vicissitudes of the "reverential feelings" for the opposite sex would surely have to be spelled out a little more to do justice to the Freudian and post-Freudian insights of the twentieth century. The reverence that De Quincey talks about would have to be tempered in the crucible of experience, the overidealization squeezed out of it as the ego ideal and all the other psychic structures reap the benefits of the adolescent passage (Blos 1979). If it is true that inside every male there is a female trying to get out (Freud went so far as to suggest that denial of femininity could be considered the universal kernel of neurosis in both sexes), adolescence is the seance that allows the exorcism to take place. This is a poor metaphor unless one considers the exorcism not as a getting rid of the female persona but as a getting in touch with affects and identifications that are repressed and disavowed under the aegis of neurosis. When a

The Contribution of Adolescence to Male Psychology

young male throws aside the chauvinism that years of latency development seem to demand of him, he has embraced the true meaning of gender, rejected "the fierce order of virility," and is well on the way toward becoming a man.

BIBLIOGRAPHY

Blos, P. 1979. *The adolescent passage.* New York: International Universities Press.

De Quincey, T. 1889. Autobiography from 1785 to 1803. In *The collected writings of Thomas De Quincey,* ed. D. Masson, pp. 316–325. Edinburgh: Charles Black.

Erikson, E. 1959. The problem of ego identity. *Psychological Issues* 1:110–111.

Flavell, J. H. 1963. *The developmental psychology of Jean Piaget.* New York: Van Nostrand Reinhold.

Freud, A. 1958. Adolescence. *Psychoanalytic Study of the Child* 13:255–268.

Freud, S. 1923. The ego and the id. In *The standard edition of the complete psychological works of Sigmund Freud,* ed. J. E. Strachey, vol. 19 (1961), pp. 3–66. London: Hogarth Press, 1953–1974.

Galenson, E., and Roiphe, H. 1971. The impact of early sexual discovery on mood, defensive organization and symbolization. *Psychoanalytic Study of the Child* 26:195–216.

Jones, E. 1922. Some problems of adolescence. *British Journal of Psychology* 13:31–47.

Kaplan, L. 1984. *Adolescence: The farewell to childhood.* New York: Simon and Schuster.

Kiell, N. 1964. *The universal experience of adolescence.* New York: International Universities Press.

Kleeman, J. A. 1965. A. boy discovers his penis. *Psychoanalytic Study of the Child* 20:239–266.

Leiris, M. 1984. *Manhood: A journey from childhood into the fierce order of virility.* San Francisco: North Point Press.

Mahler, M. S. 1967. On human symbiosis and the vicissitudes of individuation. *Journal of the American Psychoanalytic Association* 15:740–763.

Rice, J. A. 1942. *I came out of the eighteenth century.* New York: Harper and Brothers.

Sarnoff, C. 1976. *Latency.* New York: Jason Aronson.

IV

Men Seeking Change:
Men and Women
Treating Men

11

The Male–Male Analytic Dyad: Combined, Hidden, and Neglected Transference Paradigms

DONALD I. MEYERS AND ARTHUR H. SCHORE

Introduction

It is the purpose of this chapter to illuminate transference phenomena in the male–male analytic dyad that in our experience are often insufficiently emphasized or missed or go undetected as part of a larger transference picture. These hidden, combined, or neglected transference elements seem to have in common a relationship to certain resistances in our field to the full acknowledgment of the developmental role of early paternal and, perhaps to a lesser degree, early maternal factors in frequently encountered neurotic structures.

Specifically these transference elements involve the early nurturant and facilitating role of the preoedipal father, the facilitating role of the oedipal father, the transference of early maternal imagos to the male analyst by the male patient, and the impact of the early maternal imagos and paternal imagos on each other.

Complexity is added to these trends when we consider the activation in the transference of early, ill-defined, composite imagos in which early maternal and paternal elements are not clearly distinguished or are condensed due to the child's perceptual and conceptual immaturity and/or by projective and introjective processes whereby elements of self, mother, and father are combined. Further complicating our efforts to define these transference elements and their interrelationship and to reconstruct perceptions of early family configurations is the hidden or latent impact on the child of interactions between the "other parent" and the parent who is directly doing the parenting.

We are dealing then with preoedipal father and mother internalizations and how they are integrated with each other, as well as how these preoedipal internalizations are integrated with the oedipal—that is, with condensations of mother, father, preoedipal, and oedipal representations.

Awareness of these early transferences and their impact on constellations derived from later developmental stages has depended on enlightenment regarding complex early developmental processes from preverbal or paraverbal phases—information that has more recently been offered by child analytic workers, infant researchers, and researchers of early family interaction, particularly by those investigators studying early psychotic processes. We believe, however, that the insufficient emphasis on these transference aspects is a clinical reflection of personal and societal attitudes regarding the sexes. These attitudes have been loosening with the recent reappraisal of female psychology—a reappraisal that seems to have been an outcome of the postwar rise in humanism and individualism that, along with the civil rights movement, gave impetus to feminists and to the reevaluation of the female's role in our culture. The reappraisal of woman's role and the related efforts to look behind the "phallic illusion," as John Munder Ross so aptly refers to it, have led to similar efforts at reappraisal of male psychology such as is being attempted by this volume.

That research into the primary paternal role of the affectionate, supportive, noncompetitive, and facilitating preoedipal father has been neglected in favor of studies of the paternal role of the aggressive, threatening, competitive oedipal father has been amply documented by Blos (1984), Abelin (1971, 1975, 1980), and Ross (1979, 1982). This has occurred despite the fact, as Blos (1984) points out, that, without developing his ideas, Freud pointed the way to the consideration of these issues and to the need for further investigation in this area (Freud 1925; Mack Brunswick 1940), and despite the subsequent attention called to this area as early as 1951 by Loewald and later by such observers as Greenacre (1966), Mahler (1955, 1975), and Benedek (1959). It is only recently, with the further efforts of such investigators as Blos, Abelin, and Ross and in response to the recent reexamination of female psychology, that we seem to be achieving the critical mass with which to move forward in our explorations of this aspect of paternity and are focusing more on questions regarding the phallic-oedipal bias when viewing the father/son relationship.

One last speculation regarding the impact of a phallocentric bias on our theoretical and technical perspective: A number of problems seem to generate from a certain rigidity and "dominance bias" with which the developmental model used to approach our clinical material is viewed. This emphasis on dominance interferes with a clearer perspective on preoedipal development and its impact on later development.

Some have applied our developmental model, which was borrowed from turn-of-the century embryology, in a static, too-concrete way, insufficiently taking into account the refinements in the epigenetic perspective emphasized by modern developmentalists such as Piaget (1952), Werner and Kaplan (1963), Spitz (1939), and Erikson (1963), particularly when it comes to phase dominance, interpenetration or interweaving of phase constellations, and the integration of early affectomotor preverbal and paraverbal experience with later developmental constellations. The emphasis on phase dominance over the interweaving or interpenetration of phase constellations is perhaps nowhere more dramatically exemplified than in the tendency toward "genitalization" of earlier developmental constellations.

CASE EXAMPLE[1]

The following case example demonstrates the use of the genital metaphor by a disturbed child to represent object loss.

A seven-year-old girl in a residential treatment center responds to the transfer of her favorite counselor from her unit with a plea "don't touch my penis." Her mother, a shy, fragile woman, had suffered a postpartum depressive withdrawal and the girl's father had served as the nurturing object since birth. There was much seductive lap holding. The child's fantasies were rife with penis/breast representations, representations of body and self-dissolution, and preoccupation with object loss.

The fear of loss or damage to the illusory penis here represented the anxiety over the lost primary object and was a way of representing concerns about body intactness. One may argue that this was a child with impaired ego function; however, such observations combining studies of intrapsychic process and family observation have alerted workers in the field of analytically oriented child and family observation to be sensitive to more subtle forms of this use of the phallic metaphor in patients commonly seen in practice. The body as phallus (Lewin 1933) and castration fears as a metaphor for fear of body dissolution or disintegration are well-documented phenomena.

The phallocentric view that emphasizes oedipal dominance and primary castration anxiety and overlooks secondary castration anxiety conditioned by earlier anxiety about intactness and object loss is as much in error as what Shapiro (1977) has called "the great oralizing fallacy," which views the first year of life as "all determining" of later organization.

Presymbolic experience organized into sensorimotor schemata and expressed on an affectomotor level is subsequently integrated at higher cognitive levels, ultimately gaining symbolic representation. Piaget's work and its application by such

1. This case was originally reported by Green (1970) and subsequently discussed by Meyers (1974).

analytically oriented observers as Abelin (1980) to early triangulation between mother and father and child are examples of careful attempts at understanding the complexities of developmental transformations. Working in collaboration with Mahler, Abelin (1971, 1975, 1980) describes how the young child, emerging from symbiosis, moves from imitative identification on a sensorimotor level to a perception of a separate self through perceiving the mother/father dyad. He further documents the early preoedipal father role in consolidating self constancy, in helping the child "disidentify" with the mother, and in establishing generational and gender identity. This is in line with the views of others such as Mahler (1955, 1975) and Loewald (1951) regarding the father's early role in counterbalancing the regressive pull toward the mother, neutralizing the threat of maternal engulfment, and mitigating the intensity of the rapprochement crisis. The important contributions of Peter Blos (1972, 1974, 1984) should be mentioned in this context. Blos underlines the necessity of differentiating developmentally between the dyadic and the triadic father/son complex, with the resolution of the negative complex taking place in adolescence. According to Blos, the facilitation of the entry into adulthood, through the deidealization of the father with divestiture of infantile dependency needs and the organization of the ego ideal, takes place at this time. This may imply the reworking of the attitudes around the deflation of omnipotence, both the child's and that delegated to the mother, during earlier separation-individuation.

Analytic Case Material

We will present material from four analytic cases in an effort to demonstrate some of the issues we have touched on and to provide a basis for further elaboration of these issues.

CASE 1

The first case we will present, reported in more detail elsewhere (Meyers and Schore 1985), is of a successfully analyzed claustrophobia in which, by accident rather than by design, the focus was first on the oedipal and then on the preoedipal elements. This shift in focus was occasioned by the presentation of the case in a Continuous Case Seminar in late-middle phase.

Mr. A., a thirty-two-year-old businessman, separated from his wife of seven years and currently involved with another woman, entered analysis for symptoms of diffuse anxiety precipitated by his wife's decision that she wanted him back. He had guilty fears that if he did not oblige her she would direct her formidable rage, which had always paralyzed him, onto their three-year-old adopted son.

The analytic focus was on themes of oedipal anxiety and guilt acted out in Mr. A.'s uncertain courtship of his lover, a woman much warmer and more responsive than his wife. This focus led to an improvement in his relationship with women and, finally, in the ninth month of analysis, to the onset of a tunnel phobia when his parents were away on vacation. This claustrophobia became more intense when, during the analyst's second summer holiday, Mr. A. called his lover, with whom he had broken off, because of a fantasy that the analyst had not approved of the relationship and wanted him to return to his wife. This massive attack of claustrophobia led to his ending the relationship with his lover entirely. Upon the analyst's return, exploration of this acting out led to interpretations stressing castration anxiety, with considerable improvement. When the patient brought up termination, there was a recrudescence of the phobia. What was missing in the previous analytic work was attention to a subtle but persistent theme of formality and containment in dream material, associations, and the transference. For instance, an early dream depicted Mr. A. as alternately witnessing and participating in a great sword duel. It was unclear to him whether the fight was real or a stylized ritual, and he associated to the fictionalized historical novel *Shogun* (about medieval Japan), in which his favorite character gained power through stealth. Such material was approached through its oedipal content. It was only later, when the "formality" or "ritual" theme was focused on in the transference, where its subtle manifestations were hidden behind Mr. A.'s affable façade, that the patient's wish-fear of opening up to a distant, formal, absent father was recognized, and that the analysis progressed to a successful conclusion. The patient's father had been away in the army for two years when the patient was in his second and third year—and thus was not available to help him deal with a controlling, overly containing yet stimulating mother. It should be added that the mother kept the patient on a halter when he was a child and taught him to urinate on the side of the toilet bowl so as not to make splashing sounds. The father was not demonstrative. He was a formal and controlled man who disciplined the patient in a ritualized way by affectless, methodical, measured spanking strokes, using a hand-shaped wooden paddle.

When interpretations of Mr. A.'s tunnel phobia were extended from the fear of the castrating vagina to perception of his early (and current) self as filled with feelings he was fearful of expressing, needing to contain his feelings at all costs, and having an associated, conflicted longing for a father to help him deal with the containing mother who didn't allow stepping out or expressing emotion, the course of the analysis changed and his claustrophobia was resolved.

Here the containment issue involved both the mother and father transference inhibiting and/or not facilitating the stepping out—the self-assertion of the individuating toddler—although in the transference the plea was more for openness and strength from the father. (The mother theme was worked through, also extratransferentially, with an open and accepting woman whom the patient subsequently married.) Oedipal fears were superimposed or condensed with this earlier paradigm.

A dramatic representation of the conflict around rapprochement with the preoedipal father was a fantasy or, more accurately, an affectomotor experience Mr. A. had on the couch, where he sometimes felt encased inside "something," the closest approximation of which was a sleeping bag. Mostly he wished either the analyst would get inside or he outside, but sometimes he felt more comfortable with the experience of being sealed up and impenetrable. Examination of this state did stir up homosexual fears and memories of adolescent homosexual activities at camp in a sleeping bag, but more frightening was the feeling that he could not get out of the bag, that the insulation was so adhesive as to prevent the analyst and him from touching. While insulated, his own feelings were experienced as "through a film," and thus were not immediate to him. Associations were to the emotional restraint of both parents. Mr. A. recalled, for example, the proud yet very restrained, stiff handshake he received from his father when, at age sixteen, he won a major athletic award. When he was nine years old he developed a scalp infection that necessitated his mother applying medicated shampoos. He remembered how on one such occasion he saw his mother from the corner of his eye, averting her own eyes from him, her face contorted in disgust.

Rather than emphasizing a defended-against homosexual retreat from oedipal anxieties and guilt, the analysis of the conflicted wish to open up and take in the affectionate, facilitating preoedipal (and negative oedipal) father was stressed. With the acknowledgment of this wish for the father-analyst, Mr. A.'s claustrophobia began to dissipate.

CASE 2

The following case material contains examples of condensations of mother and father imagos, primarily on a preoedipal level but with some preoedipal/oedipal condensation.

Mr. B. was a twenty-four-year-old postgraduate student with a closely bound, all-encompassing, intrusive mother who, during his childhood, acted as if she could read his thoughts, and with a devalued, warm, but somewhat distant, intimidated, preoccupied father. The patient at times acted out the role of the oedipal victor seemingly secondary to the early exclusion of the father by mother and child, a behavior that alternated with competitive fears, mild depersonalization, and withdrawal into passive-aggressive behavior. Revealed as an important issue in his analysis was the painting of the warm but passive father with the same brush as the intrusive, controlling mother. The father's passivity and absence allowed Mr. B. to project the aggressive, intrusive traits of the mother and of the self onto the father without enabling Mr. B. to work this through with his father. Similarly, the father's passivity and retreat to his busy medical practice seemed to allow an intensification of both the patient's early separation/individuation conflicts and later oedipal fears. There was no active paternal ally to balance the regressive pull of the mother, the identification with the early mother, or the rapprochement ambivalence in Mr. A.'s relationship with his mother. He wished the father to be more active and had repeated wishful fantasies of the father and himself working on automobiles, which were associated to the female body. He had dreams of viewing the underside of an auto, the father showing him how to use tools, and he expressed this in transference wishes where he ambivalently struggled with the analyst around using analytic tools. He had much difficulty disidentifying the father from the controlling, narcissistically invasive mother, a fact that interfered with working through conflicts with mother and father on both preoedipal and oedipal levels. His wishes for rapprochement with the father came into conflict with the expectation that if he let the father in, the father would also turn out to be invasive, controlling, and humiliating. At one point Mr. B. dreamed of a somnolent octopus that, if awakened, would entangle him with its many arms, blind him, and engulf him, a fantasy that condensed or did not differentiate clearly mother and father imagos and that also condensed related oedipal and preoedipal conflicts. He would desire the analyst's interventions but then would feel overwhelmed, taken over, and humiliated by the analyst's comments. His ambivalent longing for paternal help was at one point expressed in a dream that also seemed to combine early maternal and paternal imagos. While the analyst observed him stroking the couch, Mr. A. reported:

> I am in a peculiar space capsule, alternately a round globe with soft upholstery and an oblong airplane-shaped object. It was comfortable

inside but lonely and I cling to the sides. There are numerous rocket pods around the outside which are loosely attached. Some seem to disappear and then reappear. There is a person in a spacesuit, I assume a man, but I can't tell because the glass of the helmet is dark. [Uncertain gender of object.] I am not sure but I hope he is friendly because I want his company and his help.

CASE 3

Mr. C. was forty-one years old when he entered analysis for symptoms of premature ejaculation and a worsening of his chronic feelings of depersonalization. In the six months prior to analysis Mr. C.'s chain of retail stores suffered major financial reverses and his previously sexually passive wife began demanding more regular and involved coitus as a result of improvement stemming from her own psychotherapy. Mr. C.'s history revealed an intensely ambivalent relationship with his chronically depressed, possibly borderline, and periodically seductive mother. He had long attempted to make his hypermasculine, industrialist father proud of him by being "a real man"—that is, athletic, driven toward financial gain, and emotionally restrained. Through early analytic work it became apparent that his business difficulties were related to unconscious wishes to obtain continued financial aid from his wealthy father and from a hypomanic denial of the limits of his own ability to create a financial empire.

Mr. C.'s sexual difficulties cleared rapidly after analysis of his competitive, rivalrous oedipal feelings in the transference, but his depersonalization and need to defend against deep affective bonds and experiences remained formidable analytic obstacles.

Early in the fourth year of the analysis Mr. C. had the following dream:

My wife and I are motoring in France, looking for a particular restaurant. We have no map and no directions. Finally we stop at an old inn to ask directions. To my surprise the owner is a woman who speaks English. She is in a warm kitchen and has a big mixing bowl. I'd like to stay there. It looks appetizing. My wife insists we drive on. I agree but very reluctantly. The road is very dark, long, and narrow.

The Male–Male Analytic Dyad

Since Mr. C. was the driver in the dream, he wondered why he let his wife overrule him. Certain features of the woman innkeeper reminded him of the analyst. He concluded that his wife's presence in the dream was meant to buffer him and to keep him from lingering in the dream's warm kitchen.

On the following morning Mr. C. presented this dream:

> I am playing handball with my friend K. on a long, narrow court. The lights are getting dimmer and dimmer. The competition is ferocious, even though by this time I can barely see the ball. I can feel myself wanting to give up and fade out. Throughout the dream there is the sense of disquiet and agitation. The long, narrow court reminds me of the road in yesterday's dream.

Mr. C. began associating by wondering why he "blew" a tennis match to his business partner several days earlier. His partner was much the inferior player. He continued:

> I was always a good athlete. Sports like handball are tight one-on-one, head-on-head competitive. In the beginning K. and I are really close and then what I want is to kind of sink into the darkness. I want to break off the competition. . . . I know what I am afraid of! I am afraid of the physical contact, rubbing against each other. We are both down low. It's hot and sweaty. It was too hot—just like it was too hot at the inn. That's why I want to leave.

When the analyst pointed out that Mr. C. was terrified of his desire to have a physical relationship with the analyst, Mr. C. could acknowledge that in recent sessions he had wished to brush up against the analyst when the session ended. "And who knows where that would end," he added. "We could wind up in each other's arms!"

The analyst now interpreted that Mr. C. wished and feared to be held in the kitchen and on the athletic court, such wishes and fears being stirred up both when he felt competitive with the analyst and when he wanted the analyst to feed him.

On the next day Mr. C. presented the following dream:

> You and I are playing a game. There is a long corridor with a line down the middle but no net. We are running in tandem on either side

of the line, passing a ball quickly back and forth, as if it were a hot potato. It was as if neither of us wanted to hold the ball. Yet there is a togetherness as we run along the line. We are running in a parallel. There is a definite grace to the game.

Mr. C. averred that the dream was about a wish for togetherness with the analyst without "the messy and steamy heat of the other two dreams." He noted how he experienced the analyst simultaneously as being afraid to get close to him and also as being seductive with him. He said:

What's all-important with you is that I bottle up the intensity of my needs for you. . . . Just then when I said you were seductive I thought of my mother. Mostly she was out of it, but there were times she tried to give me these enormous hugs. All I wanted to do then was wriggle away. She'd come at me though and I would feel like I had to brace myself. I feel the same way when my wife gets passionate and recently here with you. It's like I have to fight you off and hold myself in. I am afraid of the homosexual stuff, yes, but there is more to it. I also fear being overwhelmed. Those fears get centered on you. I feel like it's all layered. Part of it is anger. That builds up in me . . . and I am afraid of what I'll have to give you in return. You could drain me or I could drain you. So that's why I keep myself under wraps. It's a way of holding myself together. Sometimes it feels like I am made of cardboard, and I could easily collapse or explode.

Analysis of this material revealed a complex interweaving of preoedipal maternal and paternal elements with the oedipal maternal and paternal imagos.

Although Mr. C. expressed homosexual desires and fears focused on the analyst as oedipal father as a defense against competitive oedipal yearnings for the oedipal mother analyst, the material directs us to the neurosogenic importance of conflicted desires for the analyst as preoedipal mother *and* father.

His fears of intimacy with the analyst in addition to oedipal guilt and fearful homosexual retreat, combined the fears of being stimulated on both a pregenital and genital level to the point of exploding, both from the intensity of sexual stimulation and from rage over maternal deprivation at the hands of his overwhelmingly demanding, orally needy, draining mother. Further, these fears of intimacy included a fear of desertion by the father who would go off, leaving the patient to deal with the mother alone. The lack of direction and of maps in the dream appeared to apply, at times, to both parental imagos. As expressed in his dream, Mr. C. looked for warmth, nurturance, intimacy, and direction but defensively evoked a distant maternal-wife imago who was willing to travel on without directions. (One of the factors that precipitated his seeking analysis was a shift by his wife from a more removed stance to one of wishing greater intimacy.)

The picture was further complicated by memories of the father periodically filling in as the maternal figure when the mother's withdrawal and depression were more severe, making the boundaries between the early nurturant and facilitating maternal and paternal imagos more uncertain.

The playful passing of the "hot potato ball" as he and a male friend run in tandem down the narrow handball court in our view represented a wish for a friendly combination of competition and facilitating cooperation between the patient-son and the father-analyst on both a preoedipal and an oedipal level as they dealt with the hot-potato mother. The line drawn between them on the court served, as did the net in the tennis match, to ensure continued separateness of self and object as they are aggressively involved in competition and to defend against sexual contact. It ensured interaction and cooperation without overwhelming, confusing, destructive, and explosive intensity and crushing encirclement. It provided limits in their interaction for both libidinal and aggressive impulses.

CASE 4

Mr. D., a forty-three-year-old businessman who entered analytic psychotherapy with the fear that he would develop AIDS because of his promiscuous homosexual involvements, expressed strong urges to remain detached and removed from the analyst, speaking in a kind of unfollowable singsong, fragmented manner.

At times, his speech seemed indicative of a thought disorder, but the analyst successfully interpreted it as Mr. D.'s need to keep the analyst confused and out of the picture. As work was done on exploring the patient's need to distance himself, he reported seeing a play in which a character, a girl, voluntarily allows herself to be swallowed up by a man-eating plant. He became anxious at this point. The analyst interpreted that his needs for distance were in part motivated by his fears of being devoured by or of devouring the analyst in a close, merging kind of connectedness. Mr. D. responded by recalling late latency-early puberty activities in which he would dress in his mother's clothes as he lay in bed holding himself while his parents were out. Regressive behavior followed at this point, with the patient relapsing into his negativistic, mute, or singsong kind of phraseology.

After missing a session, the patient began the next session with a memory of how he was "adopted" by an older boy who taught him how to ride a bicycle. He recalled with warmth and happiness how they would run together in a kind of balanced harmony, with the patient pedaling and the older boy behind him providing support and balance. Right after he recalled this memory, which had been dormant for twenty-five years, he mentioned that he thought of the analyst and felt a desire to be close to him. Rather than emphasizing the genital or homosexual implications of the push-from-the-rear bike-riding-lessons memory in the context of oral-vaginal castration by the man-eating plant, the analyst focused on the patient's fears and desires as he faced the issues to be worked out in the analysis: that Mr. D. was struggling to maintain an ability to be close to, work with, and get assistance from the analyst yet to remain differentiated from him rather than being engulfed, as was the girl in the play.

In response to the patient's association, the analyst further emphasized that the two of them were working with somewhat different tasks but together, in cooperation. This was contrasted to Mr. D.'s fear that closeness to the analyst would involve giving up himself, as the girl did to the plant. At this point the analyst saw himself alternately as the supportive, older boy-father and the early mother whom the patient unconsciously perceived as devouring through projection of his own intense oral needs.

Of genetic import in this case is the fact that this man is the eldest of nine children, and by age five had three siblings. He recalled his mother as having her hands full and "always changing someone else's diaper." Just as important is the fact that his father was a manic-depressive who, when hypomanic, would treat the patient as his number-one son, urging him on, sometimes encouraging him to perform feats that were beyond his capacity. For example, when the patient declined to take the singing lead in the school play at age eleven due to performance anxiety, his father refused to speak to him for an extended period. The father would become depressed and would essentially drop out of the picture. At such times the father could barely go to work and would have to be pampered and babied by the already overwhelmed mother.

We postulate that the patient had to compete with his father not only on an aggressive level but also, when his father was depressed, to get nurturing and care. The facilitating older male in the bicycle memory who is running along behind giving him support involves elements similar to those discussed in Mr. D.'s hot-potato dream. It emphasizes a modulated, mutual, phase-appropriate working in tandem with a facilitating paternal figure who neither pushes too hard and fast nor withdraws his support. Here again, to focus primarily on the genital level in this homosexual man would be to deprive the patient of the therapeutic impact and importance of knowledge of the pregenital precursors, which in the analysis at that point seemed more experience-near than the genitally represented fantasy of anal incorporation.

Conclusion

It is not our purpose to provide a more extensive review of the many transference condensations seen involving preoedipal and oedipal paternal and maternal imagos that are encountered in clinical work with neurotic patients. Nor does space permit an extensive review of perspectives on the early father/son relationship. Rather our purpose is to indicate that in everyday clinical work there is plentiful evidence of important neurosogenic factors relating to internalizations of the preoedipal father (and mother) relationship that are often eclipsed or too readily deemphasized in favor of the oedipal, or seen primarily as defensive regressions from oedipal conflicts. As we have pointed out, sometimes they appear in relatively pure form in the transference, sometimes they are integrated with phallic oedipal complexes or in close sequential relationship to oedipal material, and often they are seen as simple homosexual retreats from oedipal conflict rather than as representing the natural associational flow back to important preoedipal, conflictual precursors that remain to be worked through. We wish to emphasize that when oedipal material is brought to light and interpreted, the flow of associations may lead back to earlier unresolved, neurosogenic precursors in the service of potential mastery of these conflicts. That is, regression in the service of ego growth, a phenomenon upon which the therapeutic action of psychoanalysis is based. The back-and-forth flow between oedipal and preoedipal organizations approximates the experience of the developing child who is dealing with multiple developmental levels simultaneously or in close sequentiality. Indeed, this progression and regression contributes to the formation of condensed complexes with elements of earlier and later developmental phases, an intermeshing or interweaving in which oedipal solutions are sought for preoedipal unresolved conflicts and vice versa.

We have pointed particularly to a few commonly found transference condensations involving preoedipal and oedipal mother and father imagos and emphasized the early facilitating role of the father as expressed in certain transference paradigms. We believe there is a need to underline this issue in light of the current interest in and review of male and female psychology. Further, such emphasis provides for a richer understanding of the many roles the male analysand and male analyst face together in their analytic work.

The Male–Male Analytic Dyad

BIBLIOGRAPHY

Abelin, E. 1971. The role of the father in the separation-individuation process. In *Separation-individuation,* ed. J. B. McDevitt and C. F. Settlage, pp. 229–252. New York: International Universities Press.

———. 1975. Some further observations and comments on the earliest role of the father. *International Journal of Psycho-Analysis* 56: 293–302.

———. 1980. Triangulation, the role of the father and the origins of core gender identity during the rapprochement subphase. In *Rapprochement,* ed. R. Lax, S. Bach, and J. A. Burland, pp. 151–171. New York: Jason Aronson.

Benedek, T. 1959. Parenthood as a developmental phase. *Journal of the American Psychoanalytic Association* 7:389–417.

———. 1970. Fatherhood and providing. In *Parenthood: Its psychology and psychopathology,* ed. E. J. Anthony and T. Benedek, pp. 167–183. Boston: Little, Brown.

Blos, P. 1972. The function of the ego ideal in adolescence. *Psychoanalytic Study of the Child* 27:93–97.

———. 1974. The genealogy of the ego ideal. *Psychoanalytic Study of the Child* 29:43–88.

———. 1984. Son and father. *Journal of the American Psychoanalytic Association* 32:301–324.

Erikson, E. 1963. *Childhood and society,* 2nd ed. New York: W. W. Norton.

Freud, S. 1925. Some psychical consequences of the anatomical distinction between the sexes. In *The standard edition of the complete psychological works of Sigmund Freud,* ed. J. E. Strachey, vol. 19 (1961), pp. 243–258. London: Hogarth Press.

Green, A. 1970. The effects of object loss on the body image of schizophrenic girls. *Journal of the American Academy of Child Psychiatry* 9:532–547.

Greenacre, P. 1971. *Emotional growth: Psychoanalytic studies of the gifted and a great variety of other individuals,* vol. 2. New York: International Universities Press.

Lewin, B. 1933. The body as phallus. *Psychoanalytic Quarterly,* 2:24–47.

Loewald, H. 1951. Ego and reality. *International Journal of Psycho-Analysis* 32:10–18.

Mack Brunswick, R. 1940. The preoedipal phase of libido development. In *The psychoanalytic reader,* ed. R. Fliess, pp. 261–284. New York: International Universities Press.

Mahler, M. S. 1955. On symbiotic child psychosis. *Psychoanalytic Study of the Child* 10:195–212.

Mahler, M. S., Pine, F., and Bergman, A. 1975. *The psychological birth of the human infant.* New York: Basic Books.

Meyers, D. I. 1974. The question of depressive equivalents in childhood schizophrenia. In *Masked depression,* ed. S. Lesse, pp. 165–173. New York: Jason Aronson.

Meyers, D. I., and Schore, A. H. 1985. The effects of a shift in emphasis on the course of a successful analysis. Paper presented at the scientific meeting of the Association for Psychoanalytic Medicine, New York Academy of Medicine, New York, April 2.

Piaget, J. 1952. *The origins of intelligence in children.* New York: International Universities Press.

Ross, J. M. 1979. Fathering: A review of some psychoanalytic contributions on paternity. *International Journal of Psycho-Analysis* 60:317–328.

———. 1982. In search of fathering: A review. In *Father and child: Developmental and clinical perspectives,* ed. S. H. Cath, A. R. Gurwitt, and J. M. Ross, pp. 21–32. Boston: Little, Brown.

Shapiro, T. 1977. Oedipal distortions in severe character pathologies: Developmental and theoretical considerations. In *Psychoanalytic Quarterly* 46:559–579.

Spitz, R. 1939. *A genetic field theory of ego formation (with implications for pathology).* New York: International Universities Press.

Werner, H., and Kaplan, B. 1963. *Symbol formation: An organismic-developmental approach to language and the expression of thought.* New York: John Wiley & Sons.

12

How Do Women Treat Men?

HELEN MEYERS

The somewhat ambiguous title of this chapter means to refer to the treatment situation in which a female therapist treats a male patient, not to the world of men and women at large. And yet, of course, the treatment situation is a reflection of that world at large. Since our concern in this volume is the psychology of men, the aspect of most interest to us is how the man perceives how the woman treats him, his fantasy of what he expects from her, what he wants from her, and what he fears from her, as reflected in the transference in the treatment situation with a woman. Since I will be stressing transference and countertransference throughout, I should say here that my observations apply to psychoanalysis and psychoanalytic or expressive therapy only, as my ideas are based on the forms of treatment in which transference plays a key role.

Does the Therapist's Gender Have an Impact?

What actually goes on in the treatment of a male by a female therapist or analyst? "Everything" might be the answer—everything, that is, that should go on in any well-conducted therapy or analysis. The impact of the actual gender of the therapist is a currently much-debated question. Is there an impact? If so, how much? And what is its nature? My own clinical experience and discussion with colleagues and supervisees leads me to believe that the gender of the analyst does affect the treatment, but only in certain ways—namely the sequence, intensity, and inescapability of certain transference paradigms in both therapy and analysis. I intend to spell out the details of some of these transferences in this chapter. At the same time, concentration on the gender issue can lead to blind spots and countertransference problems on the part of the therapist, which I will also try to describe in these pages. Obviously, the therapist's gender, or rather the unconscious fantasy related to it, is only one of many variables. And the variables in individual patients are so vast—their character, dynamics, and environment are so individually different—and the variables in the therapist are so many—depending on character, background, experience, training, and style—that the small part played by the therapist's gender is difficult to tease out. Thus probably the therapist's gender makes more of a difference in dynamic therapy, which is more reality linked than is analysis and where not all transferences are established and worked through. The same would apply to incomplete analyses. Chasseguet-Smirgel (1984) and others have suggested that the effect related to actual gender is probably greater with more regressed patients who have a less secure sense of self-identity, are not sure of their sexual identity, and who need, therefore, to cling more concretely to the reality of the sex of the analyst as an organizer.

In theory, in a full and well-conducted analysis, the actual gender of the analyst, like all other reality issues, should make less difference in the long run, since all transference paradigms (paternal and maternal) are established during the course of an analysis and worked through eventually. In fact, this gender question as such seems not to have come up in the writings of such eminent female analysts as Edith Jacobson or Annie Reich, who surely treated many men.

Can Woman and Man Empathize with the Other?

But Freud (1931) himself felt that, as a man, he was at a disadvantage in analyzing women compared with his female colleagues. And a considerable number of contributors to the current literature have suggested that male therapists might have difficulty in empathizing with and understanding specifically female experiences such as pregnancy and childbirth, as well as with female roles and female attitudes. One might equally ask if female therapists could properly empathize with some uniquely male experiences and attitudes. How can women treat men? I believe that, in order to empathize with another, one needs not to have shared the same actual experience but needs only to be able to relate to common elements in the experience. Basic needs, drives, desires, guilt, fears, and dangers are the ingredients of all human experience and are universals, common to all. Further, both men and women internalize aspects of both mother and father, identify with both, in the course of developing their own self-identity. Specifically, confirmation and solidification of one's gender role and identity would appear to involve some internalization of the needs and attitudes of the opposite sex as well. In order to experience fully our own gender we must also experience the other, what the partner feels (see chapter 2). Kernberg (1980) has pointed out that for complete pleasure in the loving sexual union one must cross boundaries temporarily and feel the other sex's experience simultaneously with one's own. Or as Limentani (1984) has said: "The idea of penetration requires a full comprehension and appreciation of the idea of being penetrated."

To say that man should be able to empathize with woman, and woman with man, is not, of course, to say that the final content of self and object representations, of ego ideal and superego, does not vary with gender as well as from individual to individual. The content of our ego ideal and superego is influenced by identifications with our parents' values and self-images and by cultural values, as well as by innate biological needs. Clinical findings have suggested, for example, that female values are oriented toward relationships, caring, and "field dependence," while male values lie in the direction of achievement and power (Gilligan 1982). Both men and women have in common a need to be satisfied in work, love, and play, in their relationships with others, and in their self-esteem. What is different is what constitutes a satisfactory love relationship for them, what reward they want out of work, what raises their self-esteem.

Transference Development in Male Patients with Female Analysts

Thus the gender of the therapist in relation to the gender of the patient does affect the course of treatment. As I suggested earlier, the therapist's gender affects the sequence, intensity, and inescapability of certain transference paradigms in both therapy and analysis. A man in treatment with a woman will more often start with transference reactions related to women—that is, mother. He will have more intense transferences related to the maternal than to the paternal image, whatever its content or affective valance. And he will be less likely to be able to resist the awareness of such transferences, which may be missed in the male-male pair. This difference is, I think, due to both the obvious reality pressure on the patient in seeing a woman as well as the female therapist's greater ease in seeing herself as the female object in the transference.

In terms of sequences and intensity, several male patients I know of started with explosive erotic transferences with female analysts, whereas in similar cases with male analysts such maternal transferences did not develop for years. In some of these cases of intense initial erotic transference with a female therapist, the patient had been in treatment previously with a man, with whom this type of transference had not developed. This material comes from supervisory cases and consultations with colleagues as well as from my own clinical experience.

To illustrate the point of greater inescapability of certain gender-linked transferences, let me give the following example: the patient, a man, presenting with difficulties in establishing a satisfactory relationship with a woman, was able to work out a rather subtle sadomasochistic problem with women as it forced itself on his awareness in its manifestations in a sadomasochistic transference in a reanalysis with a female analyst. This sadomasochistic issue had not come up in his previous work with a male analyst, which had focused mainly on his competitive oedipal problem. This competitive oedipal issue, equally important in his problem with women, had been the central, affect-laden transference theme with his male analyst, but its working through had not fully resolved his problem with women. I cannot state with certainty that the sadomasochistic issue emerged only because of the female gender of the second analyst—the variables mentioned earlier force me to add a qualifying "may have" here. The material might well have entered the first analysis had it continued longer than it did. Or, perhaps, countertransference issues played their part there. The first analyst, for instance, might himself have had unresolved problems with women similar to those of the patient and thus have had a blind spot. But I am suggesting that most probably the issue could be avoided with the male analyst, while it could not be avoided with a female analyst.

Countertransference: Transference Combinations in Opposite Gender Pairs

Whatever the impact on the transference of the actual gender of the therapist vis-à-vis the gender of the patient, gender-linked countertransferences are likely to be expected as well. These transference-countertransference paradigms are complex problems. Fleming's idea[1] that homosexual transferences are almost universally observed in male patients with male therapists while transferences relating to separation-individuation abound in

1. J. Fleming, 1970. Personal communication.

male patients in treatment with women will serve as an illustration. While I agree this is often clinically observable, I suggest that it is neither universal nor unavoidable, having, I suspect, more to do with frequent but not universal countertransference issues. In such instances, the male therapist, uncomfortable in experiencing himself as the loved mother of the preoedipal phase and perhaps afraid of the implied castrated state, may tend to interpret the male patient's love for him on the negative oedipal level. The female therapist, on the other hand, who may have difficulty in seeing herself as the oedipal father, will be less apt to see herself as the object of her patient's homosexual desires; she may be quite comfortable as the loved, nurturing mother and therefore may be able to address preoedipal issues more easily. I do not know, however, how much of the clinically observed phenomenon is due to such countertransference issues. How much is related to yet another consideration—namely, the extent to which the gender-related differences observed are a result of problems already existing in the patient when he chose his analyst. Does the overriding need for a loving, nurturing mother lead the patient to select a female analyst? Does the unconscious need for a loving father lead him to select a male therapist? What part, in other words, is played by unconscious anticipation in relation to the gender of the prospective therapist, what part is played by the fantasies elicited by the therapist's gender in the transference, and what part is played by gender-related countertransference?

Karme (1979) recently suggested that preoedipal maternal transferences may be established with analysts of either sex, but that oedipal transferences are always linked to the actual gender of the therapist. In other words, she suggested that while a man could experience a male analyst as either an oedipal father or a preoedipal mother, he will experience a female analyst as either an oedipal or a preoedipal mother, even a phallic mother, but not as an oedipal father. This is not borne out by my clinical material. I rather suspect that the paternal image behind the "phallic mother" image is often missed for a variety of reasons, as I will elaborate.

It would appear to me that many female therapists treating men find it easiest to see themselves as a good preoedipal mother or as the object of oedipal desire. They are somewhat less comfortable in the role of the bad preoedipal mother. But some have considerable trouble seeing themselves as the competitive oedipal father and almost never get in touch with the transference projection onto them of the homosexually loved father or the supportive preoedipal father. This phenomenon is easier to observe than to explain. It may be related to ego-ideal issues or unresolved conflicts around gender-identity issues.

Another phenomenon often observed when the genders of therapist and patient differ: male analysts almost always detect penis envy in their female patients; female analysts frequently detect pregnancy fantasies in their male patients. This is much less so in reverse—female therapists do not find penis envy as frequently in their female patients, and male therapists rarely observe pregnancy fantasies in their male patients. This presents another one of these complex transference-countertransference combinations. I would speculate that this is partly based on identification by the patient with the opposite-sex analyst, getting in touch with earlier identifications with the opposite-sex parent, and then competing for his or her sexual organ. But another part is based on an attitude of expectation on the part of the analyst as to what he or she will find, such as penis envy or envy of the inner space. This may derive from countertransference reactions leading, for example, to a phallocentric bias in the male therapist or a need to deny sexual differences due to unresolved penis envy in the female therapist. Or it may derive from an intellectual bias or understanding of male and female psychology, such as the conviction of penis envy as pivotal for female development or womb envy as a normative stage in the boy.

Advances in Theory of Male Psychological Development and Their Impact on Clinical Understanding

This brings us to the important influence of our theoretical understanding on our treatment. Our theoretical understanding informs what we hear, and what we hear affects what we do. In recent years, there have been many advances in our understanding of development of both men and women. While many of us maintain the centrality of the oedipal conflict and castration anxiety, preoedipal issues have gained in importance and have been clarified. We now see the little boy as he moves through the psychosexual stages toward manhood, at the same time establishing internal object relations as he emerges from a symbiotic union with mother, through separation-individuation stages, to autonomy and object constancy (Mahler, Pine, and Bergman 1975) and self-cohesion (Kohut 1977). We see him struggling with his ambivalent feelings toward a larger-than-life-sized mother whom he loves and hates, needs and fears; from whom he expects omnipotent protection and total love and at the same time fears punishment, abandonment, and engulfment; and whom he envies and identifies with in many aspects, including her mothering function and procreative ability (Kestenberg 1968). Chasseguet-Smirgel (1976) has even suggested that man's denegrating view of women has its roots not only in his castration anxiety but also in his need to deny the indelible picture of the overwhelming mother. She further suggests that a boy's oedipal complex includes both a wish to possess mother sexually as well as a wish to merge with the powerful mother and return into the security of her womb (Chasseguet-Smirgel 1984); and part of his oedipal anxiety is not only his fear of retaliation from father, or castration from mother, but also a fear of loss of self in merger with mother. Chasseguet-Smirgel's ideas alert us to the possibility of yet another dimension to be considered in trying to understand the transference in these circumstances—that is, the condensation of oedipal issues and issues of separation-individuation.

At the same time, the importance of the role of the father in the boy's preoedipal development has come to the fore (Ross 1985). We have begun to understand how the father in preoedipal triangulation (Abelin 1971) balances a seductive, engulfing mother; the mirroring supportive father helps in the development of the boy's self and gender identity by offering himself for identification (Kohut 1980); the nurturing preoedipal father supplements or substitutes for the inadequate maternal caring function.

The therapist aware of these developmental issues will be able to listen for their derivatives in the treatment. All of these images of mother and father, good and bad, are reflected in the transference and represent what man expects, what he wants, and what he fears from his analyst, male or female. Consciously, when a man chooses a female therapist he often will have in mind one particular transference expectation linked to the actual gender of the therapist: he may want to avoid the competition with the castrating father or the threat of homosexual desire for the yearned-for father. Actually, clinical experience suggests it may be easier to negotiate a homosexual transference with a female analyst in a somewhat lower key. Or he may want a good, caretaking, powerful preoedipal mother. Or he looks for a seductive, challenging, oedipal mother or an ambivalent preoedipal mother to help work out his "problems with women" in the treatment. Or he simply wants a female therapist in the hope of clearing up the problems left unresolved in previous work with a male therapist. Unconsciously, however, all the different mother and father representations will enter the actual transference with female therapists, though the maternal transferences will be more obvious, intense, and apparently compelling.

Some Specific Transference Issues in Male Patients with Female Therapists

I will now return to some specific issues regarding some of the more common transferences seen in male patients with female therapists. Parenthetically, I should perhaps clarify that my definition of transference is fairly conventional, that is, a new edition and experience in the treatment situation of earlier object relations, conflicts, defenses, feelings, and unconscious fantasies.

How Do Women Treat Men?

The most common, almost universal, transference established by men in treatment with women is still one where the female therapist is experienced as the oedipal mother—desired yet dangerous, seductive yet rejecting. This may manifest itself at the beginning of treatment as explosive but shallow sexual transference reactions, only to apparently dissappear and reappear much later in a more solid transference neurosis enriched by loving, longing, tender feelings together with sexual ones. Or it may start with an idealized maternal transference that remains loving but asexual for a long time only to be filled out later with intense sexual and tender yearnings. Or the appearance of the erotic transference can be delayed for months or even years. But eventually it will be there, if looked for, and must be dealt with. This transference is evidenced by dreams and associations and related memories, explicit and subtle fantasies, direct verbalization of feelings and wishes, and acting out.

One male patient, for instance, during his analyst's pregnancy, had this series of dreams indicating his involvement with the analyst as the oedipal mother: first he was responsible for a dangerous tumor growing in his mother's belly; then he dreamed of battling dragons for the fair maiden with long black hair; and finally there were dreams of the tenderest caretaking of a mother and child and happy-ever-afters. Associations and memories led to the revelation of overt sexual and loving feelings toward the analyst and, of course, led back to mother. Naturally, all this involved other transference aspects, such as destructive urges toward the "bad" mother, guilt, sibling rivalry, and identification with the maternal function, all of which were analyzed at the proper time. But at that moment most dominant was the oedipal transference—love—its emergence stimulated by a current event.

Chasseguet-Smirgel (1984) and Person (1983b) have suggested that this type of transference, the erotic transference, is relatively rare because the male patient's resistance to it is so intense. I have not found this to be so, although the resistance may be strong. These resistances may stem from fear of castration by the oedipal rival, fear of castration from the bad oedipal or preoedipal mother, fear of the wish to merge with or be engulfed by the omnipotent early mother as well as from countertransference in the therapist.

Blum (1971) and others have suggested that this Oedipus complex often has to be dealt with by extratransference interpretations, the mother or father image, or both, having been displaced outside the analytic setting—either because of the intensity of the resistance to the awareness of this transference or because the triadic nature of the oedipal complex requires an extra person. I do not agree. The oedipal mother, as I pointed out before, can always be brought into the transference with a female therapist. It is true that the rival father in the fantasy is often first displaced onto an extratransference object, a man related to the analyst— an office partner, a faculty colleague, a husband—but this is only the first step. The father too must be brought back into the transference, with the female analyst representing the hated oedipal competitor as well: on association, the dragon in the dream, as well as the fair maiden, turned out to be the analyst.

I want to stress that these transferences are not found in simple or pure form. The good mother is also the bad mother, the oedipal is infused with the preoedipal, and behind the mother is the father.

There is a constant interplay of oedipal and preoedipal issues, a mixture in each transference, but with shifting dominance, so that the dominant transference theme can be teased out and addressed at any particular time. Preoedipal issues relate to oedipal issues, of course, in a number of ways. Preoedipal conflicts affect the shape and outcome of the Oedipus but are also pathogenic in their own right. Thus in the transference, preoedipal themes can emerge as regressive defenses against the oedipal transference, just as apparent oedipal transferences can be used to hide preoedipal ones. But there also is nondefensive regression to unsolved early core conflicts.

PREOEDIPAL MOTHER TRANSFERENCE

Some of the most powerful transferences in the treatment of men by women involve the therapist as the preoedipal mother.

And just as the oedipal mother in the transference is experienced as good and bad, the preoedipal mother is perceived ambivalently. The patient wants and hopes for the good, but fearfully anticipates the bad. In the transference, he may long for holding and nurturing from the good oral mother but fears engulfment by her on the one hand and deprivation on the other. He may look for the protective mother of the second year of life, who contains and controls, but fearfully experiences the analyst as controlling, critical, punitive and guilt provoking, and holding him back from autonomy. At the same time as he wants to separate and individuate, he is afraid of abandonment by the analyst mother-of-separation. Fears and wishes for merger with the early omnipotent mother both make their appearance in the transference. This fear of losing the self in the mother may combine, as mentioned earlier, with oedipal castration fears as resistance to an erotic transference to the female therapist.

Pregnancy fantasies, the wish to have a baby and become a father, in a man in treatment with a woman may involve various combinations in the transference, of identification with the procreative nurturing preoedipal analyst/mother or with the caretaking preoedipal father and the resolution of conflicts around these early identifications, as well as resolution of oedipal conflicts.

THE HIDDEN PATERNAL TRANSFERENCES

This brings me to my final point, the importance of the subtle, more hidden paternal transferences in the treatment of male patients by a woman. The female therapist may be experienced in the transference as the competitive oedipal father, the loved father of the negative oedipal period, the supportive and nurturing or the absent and disappointing preoedipal father. This is often missed—particularly the negative oedipal and the preoedipal father image in the woman. The evidence, as always, is found in the clinical material—in fantasies and dreams, associations and memories, acting out, and direct verbalization of thoughts and feelings. In one instance, mentioned earlier, the female therapist seemed to be the desired oedipal mother, while the anger and competition was directed toward an extratransference man. It very quickly became clear that the latter was a displacement from the female analyst, who, as father, was the target of the oedipal competition and hate as well as, as mother, the target of the oedipal love. This needed to be interpreted as such in the transference for an effective resolution. In other instances, when there is evidence of a competitive, phallic, powerful image of the female therapist, it is often interpreted as the phallic mother image. This is sometimes correct, but sometimes not. The phallic mother —a defensive concept related to the boy's castration fear of the penisless woman combined with a powerful, sadistic preoedipal mother image—has to be differentiated from the oedipal father in the transference.

When the female therapist is the object of love from the male patient, she may represent, at different times, a varying mixture of the desired oedipal mother and the caretaking preoedipal mother, but also the longed-for father from the negative oedipal constellation and the wished-for supportive preoedipal father, all of which add to the love feeling. This sometimes is the case with men with inadequate fathering. By the same token, anger at the female therapist may be a combination, in varying degrees, of repetition in the transference of the battle with the preoedipal mother, defense against attachment to the oedipal and preoedipal mother, as well as the battle with the oedipal father and anger at the nonsupportive preoedipal father, the female therapist standing for the father as well.

Impact of Cultural Changes on Our Clinical Understanding

Advancement in our knowledge of the preoedipal components in male psychological development has come parallel with our culture's better understanding and acceptance of the gentle, tender, and dependent aspects of man, which may be beginning to be internalized in the male ego ideal. What is familiar is easier to accept and less frightening to deal with for both patients and therapists. Male patients seem to talk more openly about these issues, and interpretations along these lines appear to be more easily heard. Mention of sexuality in general struck fear and shame into many Victorian hearts, while homosexuality and male dependence on woman have recently become less frightening and shameful concepts. They are, in fact, now often used as resistance against even more frightening ideas and feelings. Current fears seem to center more on even earlier issues, such as fear of engulfment, dread of disintegration, and threat of loss of identity. It is not, however, that our patients are different. It is that we listen differently.

BIBLIOGRAPHY

Abelin, E. 1971. The role of the father in the separation-individuation process. In *Separation-individuation,* ed. J. McDevitt and C. Settlage, pp. 229–252. New York: International Universities Press.

Blum, H. 1971. On the conception and development of the transference neurosis. *Journal of the American Psychoanalytic Association,* 19:41–53.

Chasseguet-Smirgel, J. 1976. Freud and female sexuality: The consideration of some blind spots in the exploration of the dark continent. *International Journal of Psycho-Analysis* 57:275–287.

———. 1984. A special case: On transference love in the male. Paper presented at the London Weekend Conference, April.

Freud, S. 1931. Female sexuality. In *The standard edition of the complete psychological works of Sigmund Freud,* 24 vols. (hereafter *S.F.*), ed. J. E. Strachey, vol. 12 (1961), pp. 225–243. London: Hogarth Press, 1953–1974.

Gilligan, C. 1982. *In a different voice: Psychological theory and women's development.* Cambridge, Mass.: Harvard University Press.

Karme, L. 1979. The analysis of a male patient by a female analyst: The problem of the negative oedipal transference. *International Journal of Psycho-Analysis* 60:253–261.

Kernberg, O. 1980. *Internal world and external reality,* pp. 277–305. New York: Jason Aronson.

Kestenberg, J. 1968. Outside and inside, male and female. *Journal of the American Psychoanalytic Association,* 16:457–521.

Kohut, H. 1977. *The restoration of the self.* New York. International Universities Press.

———. 1980. Reflections on the self. In *Advances in Self Psychology,* ed. A. Goldberg, pp. 473–554. New York: International Universities Press.

Limentani, A. 1984. Areas of darkness in male sexuality. Paper presented at the London Weekend Conference, April.

Mahler, M., Pine, F., and Bergman, A. 1975. *The psychological birth of the human infant.* New York: Basic Books.

Person, E. 1983a. Women in therapy: Gender as a variable. *International Review of Psychoanalysis* 10:193–204.

———. 1983b. The erotic transference in women and in men: Differences and consequences. Plenary address at 1983 winter meetings of the American Academy of Psychoanalysis.

13

Homosexuality in Homosexual and Heterosexual Men: Some Distinctions and Implications for Treatment

RICHARD A. ISAY

Introduction

The purpose of this chapter is to provide a clinical perspective that may enable psychoanalysts and other psychotherapists to work more effectively with their homosexual patients. This perspective is based on two premises: first, that homosexuals can live, as homosexuals, well-adjusted, productive lives with gratifying and stable love relationships. This premise, which is based on clinical experience, personal observation, and world literature, will not be discussed here, but it has important implications for the therapy of our homosexual patients. The second premise is that the effort to change the sexual orientation of most gay patients is not clinically helpful.[1]

---

1. The term "gay" is used as a synonym for "homosexual," defined later in this chapter. "Gay" probably antedates the late-nineteenth-century term "homosexual" by at least five centuries, and the etymology of the word is reviewed by Boswell (1980). I use this term in an effort to deemphasize the medical and pathological connotation of "homosexual."

There are some heterosexual men, in contrast to homosexual men, who use homosexual fantasies and behavior primarily as a defense against their conflicts about assertiveness, including heterosexual assertiveness. Since the analysis of such conflicts may be helpful in altering both the homosexual fantasies and behavior in heterosexuals but, in my experience, not in homosexuals, it is important to make clinical distinctions between these two groups of patients. In this chapter I plan to offer illustrative clinical material and a schema that may be useful in making these distinctions.

The view generally held by psychoanalysts is that homosexuality is a pathological condition. This attitude is derived from the theoretical conception that a homosexual orientation is engendered by faulty parenting, especially by binding, engulfing mothering, that results in the failure to separate from the preoedipal mother and a consequent fear of closeness to women, and/or by the inadequate resolution of oedipal stage conflict and consequent faulty identification. The homosexual object choice is one attempted solution to the conflicts engendered during these developmental stages. From this perspective those most accepting of their sexuality, the "obligatory" homosexuals, are those who are considered to have the most severe ego defects and the most severely impaired character structures because of developmental failure during the separation-individuation stage of early childhood (Bychowski 1945, 1954; Socarides 1968, 1978).

This view of homosexuality as pathology and the concomitant desire to change our patients' sexual orientation is, I believe, due to the bias that only heterosexuality is normal and to our internalization of the social prejudice against homosexuals (Isay 1985). In our work with these men "empirically subjective values are posited as if they were 'objective' and accessible to empirical validation" (Hartmann 1960, p. 67); thus, such notions as "there are no healthy homosexuals" (Bergler 1957, p. 79) or that "all homosexuals suffer from a severe degree of psychic masochism" (Socarides 1978, pp. 54–55) or that homosexuals are defended, conflicted, or inhibited heterosexuals (Bergler 1957; Bieber et al. 1962; Ovesey and Woods 1980; Rado 1949; Socarides 1968, 1978).

My early clinical efforts to be of assistance to gay patients by

Homosexuality in Homosexual and Heterosexual Men

helping them to change their sexual orientation through the analysis of early conflict failed time and time again. I noticed that even with motivated patients, behavioral change could occur only through the use of such techniques as transference exploitation or positive and negative reinforcement. My more recent work with homosexual men who had entered a second treatment after unsuccessful efforts by another therapist or analyst to alter their sexuality has suggested that, while sexual behavior may change—in most cases only temporarily—sexual orientation remains unchanged in a neutral analytic or therapeutic setting. Clinical depression may be caused by the repression, denial, or suppression of the homosexual impulses and fantasies, and anxiety and depression may result from the disruption of sexual identity formation. These clinical experiences, which I have reported elsewhere (Isay 1985), have led me to conclude that it is not in the best interest of the gay patient for an analyst or therapist to have as a goal changing his patient's sexuality.

My view of the potentially harmful affects of attempting to alter a patient's sexual orientation should not, however, be taken as a nihilistic view of analytic work with homosexuals. Aside from being able to be helpful in the same manner and for the same spectrum of problems as with heterosexual patients, analyzing the origin of a gay patient's sexuality may in itself be therapeutic. If such analysis is carried out with appropriate neutrality and with respect and regard for the patient, his sexuality may become less maladaptive and part of a positive self-image. As with any character trait, however, such analysis and understanding by the patient will not, in my experience, make the homosexuality disappear nor will it turn it into heterosexuality. It may, however, modify the sexuality by making it freer of neurotic, self-destructive conflict, if such conflict is present. That sexual orientation is modifiable in these ways, but not eradicable, suggests that it has infantile preoedipal origins, that it has a constitutional basis, or, as is likely the case, that its origins lie in a combination of the two. I will return to these issues later.

My definition of a homosexual is one who has a predominant erotic preference for others of the same sex. In adults the erotic preference can usually be recollected as being present from the latency years or early adolescence (ages nine to thirteen) and often earlier. There are some heterosexuals who for developmental reasons (adolescents), for opportunistic motives (some delinquents), for situational reasons (prison inmates), or in order to defend against anxiety may engage in homosexual behavior for varying periods of time and not be homosexual. Most homosexuals do engage in sexual activity, but one need not do so to be homosexual. There are individuals who may be homosexual and are unaware of it because of the repression or suppression of their fantasies (Isay 1985; Marmor 1980).

In this definition I emphasize that it is the erotic preference as expressed in fantasy that defines the homosexual and not his behavior, since some homosexuals, like some heterosexuals, may be inhibited by social constraints from expressing their sexuality. In homosexual men there is a relative preponderance, but not necessarily an exclusivity, of homoerotic fantasy. I am emphasizing the tenacity and longevity of the preference in adults, since the fantasy and sexual impulse are usually recollected from latency or the early years of adolescence. During the course of an analysis or analytically oriented psychotherapy, the recollection of same-sex fantasies or impulses from earlier years of childhood frequently reemerge.

Defensive Homosexuality in Heterosexual Men

The most frequent form of homosexual-like behavior and fantasy seen in adult heterosexual males serves as a defense against conflicts about assertiveness by the expression of the unconscious wish to be a woman. In these patients, "feminine" is perceived unconsciously as being passive and noncompetitive, and the expression of feminine wishes opposes the dangers inherent in striving to be masculine, seen as being competitive and assertive. The conscious expression of these feminine wishes takes the form of what the patient experiences as homosexual fantasies and homosexual behavior. The expression of the unconscious feminine wish may be derived from "culturally determined attitudes that favor the male. In our society masculinity represents strength, dominance, superiority; femininity represents weakness, submissiveness, inferiority" (Ovesey and Woods 1980, p. 326).[2] What is interesting is that the symptomatic expression of these wishes to be like a woman takes the form of homosexual fantasies, and that the nature of the fantasies expresses the unconscious perception of homosexual men as being passive and submissive and heterosexuals as being assertive and dominant.

The phenomenon of defensive homosexuality is seen most frequently in heterosexual male patients who perceive their fathers as powerful, authoritarian, and frightening and their mothers as being submissive, dominated, and demeaned by their husbands. Whether fact or fantasy, such perceptions are used by the child to solidify his oedipal wish to be his mother's ally and rescuer, and they increase his castration anxieties and fears. While the perception of these fathers as being demeaning of their wives is fueled and enhanced by the oedipal child's competitiveness and anger with his father, in my clinical experience it cannot be seen as being exclusively the product of fantasy. I will present two illustrations of defensive homosexual fantasy as seen in my analytic work and then attempt to demonstrate how these predominantly heterosexual men can be distinguished clinically from those who are predominantly homosexual.

Alan was twenty-three when he began his analysis. He had graduated from college two years before with only fair grades after excelling in high school in both academic studies and extracurricular activities, including athletics. After college he went to graduate school but dropped out during the first year because of his loss of motivation. He then worked for a magazine but quit after six months because of his loss of interest. When he started analysis he was working in a retail store. He wanted treatment because of concern about his lack of motivation and his sexual

2. Such defensive homosexual behavior and fantasy has been called "pseudohomosexuality" by Ovesey. While I agree with much of Ovesey's description of "pseudohomosexual anxiety," I do not agree with his view that these same anxieties primarily motivate the homosexual behavior of gay men (1980, p. 331). Nor do I believe, as he does, that these same concepts are applicable in the treatment of homosexuals, although they may be useful in the treatment of heterosexuals who use homosexuality defensively.

inadequacy. He had a history of premature ejaculation and impotence with a girlfriend of two years, whom he had stopped seeing about one year before beginning his analysis. Currently he was dating hardly at all. His masturbation fantasies were of erect penises, sometimes of performing fellatio, and, less frequently, of having violent heterosexual sex.

Alan's father was a wealthy and highly successful businessman. My patient saw him as competitive, powerful, and emotionally detached. As the analysis progressed, he saw him more clearly as being, like himself, ashamed of tender feelings and contemptuous of tenderness in others. He was very much aware of his closeness to his beautiful mother, who was sometimes subservient to her husband and at other times demeaning of him. Alan became increasingly aware of his sadistic and spiteful rage for her and for other women because of his frustrated sexual longings.

By the third year of his analysis Alan had successfully completed graduate school and was working for a corporation. This period of renewed success was in part motivated by both a strong positive transference and the fear that I would injure him if he did not please me. It was accompanied by renewed experiences of competitiveness and increasing homosexual fantasies both in and outside of the analysis.

He had the following dream the night after being complimented by his boss for an unusual and innovative solution to a complicated business problem: "I was underneath some blankets with my shorts on. All of a sudden this guy was rubbing his leg against me. I wanted to get out from underneath the blankets but couldn't because my shorts were off and he'd see I had a hard on. He wanted to kiss me and I wanted to kiss him too. I had this sexual feeling even though I was resisting it." His associations were of sexual feelings for me, feeling small, powerless, and helpless. There was further elaboration of the manifest dream: that his legs were spread like a woman's. He commented that his penis was small like a clitoris, that he felt helpless and unable to do anything by himself—just like a woman. He wondered what it would feel like to be anally penetrated by me.

As the analysis continued and Alan was able to permit himself greater success in different areas of his life, including increased sexual pleasure with women, his anxiety correspondingly increased and he had even more frequent conscious homosexual fantasies of fondling my or some other man's penis, of being anally penetrated, and of performing fellatio. Although these fantasies were sexually arousing to him, the only actual sexual activity occurred with some gay neighbors, when he teasingly took down his trousers and let them fondle his buttocks.

On many occasions he called my attention to his erections in a casual, offhand but playfully seductive manner, repeating exhibitionistic childhood sexual play with his mother. He wanted to be like a woman (his mother) in order to get close to a powerful man (his father) by being penetrated by him, and thereby to acquire his father's energy, vitality, and power. He was hoping to demonstrate that he was no threat to me. Throughout this time of intense transference and movement in the analysis, there was no drive to be attached to another man through sexual activity. Rather, he continued to have a pervasive heterosexual drive and increasingly satisfying sexual activity.

Another patient, Benjamin, also illustrates how a basically heterosexual man may have homosexual feelings activated by his aggressive and competitive strivings. He sought help because of his concerns about premature ejaculation, an inability to get close to women, and persistent fantasies of being forced to perform fellatio on men with large penises. His other major concerns were of his inability to do well in graduate school and to focus on any specific vocational goals. He perceived his father as being powerful, authoritarian, and distant. He felt very close to his mother, although he spoke with anger of her being too easily dominated, too weak, and too conforming of her life to his father's needs.

Unlike Alan, Benjamin's inhibition in sexual activity gave way to analysis more readily than his work inhibition. During periods of increased sexual activity and improving sexual performance, or when he had unconscious aggressive feelings toward me, he would comment on his frequent and troublesome images of erect penises and thoughts of anal penetration. He recollected that, as a child of five or six, on occasion he had put on some article of his mother's clothing, but he had no recollection of homosexual fantasies until about age fifteen. There was little or no impulse to engage in homosexual activity during his analysis, and his heterosexual impulses throughout remained strong.

In both of these patients homosexual fantasies were first activated in late adolescence by the specific threats and dangers inherent in increasingly successful and aggressive strivings. Their symptoms were largely rooted in oedipal stage conflicts and negative oedipal identifications as an attempted resolution of these conflicts. In addition, with Alan, there was important unconscious gain in perceiving himself and being perceived as being like a girl, since he felt his mother preferred her daughter from a prior marriage to him. The second patient felt his father would have preferred a daughter. In both patients there was a strong drive for heterosexual attachment, and heterosexual activity became enhanced during their analyses without direction, reinforcement, or transference exploitation. Homosexual fantasies decreased in frequency and intensity with the analysis of the transference. In both patients the unconscious fantasy was to be a woman, which was partly gratified through homoerotic thoughts and feelings. Homosexual fantasies such as being penetrated and performing fellatio are not primarily motivated to provide gratification for longings for attachment to other men, but to express the fantasies of being in a penisless state like a woman and of acquiring a penis.

Clinical Distinctions

The following characteristics may be helpful in distinguishing clinically the heterosexual man who uses homosexuality defensively or regressively from the true homosexual.

1 In the heterosexual, the homosexual fantasy usually has the unconscious meaning of being womanlike and nonmasculine. The

sexual fantasy may have that same unconscious significance at times in some homosexuals, but it is not of exclusive nor predominant significance. The meaning of the homosexual fantasy of homosexuals, like the heterosexual fantasy of heterosexuals, is dependent on many aspects of character and early conflict.

2 Homosexual behavior and fantasy in a heterosexual wards off and defends against heterosexual attachment. The homosexual behavior and fantasy of the homosexual has attachment to another man as its aim, although, as with any heterosexual, that is not the only aim of the sexual behavior and fantasy, nor is it necessarily the conscious aim. Sexualization and hypersexuality may, of course, be used by both homosexuals and heterosexuals to avoid such attachment.

3 Most, although not all, heterosexual men enjoyed during childhood stereotypical male, aggressive "rough-and-tumble" activities. Most homosexual men have a history of aversion to and avoidance of these activities in childhood (Bell, Weinberg, and Hammersmith 1981; Friedman and Stern 1980; Green 1979). They also have a feeling of being different from their same-sex peers, which is most likely based on the unconscious or preconscious perception of their sexual orientation.

4 In the heterosexual the onset of the homosexual fantasy is usually recollected as starting in late adolescence or early adulthood. The fantasies of the homosexual have their onset in childhood and are usually recollected as starting in the latency years or early adolescence (Friedman and Stern 1980).

5 In heterosexuals, the homosexual fantasy is by and large unwanted and distressing (ego-dystonic). To most, although not all, homosexual patients the fantasy and behavior feel natural (ego-syntonic).

6 In the heterosexual, the homosexual fantasy either disappears or is greatly mitigated in any therapy conducted in a noncoercive, neutral manner. In the homosexual, fantasy and sexual activity become less conflicted during a properly conducted treatment.

7 In such heterosexual men, the homosexual fantasy is most likely to appear at times of conflict around aggression and competitiveness both inside and outside of the analysis. In gay men, the same-sex fantasies and behavior remain comparatively constant in a neutral, noncoercive analytic experience. The nature of the homoerotic fantasy or of the sexual behavior may, of course, vary at times of heightened transference and may change as the patient's homosexuality becomes less distorted or less inhibited by neurotic conflict.

285

As with every patient, the clinical task with the homosexual is to enable him to be as free as possible of conflict that is inhibiting and self-destructive so that he can live as gratifying a life as is within his grasp to live. Since, in my clinical experience, the sexual orientation of these men is not mutable, this can best be accomplished if their sexuality is accepted as a given. By accepting the homosexuality as a fixed trait, I feel the analyst or therapist is in the best position to "avoid imposing his self or his values" (Poland 1984, p. 291) and, by conveying in this manner his regard for the individuality of his patient, to "sustain and nurture the patient's observing ego" (Poland 1984, p. 285). I also feel that such a stance best approximates Anna Freud's (1936) idea of neutrality as maintaining equidistance between intrapsychic structures. The analyst is then most readily able to recognize and analyze those conflicts that interfere with the patient's capacity to love as a homosexual man. I am not suggesting that the origin of the homosexual object choice, like the origin of other behavior, should not come under analytic scrutiny, for such analysis and the hoped-for insight may itself enhance the patient's freedom to express his sexual impulses in a less self-destructive manner, encourage self-acceptance, and strengthen his homosexual identity. But I do feel that in good therapeutic work with these men, empathic attention must be paid not only to internal conflict of early origin but to conflict both old and new that is caused by the difficult external, social reality that may also interfere with a fulfilling expression of their sexuality.[3]

I view those homosexual patients who come for analysis or therapy because they are dissatisfied with themselves as homosexuals and with their sexuality to be responding to the real and immense social pressures and prejudices that face them and to the conflicts engendered by these, to internal conflicts interfering

3. It is important for any therapist or analyst working with gay men to understand that our social structure, prejudice, and legal restrictions contribute to the courting and sexual customs of homosexuals. Social factors contribute to, although certainly do not entirely explain, the proclivity of some gays toward anonymous sex. They also contribute to the perception that homosexuals are only interested in quick sex. "Homosexuals were not allowed to elaborate a system of courtship because the cultural expression necessary for such an elaboration was denied them. The wink on the street, the split-second decision to get it on, the speed with which homosexual relations are consummated; are all products of an interdiction" (Foucault 1982–83, p. 18.).

with and inhibiting the acceptance and expression of their sexuality and homosexual identity, and/or to conflicts unrelated to their sexuality but displaced onto it. The analysis of such conflict should enable them, like the majority of homosexual patients who enter treatment for other than conscious conflict about their sexual orientation, to live less encumbered, more conflict-free, less inhibited, more gratifying lives as homosexuals. The analysis of Carl, a twenty-six-year-old graduate student, illustrates aspects of the neutral and accepting attitude that is essential in working with these patients as well as some of the clinical issues that arise in treatment.

Case History

Carl is tall, lanky, and clean shaven, with blond hair. He is nice looking but he has poorly defined facial features, so he is not conventionally handsome. He has a slightly feminine walk, but no other feminine features or mannerisms. This was Carl's second treatment experience, having been in therapy while in his last year of high school and first year of college. He left that treatment in part because of a perception of his prior therapist's disapproval of his homosexuality and life style. He initiated therapy again in his junior year of college because of depression and dissatisfaction with his life. He had very low self-esteem and an inability to form meaningful relationships. He had casual friendships with both women and men, and transient, usually anonymous sex with men. His sexual activity was largely confined to the bathroom of the college library or to the stalls of the pornographic bookstore, performing or being the recipient of oral sex. Occasionally he had dated women and had sex on two occasions without enjoying it to see if "he could do it." He would have liked to be able to please his mother by getting married and having children. He felt this was the "right" thing to do, but he most desired to be able to have a loving relationship with another man. His mother was described as being very attentive when he was quite young, but at the time of the birth of his younger sister when he was three and a half, Carl was sent to prenursery school, his mother got her first part-time job, and she became abruptly less attentive. He felt his father to be kind and intelligent but weak, dominated by his wife, and not living up to his intellectual or economic potential. Throughout grade school Carl did well academically, but he felt different and therefore estranged from other boys his own age. He disliked athletics and other "rough" activities of his peers. He remembered homosexual impulses from age eight or nine, when he felt attracted to some of his classmates. His first homosexual experiences were mutual masturbation in his junior year of high school. In college he had some further sexual activity that increased after a summer trip abroad before his junior year, and it was in the spring of that year that he started treatment.

My initial clinical impression was that Carl was homosexual. This impression was based on his history of homosexual impulses from childhood; the continued push, in spite of conflict and social pressures, toward homosexual activities and relationships; his childhood history of feeling estranged and being "different" from other boys of his age; and his aversion to the usual "rough-and-tumble" activities of boys his own age.

In the early hours of therapy Carl expressed conflict about his homosexual impulses. My attitude was one of interest in him and in the development of his sexual orientation, but a lack of investment in whether he was heterosexual or homosexual. For example, when he revealed dismay about his homosexual impulses and feelings, I avoided asking questions that might reveal any bias toward what his sexual orientation should be. I felt that pursuing any of his conflicted feelings about his homosexuality during these early hours with questions or comments about why he did not go out with women would be an expression of a heterosexual bias. After a therapeutic alliance was established, such questions were appropriately raised in view of the difficulty he was having in forming meaningful attachments to other men.

As the analytic material developed, it further supported my early hypothesis, based on the initial interviews, about Carl's homosexual orientation. His sexual fantasies and behavior were influenced by transference in the manner in which they were expressed but not in the sex of the object toward whom they were expressed. His initial concern about his homosexuality largely disappeared as his feelings about getting close to other men became freer of conflict. The persistence of his pursuit of attachment to other men, in spite of his difficulties in forming attachments, indicated the strength of his erotic drive, and there was no evidence of a primary conflict over being close to women. With the clinical material that follows I will illustrate how conflicts about intimacy with other men were presented, how they were manifested in the transference, and will convey how the the analysis of these conflicts contributed to Carl's enhanced self-esteem and better-integrated image of himself as a homosexual man.

Carl longed for men who were unobtainable: they were either attached to someone else, had previously rejected him, were conflicted about their homosexuality, or were heterosexual and not interested. Anyone who was available was perceived as being like him and became repugnant after the first sexual encounter. After he left college and had expanded opportunities for meeting gay men who wanted relationships, a sexual pattern emerged: if he found someone he developed affection for, he became impotent.

Throughout much of our work Carl articulated and stressed that he was not attracted to "older men"—men in their forties—feeling they were "lecherous" and that they would be taking advantage of his youth. He felt anxious and helpless if an older man approached him, a conviction that raised the unsubstantiated hypothesis of an actual sexual experience or the perception of such an experience with an older man (or woman) while he was still a child. He had intense anxiety about being the recipient of anal sex. He was often too tight to permit anal penetration, especially if he felt affection for his sexual partner. He was attracted to passive, feminine-appearing young men but had masturbation fantasies of powerful black men with large penises. These symptoms were manifestations of conflicts around passivity, identification with his mother's rage, and his wish to be dominated.

The transference was initially characterized by his appearing to be oblivious of me, in spite of his occasional seductiveness and exhibitionistic behavior on the couch. He would sometimes turn to face me if he had a point that he didn't want lost, fearful that he was too weak and insignificant to be noticed unless he did so. He would ask for advice, guidance, and direction, as though I were a source of power that he needed and lacked. At other times, he would ignore my interpretations or clarifications or focus on a relatively insignificant aspect of what I had said, to defend against feeling overwhelmed or taken over by me. As the analysis progressed, he became more conscious of both his fear and the wish that I totally dominate him. At times this repeated the perceived domination and fear of his mother. At yet other times these conflicted wishes to be dominated expressed his wish for a powerful man who would protect him from his mother. For example, at one point during his analysis he was accused by his mother of siding with his father in a financial dispute. In that same hour he complained about ways in which I dominated and subjugated him. He became so anxious about his conflicted feelings for me that he thought of looking around to see what I was doing. He recalled during this hour an occasion when his father had spanked him, one of the few signs of his father's dominance, an incident that he turned to frequently thereafter as a reminder of masculine strength and power, when he felt fearful of being overwhelmed by his mother.

The affectional-sexual split gradually began to heal as the transference was analyzed and he became more tolerant of his wishes to get close to a man he perceived as powerful. Transference wishes and fears of getting close to me began to be expressed more clearly in his dreams: "I'm in a room. It looks like a cell. Some guy comes after me. I hear his heavy breathing. I dig my heels into the floor, going backward, trying to get away." His associations were to lying on the couch, sometimes being distracted by the noises I made behind him. I interpreted that if he ran away by digging in his heels and going backward, he would bump into me. He accused me of "going a bit far." Then he got angry about my silence and how long analysis takes. "I don't know what I want from you anymore," he stated with considerable longing in his voice.

Another brief dream from the same week: "I went into a shop to have my bicycle pump repaired. No matter how hard I tried it just wouldn't work." He felt that he did not get what he needed and wanted from me; that I was not good enough or smart enough to help him. His father was also weak and ineffective.

The following week he dreamed: "I was flying my own plane but you were directing it, telling me how to take off. I couldn't get it up and you had to recommend someone, a dentist or doctor to help. To get the plane up there was a strap or something I had to hold on to. I couldn't grab the other end of the strap with both hands. I came close to crashing a couple of times." He felt that I, like his father, was not strong enough to help him. His mother always complained about both of us. He had a lot of affection for his father but was frightened of getting close to him out of fear of his mother. Getting close to me, feeling I could help him, was a frightening disloyalty to her. A few weeks later he had this clear dream expressive of his attraction and desire for closeness:

> "I meet this guy. He's selling something. I'm in a cave or some dark environment. I really want to sleep with him. I don't know if he's gay. He's tall and skinny. He has long, nonstyled hair, almost like Tarzan. His pants are open. I reach out and grab his leg. He has a bathing suit underneath. We start making out. I say something like, 'Let's take off our clothes; let me suck your dick.' There's something on the underside of his dick like a swelling or herpes. It looks like it's been cut and has scar tissue around it. I suck his cock and then I sit on it. I don't remember his coming; just the wonderful feeling. I woke up very hard and jerked off."

He associated to seeing his physician at a gay resort and having spoken with him there. He wondered what he would do if he ever saw me there. He remembered recently reading about an article I had written twenty years earlier when I was in the navy, and commented that I must have looked good in a uniform. He then acknowledged for the first time some attraction to me.

This dream occurred during his fourth year of analysis. It expressed the least disguised sexual transference wish he had ever had and was followed by affectionate feelings for me and positive feelings about our work together and the progress he was making.

It seemed to usher in an even less ambivalent, but still tentative, appreciation of a young man a bit older than he whom he had been going out with for several months and whom he was now thinking of living with.

Only some of the determinants of Carl's selection of another man instead of a woman as a love object seem clear. The homosexual object choice was in part determined by his need to establish and experience closeness to a longed-for and demeaned father while at the same time he searched for and replicated his mother by selecting androgynous partners (Socarides 1978). Some aspects of his need early in the analysis to maintain distance and to keep separate by avoiding me in the transference were due to his fear of being overwhelmed or taken over, as he was by his mother if he surrendered to these longings for attachment. In part this anxiety was caused by the fear of closeness to his mother. Furthermore, the birth of his sister and the perceived rejection by his mother probably contributed to his turning in anger from women to men.

These dynamic explanations of possible determinants of Carl's homosexual object choice are, however, not very satisfying. First, there is nothing either specific or particular to Carl's family constellation or history that one does not find in many heterosexuals. Second, the basis of such explanatory efforts is to understand why he avoids women (i.e., someone like his mother), while the natural flow of a properly conducted analysis with a gay man who is not encumbered by either realistic or neurotic anxiety about his sexuality is toward the unfolding and understanding of the conflict interfering with gratifying relations with other men. This is perhaps comparable to the analysis of a heterosexual man, where we learn little about why he avoids sex with other men. Furthermore, attempting to analyze why the patient has an aversion to sex with women has no mutative value as regards his sexual orientation, though it may alter behavior patterns (Isay 1985).

Some investigations (e.g., Leavy 1985) have claimed that the biological model best explains the origin and development of sexual orientation, but at present the evidence is not entirely convincing, and what data we do have comes largely from animal studies or is contradictory or methodologically deficient (Hoult 1984). Nor is there convincing evidence, as evolutionary biologists propose, for any advantageous factors that might account for the selective survival of genes for homosexuality, even if such genes did exist. It is true, of course, "that any biological characteristic has a genetic basis, in the trivial sense that it could not develop unless the organism has information . . . that permits the potential development of the trait." Likewise there must be an "environment in which [the genetic information] is to develop" (Futuyma and Risch, 1983–84, p. 159). We can, it seems to me, say with certainty that human beings do have an inherent capacity for flexibility in sexual response and that under certain environmental circumstances, one or another type of sexuality may become prominent. The genetic disposition for flexible sexual response and the appropriate environmental conditions are both necessary but neither is a sufficient cause for the establishment of sexual orientation. Therefore, understanding the conflict incurred by the familial environment can neither change sexual orientation nor fully explain it. Our capacity to understand those conflicts and compromise formations that contribute to the formation of a homosexual orientation should not suggest that such behavior is necessarily maladaptive, since what once originated in conflict later may become adaptive, growth-enhancing behavior.

Therapy of Bisexual Patients

Before making some summary comments with regard to analytic therapy with the gay patient, I want to briefly mention work with bisexuals, who can gain varying degrees of satisfaction and pleasure with either same-sex or opposite-sex persons. Because Freud (1905, p. 144) connected an inherited bisexual disposition with the development of inversion or homosexuality, some analysts feel that bisexuals are either sick heterosexuals, who use their homosexuality to ward off anxiety-provoking heterosexual impulses, or that they are, in fact, homosexuals and that proper treatment will enable them to become functioning heterosexuals. Although there are, indeed, those who appear to be bisexual who may clinically be defending against one or the other aspect of their sexual orientation, my experience again suggests that the sexual arousal patterns are established from such an early age that only behavior can be modified by therapeutic endeavors. An important distinction between these patients and gay patients is that the suppression of one or the other of their sexual impulses in order to adapt to a life style they prefer does not appear to produce the same adverse psychological and social consequences. My experience, however, has only been with bisexuals who wanted to get married or remain married and who entered treatment because they feared that their homosexuality would be harmful to their marriage.

Most bisexual men and women seek treatment because the homosexual component of their bisexuality is unconscious and produces anxiety. In such patients the most important aspect of the therapeutic task is to make such impulses conscious and tolerable. Those who have a strong bisexual orientation may through a traditional, neutral psychoanalytic, or psychotherapeutic process be enabled to live a heterosexual life relatively unencumbered by their homosexuality. The comfort of their lives as functioning heterosexuals will, I feel, depend on the degree to which they are made conscious and accepting of their anxiety-provoking homosexual fantasies and impulses, which can then be used in the service of their heterosexuality and productivity. My impression is that these men have enough emotional gratification and satisfying sexual discharge that their homosexual longings do not need expression at the sacrifice of a satisfying heterosexual relationship. A bisexual may make both a satisfactory emotional and sexual adjustment in a heterosexual marriage, although of necessity it will be one based on compromise and some renunciation. Nevertheless, in our society such an adjustment would appear to be a favorable clinical outcome. However, as is true of the homosexual patient, the bisexual orientation, established early in development, remains, and there will be alterations only in the sexual behavior. The best clinical outcomes are in those patients motivated strongly to maintain a heterosexual relationship, who can tolerate the acknowledgment of their homosexual fantasies and impulses and the frustrations of some renunciation of homosexual behavior. Of course, as with homosexual men who remain in happy marriages, there are marriages where the wife is supportive of and comfortable with the expression of her spouse's bisexuality.

Discussion

My efforts in this chapter to clarify some basic aspects of the treatment of gay men, heterosexuals who use homosexuality defensively, and, very briefly, bisexuals should not lead to the idea that I feel that human beings can be categorized in the discrete clinical entities of homosexual, heterosexual, or bisexual. The complexity of human development leads to partial identification with both parents in every person as a solution to oedipal stage conflict. Such partial identifications provide depth, complexity, flexibility, and richness in all aspects of relationships, providing they do not lead to significant internal conflict. As mentioned earlier, homosexual fantasies or behavior that derive from such identifications may be used defensively in heterosexual men, and, when they are, these fantasies are usually manifestations of a wish to be nonmasculine. Homosexual fantasies and behavior may be used by men with a significant bisexual disposition in an attempt to resolve conflict associated with the fear of sex and/or relationships with women; likewise, heterosexual fantasies and behavior may at times be symptomatic and evoked by the transference in some gay patients and bisexuals (Isay 1985).

The question of the psychology of the homosexual man cannot be answered if the question is posed simply as "What is the nature of the oedipal or preoedipal conflict that determines one's homosexuality or the homosexual object choice?" I have seen homosexual men, such as Carl, with family constellations as described in the literature—namely, a strong, binding mother and a father who is perceived as weak. But I have also seen heterosexual patients with similar family constellations and many homosexual patients who appear to have had "average expectable" parenting (also see Leavy 1985). There are as many different types of homosexuals as there are heterosexuals, and these include homosexual men and women capable of forming lasting, loving relationships as well as those whose relationships are conflicted. Like heterosexuals, there are also homosexuals who are sadistic, masochistic, narcissistic, depressed, borderline, or psychotic; they too run the spectrum of psychological disturbances. Those gay patients who have such psychological disturbances dynamically resemble their heterosexual counterparts more closely than they do each other. The nature and origin of their object relations, the manner in which they express their sexuality and conflicts about their sexuality are determined by the nature of whatever pathology may coexist with the homosexuality and by those developmental conflicts that have contributed to this coexisting pathology. The ways in which same-sex love relationships are affected by such conflict deserve the same clinical and theoretical efforts that we have made in our attempts to understand the distortions and inhibitions of our heterosexual patients' sexuality. Questions about the origin of these patients' sexuality and the nature and origin of their psychopathology must be separated if we are going to understand our gay patients and be of adequate therapeutic assistance to them.

I have avoided the use of the term "fixation" to describe the true homosexual when attempting to distinguish him from the heterosexual's defensive or regressive use of homosexuality. This term carries the implication of being stuck in an immature developmental stage, a stage that should have been progressed beyond, a stage of developmental arrest. "Fixation" has the clinical connotation that there is a "persistence of primitive ways of satisfaction, of relating to people, and of reacting defensively to old, even outmoded dangers" (Moore and Fine 1968, p. 47). Like all behavior, including heterosexuality, the homosexual orientation may evolve at least in part as a solution to early conflict, but it acquires, also like heterosexuality, an autonomy from early conflict and the defensive role that it may have initially played. For neither heterosexuality nor homosexuality does conflict solution and compromise formation appear to be a sufficient explanation for the development of sexual orientation.

I have also avoided in this chapter emphasizing constitutional factors or inherited biological predispositions to homosexuality. Although I do feel that biological factors play an important role and that future research will clarify the nature of this role, I have deemphasized the biological because I feel that appeals to biology are based on the fallacious assumption that only what is constitutional must be accepted as a given by the analyst, and, by inference, that what derives from early conflict necessarily can and should be changed. I want to emphasize that the appropriately neutral analytic attitude can be maintained only if the analyst or therapist has neither the explicit aim nor an implicit interest in converting the homosexual love object to a heterosexual love object. It is not conceivable to me that an analyst can accept the sexual object choice of his gay patient, working empathically with the neurotic vicissitudes of his relationships, while at the same time conceptualizing that patient's sexuality as being "perverted."[4] Neutrality with these men can be best approximated, it seems to me, only if the homosexual arousal pattern is viewed as being structured so early in life by constitutional and/or developmental factors that it is conceptualized as a fixed trait.

When it comes to our clinical formulations about homosexuality, we must remind ourselves that value judgments based on social mores should play no role in our analytic work with these patients. The judgment that it is both possible for homosexuals to become heterosexual and that it is in their best interest to do so reflects, I feel, a "certain lack of clarity in distinguishing the sphere of 'health' from the sphere of 'morals' " (Hartmann 1960, p. 69). It is also a value judgment to believe that gays should behave like heterosexuals not only in their object choice but in the ways they enact their homosexuality. The healthy individual may, but does not necessarily, conform to current social values

4. "Perverted" derives from the Latin verb *pervetere*, which means "to deviate from what is considered right and correct"—that is, heterosexuality—according to the *American Heritage Dictionary*. This term and the noun "pervert" are frequently used in the psychoanalytic and psychiatric literature. These words are by definition moralistic and have acquired a pejorative connotation that reflects social bias.

that often vary from culture to culture (Ford and Beach 1951) and epoch to epoch (Boswell 1980). I believe that the essential clinical issues for us as analysts and therapists is the extent to which we may lessen the burden of the sacrifices that society imposes on these men (Freud 1961) and the degree to which we are able to help them resolve those conflicts that interfere with the fullest and most gratifying expression of their sexuality.

BIBLIOGRAPHY

Bell, A., Weinberg, M., and Hammersmith, S. 1981. *Sexual preference: Its development in men and women.* Bloomington, Ind.: Indiana Universities Press.

Bergler, E. 1957. *Homosexuality: Disease or way of life?* New York: Hill and Wang.

Bieber, I. et al. 1962. *Homosexuality: A psychoanalytic study.* New York: Basic Books.

Boswell, J. 1980. *Christianity, social tolerance and homosexuality.* Chicago: University of Chicago Press.

Bychowski, G. 1945. The ego of homosexuals. *International Journal of Psycho-Analysis* 26: 114–127.

———. 1954. The structure of homosexual acting out. *Psychoanalytic Quarterly* 23:48–61.

Foucault, M. 1982/83. Interview in *Salmagundi,* 58–59: 10–24.

Ford, C. S., and Beach, F. A. 1951. *Patterns of sexual behavior.* New York: Harper and Brothers.

Freud, A. 1936. *The ego and the mechanisms of defense. Writings 2.* New York: International Universities Press, 1966.

Freud, S. 1905. Three essays on the theory of sexuality. In *The standard edition of the complete psychological works of Sigmund Freud,* 24 vols. (hereafter *S.E.*), ed. J. E. Strachey, vol. 7 (1953), pp. 125–245. London: Hogarth Press, 1953–1974.

———. The future of an illusion. In *S.E.,* vol. 21 (1961), pp. 3–56.

Friedman, R. C. and Stern, L. O. 1980. Juvenile aggressivity and sissiness in homosexual and heterosexual males. *Journal of the Academy of Psychoanalysis* 8:427–440.

Futuyma, D. J., and Risch, S. J. 1983/84. Sexual orientation, sociobiology and evolution. *Journal of Homosexuality* 9:157–168.

Green, R. 1979. Childhood cross-gender behavior and subsequent sexual preference. *American Journal of Psychicatry* 36:106–108.

Hartmann, H. 1960. *Psychoanalysis and moral values.* New York: International Universities Press.

Hoult, T. J. 1984. Human sexuality in biological perspective: Theoretical and methodological considerations. *Journal of Homosexuality* 9:137–155.

Isay, R. A. 1985. On the analytic therapy of homosexual men. *Psychoanalytic Study of the Child,* 40:235–254.

Leavy, S. A. 1985–86. Male homosexuality reconsidered. *International Journal of Psychoanalytic Psychotherapy* 11:155–174.

Homosexuality in Homosexual and Heterosexual Men

Marmor, J., ed. 1980. *Homosexual behavior: A modern reappraisal.* New York: Basic Books.

Moore, B. A., and Fine B. P. 1968. *A glossary of psychoanalytic terms and concepts.* New York: The American Psychoanalytic Association.

Ovesey, L. and Woods, S. M. 1980. Pseudo-homosexuality and homosexuality in men: Psychodynamics as a guide to treatment. In *Homosexual behavior: A modern reappraisal,* ed. J. Marmor, pp. 325–341. New York: Basic Books.

Poland, W. S. 1984. On the analyst's neutrality. *Journal of the American Psychoanalytic Association* 32:283–299.

Rado, S. 1949. An adaptational view of sexual behavior. In *Psychosexual Development in Health and Disease,* ed. P. Hoch and J. Zubin, pp. 159–189. New York: Grune & Stratton.

Socarides, C. W. 1968. *The overt homosexual.* New York: Grune & Stratton.

———. 1978. *Homosexuality.* New York: Jason Aronson.

INDEX

Index

Index

Index

Index

Man of Flowers (Paul Cox), as illustration of dynamics of male perversion, 158–62

Manhood: adolescence and, 232; childhood and, 236

Manhood: From Childhood to the Fierce Order of Virility (Michel Leiris), 236

Marmor, J., 183n3, 280

Masculinity: defined in relation to women, 9–10; female clothes as disguise of, 90; heroic, in *Tough Guys Don't Dance* (Norman Mailer), 4; martial, hypertropy of, 53–4; men and, 12

Mastery, fantasies of, 74

Masturbation: sexual fantasies in, 178–79; vulvar fantasy and, 137–38

Masturbation tactics, maternal identification and, 67

Maternal figure, incestual fantasies and, 87

Maternal identification: inner reality and, 107; masturbation tactics and, 67

Maternalism, sublimated, men and, 50

Mavissakalian, M., 86

May, R., 74

McDougall, J., 80, 87–88, 116, 155

Meleager, 188

Men: feminism and, 12; femininity and, 11; heterosexual, homosexuality in, 21; homosexual, homosexuality in, 21; infantile psychosexuality and, 11–2; masculinity and, 12; sentimentality in, 15–6; sublimated maternalism and, 50

Menarche, induced ejaculation and, 67

Mental life, of men, and penis envy, 92

Meyers, Donald I., 20, 248n1, 250

Meyers, Helen, 20–1

Michelangelo Buonarroti, 199, 201

Middle Ages, homosexuality in, 196–98

Money, J., 9, 184n5

Moore, B. A., 296

Moore, J. C., 196n12

Morgenthaler, F., 174

Mother: as castrator, 81; father, self in triangular relation, 51–2; identification with, and struggle against sentimentality, 103–04; as parental universe, 63; primary caregiver and, 221; search for, and multiple caregivers, 220

Mother-child bond, psychopathology and, 10

Mother-child interaction: father and, 213–14; object-self organization and, 214

Mother-son interaction, male sexuality and, 72, 92–3

Multiple function, principle, and daydreaming, 101

Murphy, T. F., 182n2

Narcissism: castration anxiety and, 119; healthy, in adult life, 9; malignant, 169; malignant, perversion in, 172; oedipal complex and, 7; *see also* Sexual narcissism

Narcissistic identification: oedipal fantasies and, 157; preoedipal fantasies and, 157

Narcissistic pathology, with perversion, 171–72

Narcissistic personality structure, homosexual identification and, 167–69

Neoplatonism, homosexuality and, 198–199, 201

Neosexuality, preoedipal idealization and, 155

Neubauer, Peter B., 19, 222

Neurotic personality organization: homosexuality in, 163–65; organized perversion at level of, 170

Neutrality, technical, and patient's sexual orientation, 176–77

New Testament, prohibition of homosexuality in, 196

Object choice: homosexual analysis of, 286; sexual orientation and, 177

Object constancy, oedipal complex and, 8

Object loss, genital metaphor for, 248

Object relations: early, character formation and, 9; multiple, and primary objects, 217; multiple, triangularity of, 218; oedipal complex and, 8; perversion and, 153–54

Object-self organization, mother-child interaction and, 214

Odyssey, The (Homer), 206–07

Oedipal competition, resolution in: homosexuals, 89; transvestites, 89–91

Oedipal complex: anality and, 7; bisexuality and, 7; ego autonomy and, 8; father and, 218; narcissism and, 7; object constancy and, 8; object relations and, 8; orality and, 7; penis envy in boys and resolution of, 90; positive, and male gender role identity, 147; self-cohesion and, 8; separation-individuation and, 8

Oedipal conflict: homosexual solution of, 73; infantile, homosexuality and resolution of, 165; transvestite solution of, 73

Oedipal determinants, of perversion, 154

Oedipal father: castration anxiety and, 166; male psychology and, 10

Oedipal figures, identification with, 155

Oedipal phase, father's sexual role and, 66

Oedipal resolution, sexual identity and, 7

Oedipal rival, of childhood and lesbian fantasies, 88

Index

Oedipal themes: negative, and homoerotic wishes, 141; in sexual fantasies, 79–80

Oedipus complex, negative: and genital envy complex, 149; heterosexuality and, 66; and male ego ideal, 234; and male gender role identity, 147

"On Narcissism" (S. Freud), 156

Orality: oedipal complex and, 7; sentimentality and, 102

Ovesey, L., 89, 90, 91, 147, 184n5, 278, 281

Paradoxical unity, of heterosexual impulses in men, 52

Parental universe, mother as, 63

Paternal role, primary, and preoedipal father, 246–47

Patience (Gilbert and Sullivan), 99

Penis: erotic idealization of, 157; of father, in boys' unconscious imagery, 66; male fears and adolescent's sense of lack of control over, 83; sexual mastery and control over, 84

Penis envy: in boys, and resolution of oedipal complex, 90; castration anxiety and, 133; mental life of men and, 92; normal development in girls and, 131; phallic woman and, 147; therapist's gender and, 268; vulvar envy and, 132

Person, Ethel S., 14–5, 74n3, 79, 89, 90, 91, 147, 184n5, 271

Personality organization: borderline, perverse sexuality as part of, 171; borderline, with structural perversion, 171; perversion at neurotic level of, 157–63

Perverse infantile sexuality, polymorphous, and normal sexual behavior, 152

Perverse sexuality: normal polymorphous, 170; polymorphous, normal functions, 154–57; polymorphous, as part of borderline personality organization, 171

Perversion: character formation and, 8; definition, 152–53; genitality and, 153; in malignant narcissism, 172; narcissistic pathology with, 171–72; at neurotic level of personality organization, 157–63; object relations and, 153–54; oedipal determinants, 154; organized, at level of neurotic personality organization, 170; organized, prognosis of treatment, 166; preoedipal determinants, 154; psychoanalysis of, 176–79; in psychosis, 172–73; sexual inhibition and, 163; structured, in borderline personality, 171

Perversion, male: classification, 170–73; conceptual model, 152–79; diagnostic frame for, 169–73; *Man of Flowers* (Paul Cox) as illustration of dynamics of, 158–62

Phallic development, gender identity and, 64

Phallic illusion, in description of intercourse, 52

Phallic narcissism: phallic vulnerability and, 79; of proto-phallic phase, 65

Phallic narcissistic defenses: against ambisexual identity, 53–62; clinical overview, 53–4; illustration, 54–59, 60, 62

Phallic-oedipal bias, in father-son relationship, 247

Phallic oedipal phase, 65; in boys, 7; father and, 211–12

Phallic phase: in boys, 231; castration anxiety and, 119; Freud, S. on, 133; sexual development in, 133; upright urination in, 65; *see also* Proto-phallic phase

Phallic vulnerability, phallic narcissism and, 79

Phallocentric bias: in culture, 20; in psychoanalysis, 49–50, 51; in psychoanalytic theory, 14–5; psychoanalytic theory of male psychology, 7

Phallocentrism, male psychology and, 12

Piaget, J., 64, 233, 234, 235, 247, 248

Pindar, 204n7

Pine, F., 51, 269

Plato, 52

Platonic love, 198n13

Pomeroy, S. B., 206n19

Pontalis, J. B., 152–53

Pornographic movies, lesbian sex in, 85–6

Potency anxiety, threesome sex fantasy and, 86

Preconscious mental processes, psychology of, 96

Pregenital stage, castration anxiety and, 116–17

Preoedipal conflicts, character formation and, 9

Preoedipal determinants, of perversion, 154

Preoedipal development, dominance bias and, 247

Preoedipal idealization, neosexuality and, 155

Preoedipal issues, in male psychological development, and culture, 274–75

Preoedipal phase, castration anxiety and, 118

Preoedipal terrors, castration anxiety and, 129

Prephallic factors, in castration anxiety, 73

Primal father, identification with, 103

307

Index

tion, 157; oedipal themes in, 79–80; omni-available woman, 75–9; omni-available woman and mother, 73; omni-available woman and prostitution, 76; phallic woman, 134; pregnancy, and therapist's gender, 268; preoedipal and narcissistic identification, 157; of rape, 74; sadomasochism in, 76; simultaneous orgasm, 78–9; of submission, in women, 74; threesome sex, 85, 86; of transgression, 74; vagina dentata, 77; vulvar, 145–46; vulvar, linguistic reference, 141; vulvar, and masturbation, 137–38

Sexual fantasies, lesbian, 85–91; and feminine identification, 89; and maternal envy, 73; and oedipal rival of childhood, 88; and transvestite men, 89; and wish for feminine identification, 73

Sexual fears: castration anxiety and, 79–80; male, fantasies and, 77

Sexual identity: male, and failure of men to act as fathers, 67; oedipal resolution and, 7

Sexual inadequacy, developmental sources for feelings of, 79–85

Sexual inhibition, perversion and, 163

Sexual love: art and, 155; religion and, 155

Sexual mastery, control over penis and, 84

Sexual orientation: biological model, 292; change, through analysis, 278–79; constitutional basis of, 279; object choice and, 177; of patient, sexual behavior and, 279; sexual response and, 293; and technical neutrality, 176–77

Sexual response, sexual orientation and, 293

Sexual wishes, anxiety and, 114

Sexuality: female, in fantasies, 77–8; infantile, and adolescence, 233; male, and castration anxiety, 91; male, and mother-son interaction, 92–3; normal, homosexual tendencies in, 173–76; normal, and male homosexuality, boundary, 173–76; ontogeny of, fatherhood and, 62–8; struggle against sentimentality and, 97; see also Female sexuality; Machismo sexuality

Shapiro, T., 248

Shogun (James Clavell), 250

Simon, B., 206n19

Simultaneous orgasm, fantasy, 78–9

Slater, P. E., 206n19

Socarides, C. W., 278, 292

Social conditioning, sentimentality and, 97

Social order, homosexuality and, 204–05

Social structure, homosexual potential and, 203

Solnit, J. A., 222

Sons, psychic health of, fathers and, 13

Spelke, E., 219

Sperling, M., 134

Spitz, R., 51, 247

Stade, George, 14, 113

Starcke, O., 115

Stehling, T., 197

Stereotypes, sexual, 3, 5; theoretical models and, 5

Stern, L., 184n5, 285

Stevens, Wallace, 98–9

Stewart, W. A., 131

Stoller, R., 147, 184n5

Studies in Hysteria (S. Freud), 114

Submission, fantasies of, in women, 74

Summa Theologica (Thomas Aquinas), 198

Symposium, The (Plato), 53, 190n9, 198n13

Tearfulness, struggle against, 107

Tenderness, and genital excitement, in homosexuals, 164

Theoretical models, sexual stereotypes and, 5

Thomas, K., 196n12

Thorne, E., 75

Three Essays on the Theory of Sexuality (S. Freud), 182n1, 203n16

Threesome sex, fantasy: and lesbian sex fantasy, 85, 86; and potenecy anxiety, 86

Thucydides, 188

Tourney, G., 184

Transference: analysis of, and key words, 97; analyst's sex and, 20–21; erotic, with female analyst, 265; erotic, oedipal, with female analyst, 271–72; hidden paternal, with female analyst, 273–74; homosexual, with female analyst, 270; in male patients, with female therapist, 262–75; in male-male analytic dyad, 20, 245–60; maternal, with female analyst, 270, 271; oedipal, and therapist's gender, 267; preoedipal mother, with female analyst, 272–73

Transference development, in male patients, with female analysts, 265–66

Transgression, fantasies of, 74

Transvestic men, lesbian fantasies and, 89

Transvestite solution, of oedipal conflict, 73

Transvestites, resolution of oedipal competition in, 89–91

Transvestitic syndrome, 89

Triangular relation, of mother, father, self, 51–52

Triangularity: early, 219; of multiple object relationships, 219; see also Object relations